New Zealand Under MMP: A New Politics?

Jonathan Boston, Stephen Levine,
Elizabeth McLeay, Nigel S. Roberts

AUCKLAND UNIVERSITY PRESS
BRIDGET WILLIAMS BOOKS

First published 1996 by Auckland University Press with
Bridget Williams Books, University of Auckland,
Private Bag 92019, Auckland, New Zealand.

ISBN 1 86940 138 7

Cover design by Mission Hall Design Group, Wellington
Internal design by Afineline, Wellington
Typeset by Archetype, Wellington
Printed by GP Print, Wellington

Contents

Acknowledgements

The completion of this book would not have been possible without the assistance of numerous people and organisations. We owe a great many thanks to two institutions in particular. The New Zealand Foundation for Research, Science and Technology (FoRST) has funded the bulk of this study via the substantial research grant it provided to Victoria University for a major three-year project on the 'behavioural, institutional and policy consequences of MMP'. This project is officially entitled 'The New Zealand Political Change Project: the Impact of Electoral System Change in a Small Democracy' and is based within the Politics Department and Public Policy Group. By virtue of this grant, we have been able to employ research assistants and acquire teaching assistants to relieve us of some of our lecturing and assessment obligations. Without the generosity and foresight of FoRST, a major research project of this nature would not have been possible.

In addition, Victoria University has been unstinting with its advice and practical help. Considerable assistance was given to us in the preparation of our FoRST application, especially by Professor Warren Young (Assistant Vice-Chancellor, Research), Professor Margaret Clark (former Chairperson of the Politics Department), and Dr John Morrow (Associate Dean (Research) within the Faculty of Arts). Throughout the project we have received very welcome support and advice from Rowland Woods, Mike Doig, and Doreen Brown (all from the University's Office for Research – or Victoria Link Ltd). Victoria University (including the Research Committee of the Faculty of Commerce) has also provided us with some additional funds for employing research assistants.

We have been blessed with some very capable research assistants since we officially began the project in mid-1995. Pauline Ngan, our first research assistant, set a very high standard of performance. In particular, she ably administered a major survey involving some 1,600 people during the latter part of 1995. Evan Roberts computer-coded nearly 1,200 questionnaires with great speed and accuracy. Simon Sheppard was a mine of information about the development and structure of the political parties during the transition to MMP, and assisted with the preparation of the appendices. Virginia McLean (formerly of Parliament's Select Committee Office within the Office of the Clerk) joined us in March 1996 as our full-time research assistant – just in time to provide invaluable assistance with the editing, proofreading and completion of the text and the preparation of the index.

We would also like to extend our appreciation to the many people who provided comments on draft chapters, including Rob Eaddy, Robert Gregory, Mary Harris, Milton Hollard, Andrew Ladley, Simon MacPherson, John Martin, Caroline Morris, Donna Tunnicliffe and Nicola White. Brenda Bongiovanni (Secretary of the Public Policy Group) and Adrienne Nolan (Secretary of the Politics Department) also provided invaluable secretarial and administrative assistance at various stages during the life of this project. The authors, of course, take full responsibility for the entire text of the book.

Jonathan Boston
Stephen Levine
Elizabeth McLeay
Nigel S. Roberts
30 April 1996

Abbreviations

ACT	Association of Consumers and Taxpayers, ACT New Zealand party
CD	Christian Democrats [New Zealand]
CDU	Christian Democratic Union [Germany]
CE	chief executive
CER	Closer Economic Relations
CHP	Christian Heritage Party of New Zealand
CIR	citizens-initiated referenda
CSU	Christian Social Union [Germany]
DLP	Democratic Labor party [Australia]
FDP	Free Democratic Party [Germany]
FPP	first-past-the-post
GATT	General Agreement on Tariffs and Trade
KRA	key result area
MMP	mixed member proportional [representation]
MP	member of Parliament
OECD	Organisation for Economic Co-operation and Development
PEB	post-election briefing
PPTA	Post Primary Teachers' Association
PR	proportional representation
PV	Preferential Voting
RoC	Right-of-Centre party [now formally called the New Zealand Conservative Party or Conservatives]
SM	Supplementary Member
SO	Standing Orders
SRA	strategic result area
SSC	State Services Commission
STV	Single Transferable Vote

List of Tables and Figures

Tables

Figures

Preface

'. . . explain New Zealand and the world falls into place . . .'[1]

It is rare for democratic states to change their electoral systems. Yet in the mid-1990s, three reasonably long-established democracies – Italy, Japan, and New Zealand – embarked upon significant electoral reforms. In New Zealand's case, a majority of electors in a referendum held in late 1993 voted to introduce a new electoral system known as mixed member proportional (MMP). This move continues to generate controversy. Supporters of MMP claim that it will reduce the power of the cabinet, enhance the role and influence of Parliament, increase public consultation, and replace the old adversarial style of politics with a new era of consensus. Critics, however, fear that it will generate political uncertainty, governmental instability, policy paralysis and economic stagnation.

This book examines the changes already brought about by MMP and assesses its likely long-term impact on New Zealand's political system. Drawing on a range of survey data, comparative perspectives and international models, we consider how the new voting system will operate, how the party system is altering and could evolve, how governments will be formed, and what changes can be expected to the roles and influence of the cabinet and Parliament. Attention is also given to the implications of MMP for voters, as well as the effects of the new system on the public service, pressure groups, and policy-making.

New Zealand Under MMP outlines our views of the likely effects of proportional representation on New Zealand politics. The book also presents the findings from a survey we conducted in late 1995 on the views of other people – including politicians, business leaders, senior public servants, economists and lawyers, as well as leading figures from the Maori community, pressure groups and the media. Among the topics included in the survey were expectations about the composition of the first MMP Parliament, the likely kinds of government under MMP, the structure and operations of the executive and of Parliament, the likely implications of MMP for the role of other participants in the political system (such as interest groups and the public service), the possible impact of MMP on the policy process and policy outcomes, and possible future changes to New Zealand's constitution.

This book has been prepared as part of a three-year research project (begun in mid-1995) based at the Victoria University of Wellington, and known as 'The New Zealand Political Change Project: the Impact of Electoral System Change in a Small Democracy'. The project is supported by the Foundation for Research, Science and Technology. Over the next few years we will be presenting and publishing a series of conference papers, articles and book chapters on various aspects of MMP. Our intention is also to complete a major study of the first few years of proportional representation in New Zealand for publication in about 1999. Through these publications (and in other ways) we hope to contribute to an enhanced understanding of New Zealand's political system in all its dimensions.

Note

1 G. Nelson, 'Biogeography, the Vicariance Paradigm, and Continental Drift', *Systematic Zoology*, 24, 1975, p.494.

CHAPTER 1

New Zealand's changing political identity

New Zealand no longer stands on the brink of 'a new politics' – that time has passed. The 'new politics' promised by campaigners for a new electoral system began the very night that the results were announced, when it became evident that voters had decided in favour of a new means of electing members of Parliament: mixed member proportional (MMP).

Any person, any country, any political system, undergoes experiences which cause it to opt for 'change'. Underlying most forms of political change are developments in seven areas of political, social and human activity:

- national identity
- political culture
- demography
- economic development
- social class
- political parties
- the arts, society and mass culture.

Changes can be seen in each of these areas in New Zealand, as in other societies undergoing major change. The decision to introduce a new electoral system in New Zealand can be seen, of course, as isolated from these developments, in the same way as, for instance, a study of American constitutional conventions can be made simply by concentrating solely on the new rules of governance adopted by a group of delegates meeting in Philadelphia in 1787. Such an approach permits a sharp focus on what the new rules actually state, what they mean, how successful they are likely to be.[1] At the same time, however, looking at a new set of electoral rules without giving at least some attention to wider changes taking place in a society deprives analysis of the context and background necessary for a fuller understanding of electoral system change.

National identity

As with other countries, New Zealand's attachment to a particular institutional framework forms part of the country's image of itself as an autonomous actor within the community of nations. One reason that some New Zealanders favour a move towards a New Zealand republic is that such a change, they suggest, both is compatible with a different national identity and would help to promote values and outlooks distinct from those inherited from the British colonial era. There is little scope for republicans to proceed by attacking operational flaws in the current system; the use of a Governor-General, representing the Crown, has not (in New Zealand, at any rate) caused problems or contributed to any sense of crisis. Rather, the change to a republic is seen as 'appropriate'. As with proposals to end the use of the British honours system,[2] or to terminate the link with the Privy Council in London as New Zealand's highest court,[3] the principal motivations are linked to a sense of the institutional arrangements and political symbols deemed most suited to a contemporary (and future) New Zealand national identity.

In a similar, though more muted, fashion, the move to MMP has implications for national identity. Only a country that has been gradually moving away from its British colonial origins could have considered (in the absence of political crisis or stalemate) transforming its electoral system. The first-past-the-post (FPP) electoral system was derived from British experience.[4] As New Zealand moves towards a more independent and self-conscious identity, so its political structures have come under review. A status quo whose rationale is not ideological, or consciously political, but owes more to instinct and habit, had little chance of surviving a period of sustained criticism.

It is clear, at this point in New Zealand's political and cultural development, that there are some policy initiatives whose significance transcends their specific aims and objectives. These measures, when brought to fruition, acquire meanings beyond the inevitably limited language of statute and regulation. The anti-nuclear policy, for instance, though consolidated in New Zealand legislation and international treaty, in a very short time became a core component of the national self-image.[5] When thinking of New Zealand, or speaking about its character, 'anti-nuclear' becomes a term quickly and comfortably applied. Little wonder that, within only a few years, the policy became irresistible to a National party and parliamentary caucus that had once been so strongly critical of it. If – and it is a very big if – the new electoral system also becomes a success, indeed a point of pride for its equitable character and its effects on policy-making procedure and style, the move away from FPP will be seen as a milestone comparable to the anti-nuclear stance: ending the dependence on an inherited outlook, policies and institutional arrangements, and marking a move towards an indigenously crafted style of governance appropriate to a more mature New Zealand identity.

Political culture

A nation's identity is linked to its political culture. The term 'political culture' suggests that some aspects of a nation's culture have political meanings and implications.[6] Another way of looking at the New Zealand political culture is simply to regard it as comprising the beliefs about politics held by New Zealanders. These 'beliefs' include the ideas, values, feelings and preferences of New Zealanders with respect to politics in all its manifestations – leadership, parties, elections, and, of course, policies. For most of New Zealand's history, and notwithstanding changes from time to time in important areas (including suffrage), New Zealanders seem to have regarded the broad outlines of their electoral system as a more or less immutable part of the political landscape. There is little 'evidence' of this: there is hardly any survey or anecdotal material available on New Zealanders' attitudes towards the method of electing parliamentary candidates. This silence in itself speaks of the electoral system's absence as an 'issue', or problem, through much of New Zealand's political history.

Perhaps the central feature of a nation's political culture relates to *expectations*: the goals, hopes and aspirations its citizens hold about political matters. What a people expect from their nation's politics changes over time. In New Zealand, the expectations about government and politics which people held for decades began to change, in a whole range of policy areas, from the 1970s on. The move to MMP arose out of changing expectations about how parliamentary politics *ought* to be conducted. MMP, in its turn, will undoubtedly bring about further changes in the expectations New Zealanders have about the style and substance of national politics.[7] This process began in the pre-MMP period of disenchantment with the two major parties; and it has continued to develop during the transition to MMP, as existing parties have begun to adapt and new ones have started to emerge.

Demographic changes

Demographic changes have also played their part in the move to a new electoral system. The inevitable ageing of a population whose politics was shaped by the Great Depression and the Second World War opened up the possibilities for new political ideas, factions and personalities to emerge. The weakening of existing party loyalties reflects the rise of new generations; their memories, experiences and outlooks had the effect of making some of the established political attachments seem remote and anachronistic.[8]

In addition to the inevitable attempt by younger generations to reinvent their country's politics to suit their own perceptions, New Zealand has been influenced strongly in recent years by an assertive women's movement[9] and by spokespeople for non-British-derived cultures. Immigration from Pacific Island countries and from Asia has added further complexity to New Zealand's multi-cultural mix.[10] At the same time, the attempt by many Maori – some of them women, some of them young – to assert their Maori heritage in politically meaningful directions has reintroduced (to the extent that it was ever absent) an ethnic factor into the New Zealand political setting.[11] These demographic elements – changes to the character and content of the New Zealand population itself – have also enlarged opportunities for change, making it more difficult for established political parties and institutions to proceed through the 1990s as though the world in which they were formed was destined to go on for ever.

Economic development

A perpetually prosperous New Zealand would be unlikely to experience much pressure for institutional change; boredom is rarely the primary motivating force in a revolution, even a peaceful one. The disappointments and hardships of many New Zealanders from the mid-1970s onwards have elected and unseated governments. The failure of the New Zealand economy to extend the 1960s era of full employment and cradle-to-grave social security endlessly into the future laid much of the foundation for the dissatisfaction with status quo politics which found its culmination in the two referendums endorsing MMP.[12]

Parliament had long been subject to derision; MPs' broadcast speeches, and the spectacle of 'informed debate' which they suggested, have changed little in character, and rarely cause listeners to take pride in their legislative institution. What changed from the mid-1970s – for those New Zealanders who chose not to emigrate in search of a job, a home, a better life in some other country (generally Australia) – was the willingness to take a tolerant attitude towards politicians. Unemployment, inflation and a rising national debt led many New Zealanders to question the judgement and competence of those elected to manage the nation's affairs. From expectations of security to hopes of a steadily rising standard of living, New Zealand slid – in only a very few years – to becoming apparently unable to protect and preserve the well-being of many of its citizens. Political science has often focused on economic performance in predicting and explaining the outcome of elections. In New Zealand's case, successive failures of economic management not only defeated governments but, in addition, played an important role in establishing the basis for voter rejection of the system by which those governments were chosen.

Social class

Related to the dismal performance of the New Zealand economy was the uneven way in which hardship was created. For a country whose view of itself focused sharply on egalitarian values – an important and enduring element of New Zealand's political culture[13] – there was something especially traumatic about the way in which economic dislocation fell more heavily on some groups than on others. Both the women's movement and the development of a more strident Maori political voice owe something to the uneven way in which steadily narrowing economic rewards came to be distributed among the population. Disparate outcomes in so many areas – housing, education, employment, health care, income – when associated with gender and ethnicity, could not help but undermine the credibility of established political institutions, whose ostensible role was to smooth out inequalities.[14]

The development of 'pockets of poverty' throughout New Zealand contributed to the view that parliamentary politics had become trivialised in minutiae and pointless acrimony, at a time when such discourse was self-indulgent. A compromised system of non-consultation, imposed first under one government (Labour), then under its successor (National), could have been tolerated if the economic rewards were distributed more or less equally, to old and young, women and men, Maori and Pakeha. The resentment directed towards corporate New Zealand for its failings – expressed most vividly, perhaps, during the ongoing 'winebox' saga[15] – had its counterpart in the dismay directed at political and bureaucratic New Zealand, apparently unable to introduce policies designed to reduce (rather than accelerate) the economic and social divisions among New Zealanders. An ideology that 'we are all one people', that we are all New Zealanders, seemed empty, even manipulative, set alongside evidence that some New Zealanders were suffering hardship and deprivation while others were growing ever more comfortable.[16]

Political parties

Against this background of dissatisfaction, New Zealand's established party system – acting out its differences of opinion triennially at election time and intermittently in parliamentary debates of indifferent quality – seemed not so much irrelevant as unconstructive. The Labour party was founded during the First World War; the National party was formed towards the end of the Depression. Onto their differing and essentially class-based domestic agendas was to be grafted, in time, differences of outlook on international issues. But the return of large-scale and enduring unemployment suggested that the smug satisfaction with the welfare state – the ostensible solution to mass social and economic hardship – was premature. The end of the Cold War, prefigured in New Zealand by separation from the American-led 'Western alliance', meant that ideological divisions over New Zealand's rightful stance towards the rest of the world had also outlived their usefulness.

There would have been difficulty, in any case, for New Zealanders in maintaining loyalties towards parties whose values and rhetoric dated from superseded domestic and international antagonisms. When those parties failed to deliver the results expected of them – and, in some instances, explicitly promised by them[17] – it was inevitable that people would begin to search for alternatives. New political parties have proliferated over the years: Social Credit, Values, the New Zealand Party, NewLabour, the Greens – to name some of the more intermittently 'successful' of them. The search for political alternatives ended in a cul-de-sac, less because of a return to underlying political loyalties only momentarily discarded than because of the obstacles to success imposed by FPP. New Zealand's system of political parties – now more varied and more complicated than ever before – began to change when the established parties' power to command respect and loyalty began to decline.[18] MMP ensures that, at least for some time to come, experimentation with new parties will continue – but it was the frustrations of New Zealanders already concerned about the need for change, and irritated by the institutional obstacles to it, that contributed to the move to a new electoral system in which challengers to the two long-dominant parties would be given more of an even break.

The arts, society and mass culture

Politically significant developments do not occur within a framework of discussion and competition altogether isolated from other features of a society. Changes in music, theatre, literature, education, film, the arts generally, can help to consolidate, or to undermine, existing patterns of power and influence, and the values and policies associated with them.[19] New Zealand's politics have been influenced and altered profoundly, and repeatedly, by cultural developments beginning elsewhere. This process continued, in a more wide-ranging manner, from the 1960s on.

It is commonly argued that the American voter of the 1930s and 1940s would have been unlikely to elect Franklin D. Roosevelt as President – though he is the only person to have held that office for more than two terms – had television existed at the time. Would Americans, caught up in a depression and then a world war, have been willing to turn to a man in a wheelchair? Most commentators doubt whether they would. Going back to the 19th century, only a very small proportion of the American public ever heard President Abraham Lincoln speak. With a high-pitched, even 'squeaky' voice, he might well have been unelectable, the despair of political handlers faced with selling their candidate on radio and television.

How effective would New Zealand's first Labour Prime Minister, Michael Joseph Savage, be today, faced with radio and television scrutiny as well as the Sunday tabloids? Would he or his successor, Peter Fraser, have been held in the same esteem after years of scrummaging with Paul Holmes or Kim Hill? How 'telegenic' would Premier Richard Seddon ('King Dick') have been?

The introduction of a new means of communication alters many things about a nation's social, economic and political interactions. The adversarial and competitive nature of parliamentary and party politics is complemented by the ultimately adversarial and competitive quality of the media. The capacity of those in government to withstand the sustained scrutiny of the mass media is limited; eventually all political figures have their own weaknesses, and those of their party – deficiencies of policy and personnel – exposed to public view too often for authority to be preserved.

New social movements attract new art forms – and vice versa. In both subtle and explicit ways, New Zealand-based film, television, music and art have helped to corrode and undermine the political values and institutions of post-1935 New Zealand. Although former Prime Minister Robert Muldoon sought at one point to identify himself with contemporary entertainment styles – playing a role in the *Rocky Horror Show* – ultimately the art of the 1970s, 1980s and 1990s has made allegiance to those in authority steadily less plausible. No doubt a cultural turning-point was reached in New Zealand when film audiences no longer rose to 'God Save the Queen' – and when cinema owners and managers ceased to play it.

Fundamental challenges and the future of MMP

A variety of social, economic, artistic, demographic and cultural changes contributed, each in its own way, to New Zealanders' acceptance of an unusual idea – namely, that there were problems of politics and policy which a new voting system might well remedy. The result, eventually, was a decision by the National government to offer New Zealanders an opportunity to vote for change, and a decision by a majority of New Zealanders to do so.

Political science offers various theories and conceptual systems to understand aspects of political behaviour. Among them are broad analytical frameworks to interpret major changes in the way a nation's politics works – and surely MMP, whatever its consequences, involves important changes in the way New Zealand's politics will work. One approach in the academic literature suggests that all governments, all political systems, at some stage in their lives must face, and resolve, five broad problems if they are to survive.[20] In practice these problems, or challenges, are faced not once but repeatedly, as political systems evolve and acquire their unique character and institutional definition.

These fundamental challenges include:

- identity
- participation
- distribution
- penetration
- legitimacy.

These five challenges, like the seven areas of change listed above, provide a prism through which New Zealand's move to MMP can be viewed.[21] We have already commented on identity: the move to MMP can be understood as a part of the process by which New Zealanders have come to emphasise their separateness, not only from Britain, but from the established political institutions and values of the New Zealand past.[22] The changes to our political culture – our expectations of government and politics – are linked to this process of national redefinition.

The challenge of participation derives from the effort to discover the most appropriate relationship between the governed and their rulers. In democratic societies the balance is obviously very different from what prevails in more authoritarian settings. To focus solely on the franchise, the irresistible trend in the history of democratic government has been for its extension and enlargement – from various classes of citizen (property holders, men, those over the age of 21, and so on) to virtually all residents.

The triumph of democratic values and expectations has been so complete that it is difficult, in the long run, for strategies to enlarge public participation to fail in their wider objectives. Satisfaction with the FPP system was consistent not only with a sound economic performance but also with the view that all New Zealanders, irrespective of wealth or place of residence, ethnicity or gender, had equal opportunity (at least in principle) to use their vote in an effective and meaningful manner. The enormous discrepancies between votes and parliamentary seats gained by Social Credit in 1978 and 1981 (see Chapter 2) undermined the view that FPP was 'just' and 'fair'. Once that happened – once FPP was identified as denying proper participation at the ballot box to large groups of New Zealanders – it was probably doomed, particularly when associated with the deep economic crises of the 1980s.

Whether MMP can solve the 'crisis' of participation will influence its longevity as New Zealand's electoral system.[23] If MMP appears to be responsible for denying large groups of New Zealanders the influence to which they feel entitled, because smaller parties (and those who voted for them) have gained an advantage perceived as 'unfair', the moral high ground will shift, and possibly quite rapidly.

The challenge of distribution relates to the ability of the state to ensure equitable economic and social outcomes for all its citizens. The difficulties the established parties have had in accomplishing that objective contributed to the rejection of the system under which they gained office and political power. The evolution of MMP will also be shaped by New Zealanders' perceptions about the capacity of MMP governments to ensure that economic and social rewards are distributed in a way most New Zealanders see as 'fair' and 'just'.[24]

Much of what ideological fervour remains in New Zealand politics revolves around the challenge of 'penetration' – that is, the proper role, size, and functions of the state.[25] Divisions between the major parties, Labour and National, originated in disputes about such matters. In more recent times, much more dramatic intra-party conflict – divisions within the major parties – have focused on this very point. Market liberals dream of a small state, stripped of much of its arsenal of economic and social welfare weaponry, and work to make those dreams a reality. Others see 'laissez faire' as a formula which allows those with the power to help others to escape their responsibilities.

The attractiveness of MMP in the early 1990s arose at least in part out of the stresses felt by many New Zealanders as a result of the fairly single-minded application of the politics of market liberalism. MMP appeared to offer a means by which those unhappy about those policies might yet regain some influence. There was also a measure of revenge against the established parties, held responsible for the excesses of the market liberal approach, in the vote for MMP.[26] In the transition period, new parties – United, ACT, Progressive Greens, Conservatives, Christian Democrats – have also sought to develop answers to questions about the appropriate place for government now. Although some parties are pursuing moral and ethnic agendas, much of New Zealand's politics will remain in essence what it has been for a long time – a succession of disputes arising out of the failure to develop a common view, among public and elites alike, about the proper boundary between the state, society and the individual.

All political systems, if they are to endure, need to persuade those who live under them that the fundamental arrangements for the acquisition, exercise and transfer of power are as they ought to be. The challenge of legitimacy is overcome when all of the other challenges – identity, participation, distribution and penetration – are successfully resolved. When people identify their own destiny with that of their country, when they feel they have sufficient and appropriate opportunities to participate in the making of authoritative decisions about government, when they feel that 'the system' provides reasonably equitable outcomes, there is likely to be a sense that governments have the *right* to govern.

All sorts of failings can sap a system's strength. It is far more difficult to instil a sense that a system is fundamentally fair and sound than to suggest that its defects are palpable and in need of urgent repair. That FPP endured as long as it did suggests that New Zealand, for a very long time, was more or less the way most New Zealanders wished it to be. It also suggests that, whatever dissatisfactions New Zealanders did hold with politics, the system itself, introduced from Britain, was seen as providing a means for British political values – and the British heritage of democratic governance – to be disseminated, and sustained, in a new setting.

The striving for a new political system, more sensitive to indigenous concerns, more acute in its ability to register discordant sentiments, and more skilled in its management of underlying social cleavages, seems to be part of the effort New Zealanders have been making in recent years to develop a new rationale for the political order. A once-ignored treaty has become the country's 'founding document'; from a simple 'nullity' at law the Treaty of Waitangi has developed into a principal constitutional text. A British-derived system of government sits somewhat uneasily astride a polity now committed to 'partnership'. The fading of the imperial past, in which New Zealand took its rightful place, first as colony and then as dominion, has seen the institutions and conventions of that inheritance called increasingly into question.

All of these developments represent a challenge to the legitimacy of the established order. As new generations gain influence, shaped by political and cultural experiences very different from those of the past, the effort to revalidate the existing nation-state – New Zealand, or New Zealand/Aotearoa – may be expected to intensify. By international standards this country is grappling with a crisis of legitimacy in a remarkable way: with little violence and much discussion. The introduction of a new electoral system, intended to be more receptive to minority and indigenous Maori voices, and somewhat divorced from the British adversarial approach to parliamentary politics, is part of the process of building a new polity perceived as legitimate (i.e. with a broadly accepted right to rule) by all. This may not happen. Political integration – the development of a new electoral and parliamentary system based on informed consent – may not occur. If MMP brings in its wake parties that will not co-operate and governments that cannot govern – if, in other words, the idea of government by 'consensus' proves to be a dream too far – there may be a longing for the perhaps more manageable frustrations of life under FPP and the 'pure' Westminster approach.[27]

Conclusion: the new politics – interpreting change

The move to a new electoral system, the basis for a new Parliament and in time a new executive, began formally with the Report of the Royal Commission on the Electoral System. The process by which MMP came to be introduced, and the nature of MMP itself, is reviewed in Chapter 2. Chapter 3 examines the expectations held by many sectors of society about the likely results of the new electoral system, while the following chapters discuss the anticipated effects of MMP on various aspects of the nation's politics: the party system; Parliament, and the means by which governments are formed and the way they operate; the public service; interest groups and the policy process. The final chapter looks ahead to other 'constitutional' changes which New Zealand may well experience in the coming decade, partly in response to MMP, but also as a product of the same social, economic and cultural forces that brought about electoral reform.

This book traces the effects of MMP on all these aspects of New Zealand's politics against the broader interpretive background sketched in this chapter. Where appropriate, the themes and trends, crises and challenges, which underlie New Zealand's quest for a more efficient, effective and equitable electoral system are re-examined in the light of particular developments and opportunities. No set of political rules comes with guarantees, but we can be sure that MMP, New Zealand's unique blend of proportional, constituency and ethnic representation, starts its life with at least the potential to have a major impact on the economic, social, political, ethnic and cultural life of the people of New Zealand.

Notes

1 There is a vast literature on constitutional issues, much of it pertaining to the American experience. Some studies concentrate on the meaning of the constitutional text: see, for instance, J. R. Vile, *A Companion to the United States Constitution and Its Amendments*, Praeger, Westport, Connecticut, 1993; others focus on the circumstances in which the US Constitution came to be written: see, e.g., C. Rossiter, *1787: the Grand Convention*, Macmillan, New York, 1966; while others examine the constitution in a wider context, identifying underlying causes and ongoing consequences: as in M. Kammen, *A Machine That Would Go of Itself: the Constitution in American Culture*, Knopf, New York, 1986. Our introductory chapter looks at the move to MMP in a wider context; Ch. 2 traces the steps by which MMP came to be approved; and the book as a whole describes features of MMP and its impact on various aspects of the political system.

2 See *Report of the Prime Minister's Honours Advisory Committee: the New Zealand Royal Honours System*, Wellington, September 1995.

3 See *Appeals to the Privy Council: Report of the Solicitor-General to the Cabinet Strategy Committee on Issues of Termination and Court Structure*, Wellington, May 1995.

4 The legislation establishing representative institutions for New Zealand was drafted in London by W. E. Gladstone in 1845 and enacted by the British Parliament the following year. See B. Ritchie and H. G. Hoffman, 'The Electoral Law of New Zealand: a

Brief History', in *Report of the Royal Commission on the Electoral System: Towards a Better Democracy*, Appendix A, Government Printer, Wellington, 1986, p.8.

5 A celebration of that self-image, and an account of how the policy came about, is provided by former Prime Minister David Lange in his *Nuclear Free – The New Zealand Way*, Penguin, Auckland, 1990. A contrary view is offered by Ewan Jamieson, formerly Chief of the Defence Staff for the New Zealand Armed Forces, in *Friend or Ally: New Zealand at Odds with Its Past*, Brassey's Australia, Sydney, 1990. Both authors discuss defence policy options with an eye to New Zealand's identity and values: the point is implicit in the sub-title of Lange's book, while Jamieson's opening chapter, 'The Central Issue', includes a section headed 'Sense of National Identity'.

6 The concept of political culture is explored in G. A. Almond and S. Verba, *The Civic Culture: Political Attitudes and Democracy in Five Nations*, Princeton University Press, Princeton, 1963. A useful introduction can be found in W. A. Rosenbaum, *Political Culture*, Thomas Nelson, London, 1975. An overview of New Zealand's political culture, based on survey data, is presented in H. Gold and P. Webster, *New Zealand Values Today*, Alpha, Palmerston North, 1990. Two views of New Zealand political culture are offered in A. D. Robinson, 'The Political Culture', in H. Gold (ed.), *New Zealand Politics in Perspective*, Longman Paul, Auckland, 1985, pp.12–26, and R. Chapman, 'Political Culture: the Purposes of Party and the Current Challenge', in H. Gold (ed.), *New Zealand Politics in Perspective*, second edition, Longman Paul, Auckland, 1989, pp.14–32.

7 S. Ingle discusses how MMP gained support from those who were unhappy with adversarial politics and a lack of government accountability, and hoped that a more consensual form of parliamentary democracy might be fostered through electoral system change. He suggests that such hopes might be disappointed. See S. Ingle, 'Electoral Reform in New Zealand: the Implications for Westminster Systems', *Journal of Legislative Studies*, 1, 4, Winter 1995, pp.76–92. See also R. Mulgan, *Politics in New Zealand,* Auckland University Press, Auckland, 1994.

8 See, by way of contrast, A. Mitchell's observations about 'The Kiwi as a Political Animal' in his *Politics and People in New Zealand*, Whitcombe & Tombs, Christchurch, 1969, Ch. 7, and those of Jack Vowles et al., *Towards Consensus? The 1993 Election in New Zealand and the Transition to Proportional Representation,* Auckland University Press, Auckland, 1995, in Ch. 7, dealing with 'Representation and Trust'. C. James in *The Quiet Revolution: Turbulence and Transition in Contemporary New Zealand*, Allen & Unwin/Port Nicholson Press, Wellington, 1986, draws attention to the importance of generational change not only among New Zealand's voters but among policy-makers (particularly in the fourth Labour government).

9 For an overview of gender issues and political behaviour in New Zealand, see H. Catt and E. McLeay (eds), *Women and Politics in New Zealand*, Victoria University Press, Wellington, 1993.

10 For one treatment of recent immigration patterns, see S. Greif (ed.), *Immigration and National Identity in New Zealand: One People – Two People – Many Peoples?*, Dunmore, Palmerston North, 1995. Many of P. Spoonley's publications, including *Racism and Ethnicity* (Oxford University Press, Auckland, 1993), examine the extent of tolerance in New Zealand for people of differing ethnic backgrounds.

11 The debate over the increasingly contested concept of sovereignty can be seen as a struggle over issues of identity: whose country is this, and what is its name? Recent, contrasting perspectives are found in H. Melbourne, *Maori Sovereignty: the Maori Perspective*, and C. Archie, *Maori Sovereignty: the Pakeha Perspective,* both Hodder Moa Beckett, Auckland, 1995, as well as the essays by R. Walker and A. Sharp, each entitled 'Sovereignty: Te Tino Rangatiratanga', in D. Novitz and B. Willmott (eds), *New Zealand in Crisis*, GP Books, Wellington, 1992, pp.17–33.

12 There have been numerous critiques of the New Zealand economy (in newspapers,

magazines, corporate newsletters, conference papers and presentations) over the years. Some relevant book-length studies (in chronological order) include S. H. Franklin, *Trade, Growth and Anxiety: New Zealand Beyond the Welfare State*, Methuen, Wellington, 1978; J. Gould, *The Rake's Progress: the New Zealand Economy Since 1945,* Hodder & Stoughton, Auckland, 1982; S. H. Franklin, *Cul de Sac*, Allen & Unwin/Port Nicholson Press, Wellington, 1984; L. Bayliss, *Prosperity Mislaid: Economic Failure in New Zealand and what should be done about it*, GP Publications, Wellington, 1994. Works of this kind which have political as well as intellectual interest are R. Douglas, *There's Got to Be a Better Way*, Fourth Estate Books, Wellington, 1980, and R. Douglas and L. Callan, *Towards Prosperity*, David Bateman, Auckland, 1987.

13 The persistence of beliefs that New Zealand is an egalitarian society (a 'notion firmly embedded in the national subconscious') despite much evidence to the contrary is noted in T. Simpson, *A Vision Betrayed: the Decline of Democracy in New Zealand*, Hodder & Stoughton, Auckland, 1984. The relevance and vitality of an egalitarian vision is a central focus of this study.

14 The fourth Labour government appointed a Royal Commission on Social Policy, presumably to identify ways in which the state might assist progress towards reducing hardship and inequalities in a range of social policy areas; its recommendations, however, were ignored, and its multi-volume report became a subject of ridicule among Labour MPs. See Royal Commission on Social Policy, *April Report*, Government Print, Wellington, 1988.

15 The term refers to an inquiry into the use by New Zealand corporations of Cook Islands tax laws so as to reduce their tax liability in New Zealand.

16 For a discussion of the critique by some New Zealand churches of the social cost of government economic policies, see J. Boston and A. Cameron (eds), *Voices for Justice: Church, Law and State in New Zealand*, Dunmore, Palmerston North, 1994.

17 See R. Mulgan, 'The Changing Electoral Mandate', in M. Holland and J. Boston (eds), *The Fourth Labour Government: Politics and Policy in New Zealand*, Oxford University Press, Auckland, 1990.

18 By way of contrast, see the accounts of New Zealand's parties in R. S. Milne, *Political Parties in New Zealand*, Oxford University Press, London, 1966; and B. Gustafson, 'Regeneration, Rejection or Realignment: New Zealand Political Parties in the 1990s', in G. R. Hawke (ed.), *Changing Politics? The Electoral Referendum 1993*, Victoria University of Wellington, Wellington, 1993.

19 Some of the essays in D. Novitz and B. Willmott (eds), *Culture and Identity in New Zealand*, GP Books, Wellington, 1989, draw attention to some of these relationships. See, e.g., the opening and closing essays (B. Willmott, 'Introduction: Culture and National Identity', and D. Novitz, 'On Culture and Cultural Identity') as well as J. Batten, 'Art and Identity', R. Butterworth, 'The Media', I. Snook, 'The Education System' and L. Jones, 'Versions of the Dream: Literature and the Search for Identity'.

20 The scheme is outlined in L. Binder et al., *Crises and Sequences in Political Development,* Princeton University Press, Princeton, 1971. For a comparative study using this approach, see Raymond Grew (ed.), *Crises of Political Development in Europe and the United States*, Princeton University Press, Princeton, 1978.

21 Another perspective on New Zealand's principal challenges can be found in D. Novitz and B. Willmott (eds), *New Zealand in Crisis*, which explores different views on New Zealand's identity, government, economy, race relations, and social welfare issues. An overview of New Zealand's response to various social and economic challenges is in C. James, *New Territory: the Transformation of New Zealand 1984–92*, Bridget Williams Books, Wellington, 1992.

22 There is a substantial reservoir of materials on the New Zealand 'character' and national identity. Among the more influential have been D. Ausubel, *The Fern and the Tiki: an American View of New Zealand National Character, Social Attitudes, and Race Relations*,

Angus & Robertson, Sydney, 1960; G. McLauchlan, *The Passionless People*, Cassell, Auckland, 1976; W. H. Pearson, 'Fretful Sleepers', *Landfall*, 6, September 1952, pp. 201–30. Two recent books explore themes of New Zealand identity and how it is forged: see C. Bell and J. Lyall, *Putting Our Town on the Map: Local Claims to Fame in New Zealand*, HarperCollins, Auckland, 1995, and C. Bell, *Inventing New Zealand: Everyday Myths of Pakeha Identity*, Penguin, Auckland, 1996. To these may be added the many contributions which explore the implications for New Zealand identity of a bicultural and/or multicultural commitment. When changes are made to important policy areas or political institutions, aspects of New Zealand's identity begin to be modified as well. In other words, when we alter our form of government (as in the move to MMP), we ourselves are changed.

23 New Zealanders have traditionally had high rates of voting participation and political party membership. The former has fallen somewhat in recent elections. As for parties, there are more of them yet fewer people belong to one. A weakening involvement with the country's political and community institutions, if not reversed, would suggest a dwindling 'social capital'. See R. Putnam et al., *Making Democracy Work,* Princeton University Press, Princeton, 1993.

24 For perspectives on these issues, see J. Boston and P. Dalziel (eds), *The Decent Society? Essays in Response to National's Economic and Social Policies*, Oxford University Press, Auckland, 1992, and G. R. Hawke (ed.), *A Modest Safety Net? The Future of the Welfare State*, Institute of Policy Studies, Wellington, 1991.

25 Recent contributions to that debate include D. G. Green, *From Welfare State to Civil Society: Towards Welfare that Works in New Zealand,* New Zealand Business Roundtable, Wellington, 1996, and J. Kelsey, *The New Zealand Experiment: a World Model for Structural Adjustment?,* Auckland University Press/Bridget Williams Books, Auckland, 1995.

26 See S. Levine and N. S. Roberts, 'The New Zealand Electoral Referendum of 1992', *Electoral Studies*, 12, 2, 1993, pp.158–67; S. Levine and N. S. Roberts, 'The New Zealand Electoral Referendum and General Election of 1993', *Electoral Studies*, 13, 3, 1994, pp.240–53; and J. Vowles et al., *Towards Consensus?*, Ch. 10.

27 See A. Lijphart, 'The Demise of the Last Westminster System? Comments on the Report of New Zealand's Royal Commission on the Electoral System', *Electoral Studies*, 6, 2, 1987, pp.97–103; and A. Lijphart, *Democracies: Patterns of Majoritarian and Consensus Government in Twenty-One Countries*, Yale University Press, New Haven, 1984.

CHAPTER 2

The new electoral system

In their 1989 comparative study of electoral systems, *Seats and Votes,* Rein Taagepera and Matthew S. Shugart conclude:

> Even if imperfect, a long-established existing electoral system may . . . supply a stable institutional framework for the expression of various viewpoints . . . better than could a new and unfamiliar system, even if it were inherently more advantageous. . . . Familiarity breeds stability. In contrast, introduction of a new electoral system inevitably involves a temporary reduction in stability. Parties, candidates, and voters have to learn new strategies while passing through a period of enhanced surprise, disappointment, and frustration. . . . Major electoral reforms should not be undertaken lightly.[1]

This warning has an unintended irony. New Zealand has indeed changed its 'long-established existing electoral system' – on 6 November 1993, electors voted by a margin of 54 to 46 percent to adopt a new electoral system. The irony is that New Zealand's old electoral system is used throughout the book as a prime example of how electoral systems work because it was 'essentially unchanged over eighty years'. New Zealand, the authors argued, 'is in some ways more British than Britain'.[2]

This chapter briefly examines the reasons why New Zealand discarded its first-past-the-post (FPP) electoral system in favour of a system of proportional representation (PR). It then describes the main features of the country's new mixed member proportional (MMP) electoral system, and how it will operate.

There were three distinct phases in the process of changing the voting system in New Zealand, and the reasons why New Zealand opted for PR at each stage need to be considered in turn.

1986 royal commission

The results of both the 1978 and 1981 New Zealand general elections caused considerable disquiet among various sections of the population. In both elections, the Social Credit Political League won an unusually high share of the votes but gained a low share of the seats (16 percent of the poll and one seat in Parliament in 1978; 20 percent and two seats in 1981). In addition, in both elections the Labour party failed to win power despite winning more votes throughout the country as a whole than the incumbent National government. These results underscored the fact that, on a comparative basis, New Zealand's electoral system ranked 'near the bottom on every measure' of proportionality.[3]

In its 1984 election manifesto, the Labour party promised to appoint a royal commission to examine a range of constitutional questions, including 'whether proportional representation or some other variant from the existing first-past-the-post system should be introduced'.[4] Labour won office in a snap election in July 1984, and in early 1985 the Labour government appointed a five-member Royal Commission on the Electoral System. Despite the somewhat anachronistic language surrounding its appointment – it was formally appointed under the authority of 'Elizabeth the Second, by the Grace of God Queen of New Zealand and Her Other Realms and Territories, Head of the Commonwealth, Defender of the Faith', and chaired by 'Our Trusty and Well-beloved The Honourable John Hamilton Wallace'[5] – it can be argued that the royal commission moved the country not only towards a new electoral system but arguably, in due time, towards other political and cultural changes.

The royal commission had a wide-ranging brief. Its terms of reference entitled it to investigate and report on:

- 'Whether any changes to the law and practice governing the conduct of Parliamentary elections are necessary or desirable';
- 'Whether the existing system of Parliamentary representation . . . should continue or whether all or a specified number or proportion of Members of Parliament should be elected under an alternative system or alternative systems, such as proportional representation or preferential voting';
- 'Whether the number of Members of Parliament should be increased, and, if so, how many additional Members of Parliament there should be';
- 'Whether the existing formulae and procedures for determining the number and boundaries of electoral districts should be changed . . .';
- 'The nature and basis of Maori representation in Parliament';
- 'The term of Parliament';
- 'To what extent referenda should be used to determine controversial issues, the appropriateness of provisions governing the conduct of

referenda, and whether referenda should be legislatively binding';

- 'Whether the present limits on election expenses are appropriate . . . and whether such expenses should be defrayed wholly or in part by State grants and the conditions, if any, which should apply to such grants';
- 'Any other question relating to the electoral system which you may see fit to inquire into, investigate, and report upon.'[6]

The last item emphasised the sweep of the royal commission's mandate. In its 1986 report, the commission considered each of the topics listed above and, in due course, these matters were addressed by the cabinet and Parliament and gained attention from the media, interest groups and the general public. While not every royal commission succeeds in gaining support for its recommendations, this one produced a wide range of important outcomes:

- The number of members of Parliament was increased to 120, effective at the 1996 general election.
- The basis for determining the number of Maori parliamentary seats, and fixing their boundaries, was revised by Parliament. As from 1996, the number of Maori seats will rise by one (i.e. to five) for the first time since they were established in 1867.
- A referendum was held in 1990 on extending the term of Parliament from three years to four – the proposal was defeated, overwhelmingly, as it had been once before (in 1967).
- A measure known as the Citizens Initiated Referenda Act was passed by Parliament in 1993. The first referendum to be held under this law was in December 1995, and organisers have been busy with petitions to submit other subjects to the voters for consideration by referendum.
- Changes have been made to various campaign practices, including overall limits on spending by political parties; and new rules for allocating broadcast time to parties were also put into place.
- Most significant of all, the royal commission reported back to the Governor-General and Parliament with the recommendation that 'the mixed member proportional system . . . should be adopted'.[7]

The royal commission's 10 criteria

What was the basis for this last decision? The royal commission approached its task systematically, adopting from the outset a standard for evaluating electoral systems which it then applied to the existing FPP system and the various alternatives. This embodied 10 criteria:

- '*Fairness between political parties.* When they vote at elections, voters are primarily choosing between alternative party Governments. In the interests of fairness and equality, therefore, the number of seats gained by a political party should be proportional to the number of voters who support that party.

- *Effective representation of minority and special interest groups.* The voting system should ensure that parties, candidates and MPs are responsive to significant groups and interests. To facilitate this, membership of the House should not only be proportional to the level of party support but should also reflect other significant characteristics of the electorate, such as gender, ethnicity, socio-economic class, locality and age.
- *Effective Maori representation.* In view of their particular historical, Treaty and socio-economic status, Maori and the Maori point of view should be fairly and effectively represented in Parliament.
- *Political integration.* While the electoral system should ensure that the opinions of diverse groups and interests are represented it should at the same time encourage all groups to respect other points of view and to take into account the good of the community as a whole.
- *Effective representation of constituents.* An important function of individual MPs is to act on behalf of constituents who need help in their dealings with the Government or its agencies. The voting system should therefore encourage close links and accountability between individual MPs and their constituents.
- *Effective voter participation.* If individual citizens are to play a full and active part in the electoral process, the voting system should provide them with mechanisms and procedures which they can readily understand. At the same time, the power to make and unmake governments should be in the hands of the people at an election and the votes of all electors should be of equal weight in influencing election results.
- *Effective government.* The electoral system should allow Governments in New Zealand to meet their responsibilities. Governments should have the ability to act decisively when that is appropriate and there should be reasonable continuity and stability both within and between Governments.
- *Effective Parliament.* As well as providing a Government, members of the House have a number of other important parliamentary functions. These include providing a forum for the promotion of alternative Governments and policies, enacting legislation, authorising the raising of taxes and the expenditure of public money, scrutinising the actions and policies of the executive, and supplying a focus for individual and group aspirations and grievances. The voting system should provide a House which is capable of exercising these functions as effectively as possible.
- *Effective parties.* The voting system should recognise and facilitate the essential role political parties play in modern representative democracies in, for example, formulating and articulating policies and providing representatives for the people.

- *Legitimacy*. Members of the community should be able to endorse the voting system and its procedures as fair and reasonable and to accept its decisions, even when they themselves prefer other alternatives.'[8]

These criteria – which can be used to assess not only an electoral system but the overall character of a nation's political system – encompass the five 'challenges' noted in Chapter 1. The challenge of identity – the process of forging a distinctive political and national identity, which in New Zealand has arisen gradually out of the colonial and imperial past – is bound up with ensuring 'effective Maori representation' and 'political integration': a genuine politics of inclusiveness. These virtues are also linked to the challenge of participation: ensuring that New Zealand's political institutions are consistent with the democratic values and aspirations to which the country is committed by tradition and conviction. Most of the commission's other criteria – representation of minorities and special interests, fairness between political parties (and those who vote for them), the effective representation of constituents, the effectiveness of voter participation and of political parties – are also associated with the effort to maintain a system which allows people the opportunity to take part in politics and to see their views and interests represented. But there is more to politics, and to a democratic state, than feeling oneself to be a member of a purposeful society (identity) or having opportunities to communicate one's point of view (participation). The royal commission recognised that an electoral system has an important, even decisive, role to play in determining whether the state can carry out its duties. New Zealanders may take the existence of a working political system for granted; many people in other countries do not. The royal commission was concerned, therefore, that its efforts to ensure a 'fairer' electoral and political system were not at the expense of viable government. The twin challenges associated with the use of state power for economic and social ends – distribution (the allocation of rewards and benefits) and penetration (the power of the state to regulate and, where necessary, coerce) – were implicit in the criteria for 'effective Government' ('the electoral system should allow Governments in New Zealand to meet their responsibilities') and 'effective Parliament'. As in the previous chapter, so too in the royal commission's 10 criteria: the value of legitimacy was left to the last. No doubt 'members of the community' will have no serious objections to an electoral system which satisfies the other criteria – the tenth criterion, legitimacy, is effectively achieved when the other nine are realised.

Thus the royal commission, though studying New Zealand's electoral system, did so in a manner consistent with political and theoretical analysis identifying the underlying features making for political change and continuity. In other words, its approach encouraged scrutiny of the fundamental values underpinning New Zealand's political institutions and processes of government. The commission's findings also had important implications for the entire policy-making process, affecting voters, parties, MPs, parliamentary staff, cabinet and the public service. While these themes are considered in subsequent chapters, what should be noted here is how and why MMP, an unusual hybrid system, came to be regarded by both the royal commission and the public as New Zealand's preferred alternative, the system best suited to the criteria, values and challenges noted above.

The electoral system is especially important in a country, such as New Zealand, in which there are so few constraints on the power of the executive: no upper House; no written constitution; no other units of political authority (i.e. states or provinces, as in federal or confederal systems). New Zealand's move to a new electoral system thus acquires even greater importance, since it is often argued that it is principally through the ballot-box that New Zealanders can maintain control over their government in a democratic manner.

1992 indicative referendum

After applying its criteria, the royal commission examined a range of electoral systems. It found that 'both the MMP and the STV [i.e. the Single Transferable Vote, used in Ireland and often regarded as the British form of PR] electoral systems . . . are, because of their proportionality, fair and legitimate in ways that our present single-member system can never be'. However, the commission went on to say, 'Of the [two] proportional systems, MMP and STV, it is our view that for New Zealand MMP is clearly superior', in part because MMP 'is likely to be more closely proportional', and because 'it retains single-member constituencies'. The commission was also concerned about 'the fierce intra-party competition over constituency service experienced under STV in some countries' and the possibility that this might 'seriously undermine MPs' work in parliament'.[9]

One of the unique features of the New Zealand electoral system, Maori representation, received special scrutiny. The commission concluded: 'We are certain Maori representation under MMP would be much better than under the plurality system with or without separate Maori electorates. We have no doubt the Maori people would use the flexibility and opportunities of MMP to ensure that their interests were adequately and effectively represented.'[10]

The commission also recommended that 'a referendum on the adoption of the mixed member proportional system should be held at or before the next general election after 1987'.[11] In mid-1987, at the height of the next general election campaign, the Labour Prime Minister, David Lange, inadvertently promised not only to hold a referendum on the electoral system, but also to make it binding.[12] Once the Labour government had been re-elected, however, it was beset by internal divisions and disputes, and the Prime Minister's pledge to hold a referendum was discarded. In the lead-up to the 1990 election, in an attempt to capitalise on the Labour government's broken promises – and, ironically, in an example of the adversarial politics so deplored by opponents of FPP systems – the opposition National party said that it would 'provide for a binding referendum to be held on electoral law matters prior to the end of 1992, including questions on the method of electing the House of Representatives'.[13]

The National party – which won the Treasury benches in October 1990 – did not keep its word to the letter, but it did hold an indicative (i.e. non-binding) electoral referendum on 19 September 1992. The referendum offered voters two sets of choices. In the first instance, they could say whether (to quote from the voting paper) they wanted 'to retain the present first-past-the-post system' or 'a change to the voting system'. Then, regardless of their choice on the first question (whether they were for or against change), voters could indicate a preference for one of four 'reform options': MMP, STV, preferential voting (as used, for example, to elect members of the lower House of the Australian federal Parliament), and supplementary member (roughly akin to the voting systems then in force in Hungary and South Korea).[14] The results of the September 1992 indicative referendum were dramatic and one-sided. As Labour's Mike Moore (then Leader of the Opposition) noted, 'The people didn't speak . . . they screamed.'[15] Although only 55 percent of registered electors participated in the referendum, nearly 85 percent of them voted for a change to the voting system. More than 70 percent of those who voted chose MMP as their preferred 'reform option'. Full details of the results of the referendum are shown in Table 2.1.

Table 2.1. ***Results of the September 1992 electoral referendum in New Zealand***

	Votes	Percent
Part A		
Vote to retain the first-past-the-post system	186,027	15.3
Vote for a change to the voting system	1,031,257	84.7
	1,217,284	100.0
Part B		
Vote for the supplementary member system (SM)	62,278	5.5
Vote for the single transferable vote system (STV)	194,796	17.4
Vote for the mixed member proportional system (MMP)	790,648	70.5
Vote for the preferential voting system (PV)	73,539	6.6
	1,121,261	100.0
Turnout		55.2

These results were, in large part, an inevitable consequence of strong – indeed, pervasive – anti-government and anti-politician feelings within the electorate. Many voters felt battered and betrayed by the country's major parties after eight years of economic reforms allied with broken promises. The 1992 referendum, held against a backdrop of harsh welfare benefit cuts and during an economic recession, was an opportunity for electors to exact some revenge, and the fact that MMP had been formally recommended by the Royal Commission on the Electoral System gave it an edge over all other electoral options which it was never in any danger of losing.[16]

1993 binding referendum

The results of the indicative referendum committed the government to holding a second, and binding, referendum at the same time as the November 1993 general election. It was a run-off referendum, a straight fight between the FPP and MMP electoral systems.

In both 1992 and 1993, the Minister of Justice appointed an independent Electoral Referendum Panel to ensure that the official public education campaigns for the referendums were 'impartial and unbiased'. The panels were charged with presenting 'the facts on each of the options' so neutrally that their 'task did not extend to the making of any statements on the advantages and disadvantages of each option'.[17] The net effect of such strict objectivity was to reduce the status of the existing plurality system to that of the other voting systems under consideration and, conversely, to give MMP equal legitimacy with FPP during the decisive campaign in 1993.

The 1993 referendum was contested far more strongly than the 1992 referendum. Politicians generally stayed on the sidelines (their support in 1992 for the existing plurality system having been counter-productive), but the presence of two rival pressure groups meant that the issue was highly contentious in 1993. The Electoral Reform Coalition had advocated support for MMP for more than five years; it was opposed by the Campaign for Better Government, a group formed in mid-1993 and led by the chairman of Telecom (New Zealand's largest public company). It was a case of David and Goliath. In the final analysis, the mismatched resources of the two groups worked against the Campaign for Better Government, as some voters linked financial power and vested interests with the plurality cause, and reacted accordingly by voting for MMP. More than 85 percent of electors voted in the second referendum – up 30 percent on the turnout in the referendum 14 months earlier – because it coincided with the election. The final tally in favour of MMP was close but comfortable: see Table 2.2.[18] As a result, New Zealand has now embarked on its historic course away from FPP and towards a version of Germany's system of proportional representation.

Table 2.2. ***Results of the November 1993 electoral referendum in New Zealand***

	Votes	Percent
Vote for the first-past-the-post system	884,964	46.1
Vote for the mixed member proportional system	1,032,919	53.9
	1,917,883	100.0
Turnout		85.2

How MMP works

The new electoral system is called *mixed member* proportional because there will be two types of MPs. The overall number of members of the House of Representatives will be raised from 99 to 120, with 65 MPs representing single-member electorates. There will be 16 South Island general electorates, 44 North Island general electorates, and five Maori electorates in the first MMP Parliament. While subsequent redistributions will doubtless alter the number of North Island general electorates and of Maori electorates, they will not change the number of South Island general electorates, which is a keystone in the 1993 Electoral Act. The 65 electorate MPs will all be elected by simple plurality voting (i.e. by FPP).

However, as well as having a vote for a local electorate MP, voters in New Zealand – as is the case in Germany – will also have a separate vote for a political party. The votes cast for political parties (usually known as 'party votes' or 'party-list votes') will determine their overall share of all the seats in Parliament. In addition to electorate candidates, parties are also able to nominate rank-ordered lists of candidates. A party's complement of electorate MPs will be topped up from its list of candidates until the number of seats it holds in Parliament is in proportion to its party vote. This is why the new electoral system is called mixed member *proportional.*

How the new electoral system will operate can be illustrated with a brief example. If a political party, say Labour, wins 25 percent of the party votes in an election, it will qualify for about 30 of the 120 seats[19] – i.e. a quarter of the seats – in Parliament. If the Labour party has already won 23 constituency (or electorate) seats, then it will be given seven additional seats in Parliament, and these seats will be allocated to the first seven eligible people on the Labour party's rank-ordered list of candidates. (Party-list candidates who are elected in an electorate are, of course, skipped in this process.)

Since, as the royal commission pointed out, Germany 'is the only country to use MMP',[20] it is worth briefly noting some of the similarities and differences between MMP in New Zealand and the model on which it was based. Unlike Germany, where political parties put forward separate lists in all the states (or *Länder*), in New Zealand each party will be able to field only one nationwide list of candidates. However, as in Germany, people can be nominated as candidates both at the electorate level and on their party's list. Just as in Germany, too, there is a five percent threshold which political parties in New Zealand must clear in order to win list seats in Parliament. There is an 'escape' clause to this rule in both countries: in Germany a party which wins at least three district seats qualifies for list seats in the Bundestag, while in New Zealand a party needs to win only one electorate seat in order to acquire additional list seats in the House of Representatives. It should be borne in mind, though, that there are significant differences between the German and New Zealand political systems. For instance, Germany is a federal system, New Zealand is not; Germany has a bicameral legislature, New Zealand's Parliament is unicameral. In addition, of course, there is no German equivalent to New Zealand's separate and parallel system of representation for Maori.

There are also significant similarities between MMP and electoral systems other than Germany's. Indeed, MMP falls into a distinct category of electoral systems: two-tier compensatory member PR systems.[21] As Arend Lijphart notes in his new book, *Electoral Systems and Party Systems*:

> . . . twenty-one PR systems . . . use . . . two-tier districting . . . to combine the advantage of reasonably close voter-representative contact offered by smaller districts with the advantage of greater proportionality and minority representation offered by larger districts.
>
> . . . In . . . fourteen systems . . . the districts at the lower level are used for the initial allocation of seats, but the final allocation takes place at the higher level on the basis of all of the votes cast in all of the lower-tier districts that together make up the higher-tier district. Most commonly, a certain number of adjustment seats are provided at the higher level in order to even out the disproportionalities that may have occurred at the lower level.[22]

In New Zealand this means that 'the initial allocation of seats . . . at the lower level' takes place in 65 electorates (i.e. 60 general and five Maori seats). The 'final allocation . . . at the higher level' is on the basis of the party (or party-list) votes received by each of the political parties contesting the election, and the 55 list seats are the 'adjustment seats . . . to even out the disproportionalities that may have occurred' at the electorate level. Similar adjustments occur in the PR systems used in Denmark, Germany, Norway, South Africa, and Sweden.

Conclusion

At the time of the 1993 electoral referendum, sweeping claims were made on all sides about the dangers New Zealand would face if it were to adopt, or reject, the new electoral system. Indeed, even though New Zealand has not yet held its first MMP election, there have already been significant changes to party and parliamentary politics (see Chapters 4, 5, and 6 in particular). It remains to be seen whether these will have lasting – and possibly deleterious – effects, or whether they are simply 'a temporary reduction in stability' (to quote Taagepera and Shugart).[23] In the next chapter, we look at what a range of opinion leaders in New Zealand consider are the likely short- and long-term effects of MMP.

Notes

1 R. Taagepera and M. S. Shugart, *Seats and Votes: the Effects and Determinants of Electoral Systems*, Yale University Press, New Haven, 1989, p.218.

2 Ibid, p.38.

3 M. Gallagher, 'Proportionality, Disproportionality and Electoral Systems', *Electoral Studies*, 10, 1, 1991, p.45.

4 See K. Jackson, 'The Origins of the Electoral Referendums', in A. McRobie (ed.), *Taking It to the People? The New Zealand Electoral Referendum Debate*, Hazard Press, Christchurch, 1993, p.17; and G. Palmer, *Unbridled Power: an Interpretation of New Zealand's Constitution and Government*, Oxford University Press, Auckland, 1987, p.246. The promise to appoint a royal commission had also been made by Labour three years earlier – see P. Harris and S. Levine (eds), *The New Zealand Politics Source Book*, Dunmore Press, Palmerston North, 1992, p.172.

5 *Report of the Royal Commission on the Electoral System: Towards a Better Democracy*, Government Printer, Wellington, 1986, p.xiii.

6 Ibid, pp.xiii–xiv.

7 Ibid, p.64.

8 Ibid, pp.11–12.

9 Ibid, pp.62–63, 60.

10 Ibid, p.103.

11 Ibid, p.63.

12 Lange apparently made this commitment as a result of an error in his speech notes. See Jackson, 'The Origins of the Electoral Referendums', p.18.

13 See Harris and Levine (eds), *The New Zealand Politics Source Book*, p.205. The process by which electoral system change in New Zealand was set in motion by both Labour and National has thus been aptly characterised as not so much 'a revolution from below [as] an accident from above': Chris Rudd and Ichikawa Taichi, *Electoral Reform in New Zealand and Japan: a Shared Experience?*, Massey University, Palmerston North, 1994, p.11.

14 Further details of the electoral systems under consideration in the 1992 indicative referendum can be found in the official *Guide to the Electoral Referendum*, Electoral Referendum Panel, Wellington, 1992; and in H. Catt, P. Harris and N. S. Roberts, *Voter's Choice: Electoral Change in New Zealand?*, Dunmore Press, Palmerston North, 1992.

15 S. Levine and N. S. Roberts, 'The Referendum Results: "The People Screamed"', in McRobie (ed.), *Taking it to the People?*, p.57.

16 For further details, see S. Levine and N. S. Roberts, 'The New Zealand Electoral Referendum of 1992', *Electoral Studies*, 12, 2, 1993, pp.158–67.

17 Electoral Referendum Panel, *Report of the Electoral Referendum Panel on the Public Information Campaign organised in conjunction with the Electoral Referendum held on 6 November 1993*, House of Representatives, Wellington, 1993, p.3.

18 For further details, see S. Levine and N. S. Roberts, 'The New Zealand Electoral

Referendum and General Election of 1993', *Electoral Studies*, 13, 3, 1994, pp.240–53; and especially J. Vowles, P. Aimer, H. Catt, J. Lamare and R. Miller, *Towards Consensus? The 1993 Election in New Zealand and the Transition to Proportional Representation*, Auckland University Press, Auckland, 1995.

19 The exact number of seats each party will be entitled to in an MMP Parliament will be determined by the Sainte Laguë electoral formula. Parties that qualify for seats in Parliament will have the number of votes they receive in a general election divided by successive odd numbers — 1, 3, 5, 7, 9, 11, etc. The resultant quotients will then be ranked in order from the highest quotient (which will, of course, be exactly the same as the number of votes won by the political party with the most party-list votes in the election) to the smallest quotient (i.e. the 120th-highest quotient). These quotients will then determine both the number of seats each party is entitled to and the order in which seats are allocated to the political parties. See Appendix 2 for further details of how the Sainte Laguë formula works. Readers may also wish to consult *Referendum '93: Media Handbook*, Electoral Referendum Panel, Wellington, 1993, pp.41–44; and *The Referendum. The Guide*, Electoral Referendum Panel, Wellington, 1993, pp.12–13.

It should also be noted that there could, on occasion, be either more or less than 120 seats in an MMP Parliament. If a party wins more electorate seats than it is entitled to as a result of its party vote, it will not lose any seats. Thus, if a party wins 32 electorate seats but its party vote entitles it to only 30 seats in Parliament, it will keep its 32 seats and for the life of the next Parliament there will be 122 seats in the House of Representatives. On the other hand, there would be fewer than 120 seats in Parliament if a party's list of nominated candidates was shorter than the number of party-list seats to which it was entitled. For example, in the event that a party entitled to nine list seats in Parliament were to have a list of nominated candidates of only seven names, the overall number of seats in the next House of Representatives would be reduced to 118.

20 *Report of the Royal Commission on the Electoral System*, p.36.

21 J. Elklit and N. S. Roberts. 'A Category of Its Own? Four PR Two-Tier Compensatory Member Electoral Systems in 1994', *European Journal of Political Research*, 30, 2, 1996.

22 A. Lijphart, *Electoral Systems and Party Systems: a Study of Twenty-Seven Democracies, 1945–1990*, Oxford University Press, Oxford, 1994, pp.30–32.

23 Taagepera and Shugart, *Seats and Votes*, p.218.

CHAPTER 3

The effects of MMP: the expectations of opinion leaders

Debates about MMP suggest that there are two competing visions of New Zealand post-MMP.[1] One sees the new system as a means for promoting a more co-operative, consensus style of government, free from childish political games or the ruthless exercise of power. This view of MMP sees the policy process, in Parliament and other settings, being characterised by consultation, compromise and consent. The competing view, emphasised by those unhappy with the possibility that smaller parties may gain power and influence far in excess of their support in the New Zealand electorate, is that under MMP politicians and political party functionaries are going to become even less accountable than under FPP. This vision of MMP foresees pre- and post-election deals, broken promises, unanticipated coalition agreements, small parties extorting power from larger ones – 'a state', as Sophocles wrote in *Electra*, in which 'one cannot be moderate and restrained nor pious either'.

The truth probably lies not so much in the centre between these two visions, as fluctuating towards one pole, then another, depending on the election returns. At times there may be relatively little change in practice or in policy outcomes – if, for instance, National were to win the 1996 election with sufficient support to govern on its own, or with a junior partner with whom it shared a broad ideological affinity. At other times, however, there will be dramatic discontinuities as outsiders, eager for change, grasp the reins of government.

Elite expectations

All those with an interest in MMP no doubt have had some idea of what actually having MMP would be like. Of course, many people who voted in the 1992 and 1993 referendums will by now have forgotten what they thought the effects of MMP would be. At the time of those two referendums the most important set of predictions about MMP – expectations about the effects of an experiment with an electoral system – were in the minds of the voters themselves. Although largely unarticulated, those imaginings led New Zealanders to vote either for or against what was for them (notwithstanding observations on how PR works in Germany) an entirely speculative system.

Now that MMP is being introduced, possibly the most important expectations about what it will be like are in the minds of the people who will work most closely with the new system. These include MPs, cabinet ministers, senior parliamentary staff, senior public servants, and the media. What others concerned with the results of policy-making – such as economists and lawyers, bankers and insurance company officials, union representatives and ethnic community leaders, political party organisers and political scientists – expect from MMP is also now especially pertinent. As in any endeavour, what people get from a system is influenced by what they expect from it. Expectations condition behaviour: how MMP will work – whether it is more likely to fulfil the promise of the first vision above, or betray that promise, as in the less hopeful outlook of the second – depends to some extent on the view of it taken by the 'opinion leaders' most closely connected with its implementation.

As a result, in September 1995 we decided to organise a survey of selected groups of New Zealanders. This was not a public-opinion study representative of the entire electorate; rather, it was designed to elicit the views and expectations about the likely consequences of MMP among those most continually involved in the political decision-making process. Clearly, establishing a record of their expectations *before* MMP was formally introduced was important. While one could ask people about the consequences of MMP later on, it would not, at that stage, be possible to discover what they had earlier expected. Reliance on 'restored' or 'recovered' memories is apt to be an imperfect guide to the truth.

Survey themes and responses

The survey of the views of opinion leaders was carried out in November–December 1995 using a written questionnaire. The overall response rate – 71 percent – was especially high. Indeed, the participation among some groups was overwhelming: members of the executives of political parties (89 percent), chief executives of the departments and ministries in the public service (85 percent), heads of interest groups (83 percent), trade union leaders (83 percent), and education leaders (79 percent).[2]

The questions focused on the participants' expectations of political and parliamentary life under MMP. The instructions stated:

- 'This questionnaire has no right or wrong answers. We want to know *your* views – what *you* think is likely to happen under MMP.

- We recognise that a lot can change between now and the next election. We are interested in *your current views*; your expectations *as of now* about what is likely to occur under MMP.'[3]

The questions fell neatly into eight categories:

- what sort of Parliament is likely to be elected;
- what kind of government is likely to be formed;
- how cabinet will be affected;
- the consequences for the running of Parliament;
- how interest groups will fare;
- the implications for public policy;
- whether any other 'constitutional' changes are likely for New Zealand;
- whether MMP itself is likely to endure.

The themes covered by the survey correspond to those considered elsewhere in this book. Some of the questions looked at the effects of MMP on the democratic process and the opportunities for participation in policy-making. Others encouraged respondents to reflect on the likely implications of MMP for the role of the state and its potential for redistributive activity on behalf of disadvantaged groups. The reshaping of New Zealand's political identity is considered in questions dealing with other prospective constitutional changes, while a question on the future of MMP – is it likely to last? – deals directly with the theme of the new electoral system's legitimacy.

The questions also asked respondents, in effect, whether the royal commission's criteria (see Chapter 2) were likely to be achieved under MMP. The responses to these questions suggest a good deal of uncertainty about the results MMP will actually bring for New Zealanders – a reminder that every policy initiative is something of a gamble, that social policy is an inexact 'science', and that there is rarely enough evidence to determine, unequivocally and comprehensively, the consequences of a policy proposal before its implementation.[4]

Composition of the first MMP Parliament

The first set of questions focused on Parliament: in broad terms, how would MMP affect its composition? At the 1993 election, four political parties gained seats in Parliament – National, Labour, the Alliance and New Zealand First. Most of those surveyed foresaw little change in 1996: 46 percent expected four parties to be represented, and 32 percent five. If either of those views proves correct, some of the parties and individuals currently in the House will not be there after 1996, because, by mid-1995, there were *seven* parties in the New Zealand Parliament, including United, the Conservatives and Christian Democrats.

The National government improved its popularity significantly during 1995. By the end of the year there were signs that it might be able to win the next election and so, even under MMP, govern on its own. The timing of the survey coincided with that mood: 94 percent of those polled thought National would 'have the largest number of seats' in Parliament after the first MMP election.

Women and Maori

The royal commission hoped that MMP would open up greater opportunities for women and for Maori to enter Parliament. Since the commission's report, there has already been a steady increase in the number of women elected to Parliament – up from 13 percent in 1984 to 21 percent in 1993.[5] Survey participants were asked whether they thought 'the proportion of women MPs in the first MMP Parliament' would rise, fall or stay about the same. Few (5 percent) thought there would be fewer women in Parliament; in fact, a majority (53 percent) thought that MMP would have the intended effect of increasing the number of women MPs.

As for the number of Maori MPs, the previous chapter noted that the number of Maori electorates will increase by one with the introduction of MMP. In addition, a number of Maori were elected to Parliament in general electorates in 1993. The survey found that 57 percent of respondents considered it likely that the number of Maori elected in the first MMP Parliament would be 'more than were elected in 1993' – again, the effect intended by the royal commission.[6]

Likely kinds of government under MMP

Many advocates of MMP hoped that smaller parties (and those they represent) would gain a share in government and policy-making. Until 1995 there seemed little prospect of any single party gaining the necessary support to govern on its own under MMP. During the 1980s and early 1990s, when MMP and other PR alternatives were being considered, there was little expectation that the type of government to which New Zealanders had become conditioned – single-party majority government (i.e. one party in control of Parliament with a majority of the seats) – would occur under MMP. Indeed, that was the point of changing to a new electoral system for many of its proponents. Coalition governments seemed a logical alternative to the form of government New Zealand had been experiencing, a desirable alternative to the 'Muldoonism', 'Rogernomics' and 'Ruthenasia' which had characterised the previous decades.[7]

However, as detailed in Chapter 6, there is a broader range of government options. There can be single-party majority government, single-party minority government, multi-party (i.e. coalition) majority government, and multi-party (coalition) minority government. Among these four categories, which type of government is most likely under MMP?

A minority government is inherently precarious. It would seem, in theory, the least likely outcome, particularly for New Zealand, a country used (by theory and practice) to *majority* rule. Only 27 percent thought that some type of minority government was likely. On the other hand, the single-party majority administration (as New Zealand has had from the 1930s through to 1994) was considered 'most likely' by an even smaller proportion: 16 percent. The majority, 56 percent, felt that MMP was likely to bring about a coalition government – but a coalition with a majority in the House.

Most people accept that the first MMP election will usher in a settling-in period, a further time of transition under which new conventions will be established, new voting patterns become entrenched, and new party alignments gradually take shape. What about the longer term, therefore, the period beyond the first MMP election? Is it likely that the type of government in New Zealand will remain a coalition? Interestingly, most survey respondents thought it would. There is no coalition culture in New Zealand at present; coalitions are seen as an oddity, an aberration, an approach to governance which needs some thought. But 76 percent of those surveyed thought multi-party majority coalitions would become the norm in New Zealand, and there was little expectation that the country would return to single-party majority governments, at any rate under MMP.

For most New Zealanders, however, the important questions of politics are not the number of parties in Parliament or government, but what sort of policies the parties in power are likely to pursue. This in turn depends largely on the ideological direction of the government. As noted, some commentators and voters see MMP as an opportunity for small and even extreme groups to hold the government (and the public) to ransom. Was this vision common among the opinion leaders participating in the survey?

Most of them expected a centre–right government after the first MMP election: 82 percent expected National 'to form the first MMP government'. Those who expected a coalition government generally saw United (mentioned by 23 percent as likely to be part of that 'first MMP government') as National's probable coalition partner. Others saw Labour (24 percent), the Alliance (20 percent) and New Zealand First (12 percent) as possible participants in an MMP-elected government.

The picture was little different for the longer term: most of those polled saw a centre–right, or a centre, government for New Zealand in the medium to long term. Very few (about 1 percent in each case) thought that either right-wing or left-wing 'extremes' were likely to form a government either in the aftermath of the first election or subsequently.[8] On the other hand, nearly half the sample thought that under MMP 'the tenure of governments' would be 'shorter'.

The structure and operations of the executive

Many of those who supported the introduction of MMP hoped that it would reduce the power of the executive *vis-à-vis* Parliament. Certainly, the issues of a dominant executive and, within that locus of power, an overly powerful Prime Minister have been staples of New Zealand politics since at least the Muldoon years.[9] The question of cabinet's power in relation to the historic prerogatives of Parliament remains of interest to many commentators and is at times articulated in editorials and letters to the editor. Policy-making catastrophes of one form or another (such as the Cave Creek tragedy)[10] ensure that issues of ministerial responsibility always resurface for public attention.

Some exponents of MMP thought that a larger Parliament, and possibly a smaller cabinet, might be one way of reversing the drift of power towards the executive.[11] The larger Parliament is a fact; it will be achieved in the first MMP Parliament (with 21 more MPs than the current one). But will cabinet be smaller? Or will coalition agreements require the distribution of more portfolios, to satisfy backbench MPs and the ambitions of smaller parties?

Half of those who responded to our questionnaire thought cabinet would probably be not 'significantly different from its present size', but few thought that it would get 'smaller than at present' and a third that it might be 'larger than at present'. But what sort of cabinet would it be? One that maintained a unified posture on questions of policy? Or one prone to division and disunity?

Expectations were that 'the convention of collective cabinet responsibility' would be 'weakened' – 63 percent of respondents expected a very different type of cabinet from that which New Zealanders (but not residents of some other countries with coalition governments) have come to expect. A question probing the likely effect of MMP on 'the convention of individual ministerial responsibility' – a convention under siege following Cave Creek – produced a much less one-sided result. While a third foresaw little change from the present, opinion was divided as to whether individual ministers would become more 'responsible', in the traditional sense, or less.

There was little dissent, however, about the shifting power-balance between cabinet and Parliament. Most respondents expected a weaker cabinet and a stronger Parliament – 77 percent thought that under MMP 'the cabinet will have less control over Parliament'. Only 6 percent thought that the control of cabinet over Parliament might increase under MMP.

The role and operations of Parliament under MMP

But whether Parliament itself is *really* likely to change under MMP – in some respects, the whole point of the switch to MMP was to change Parliament – is problematic. Are we really on the threshold of 'a new politics'? Or is this just another case of old wine being poured into extravagantly overrated new bottles?

Questions about the role of Parliament were included in the survey. Most participants, consistent with the view of cabinet having 'less control', saw Parliament enhancing its position in the policy process. In particular, and fulfilling Sir Geoffrey Palmer's vision of the select committee system being the heart of the reform process,[12] 83 percent of respondents expected Parliament's select committees to acquire 'a greater role in scrutinising legislation', and 72 percent 'a greater role' for Parliament's committees 'in scrutinising the operations of the executive'.

Under single-party governments (when all other parties are in opposition), it is natural to expect the executive to dominate Parliament through the party's parliamentary caucus. Some commentators expect party control over MPs to increase under MMP, due in part to the power of parties over the compilation of the party list. Others, however, focusing solely on parties in government, see the power of the executive declining *vis-à-vis* MPs. Will MMP see greater autonomy for MPs? Or will party discipline need to be stronger, in order that members adhere to coalition agreements and multi-party bargains crafted by party leaders?

Amid these multiple scenarios, outcomes are inevitably difficult to predict. A plurality (43 percent) of respondents thought party discipline would be 'weaker than in the past'. But 28 percent thought it would probably be 'stronger', while 23 percent saw little prospect for change.

A more complex process of policy-making was foreseen, however. It was widely expected that opposition parties would gain 'a greater role in the making of public policy' (73 percent) and that – given the enlarged roles for opposition parties and for select committees, and the weaker role of cabinet over the direction of Parliament – 'the passage of legislation through Parliament will be slower than in the past' (79 percent). A more deliberative legislative assembly, if that eventuates, will be very different from the body described by Palmer as one which 'passes too many laws and . . . passes them too quickly'.[13]

Other participants in the political system

Under some New Zealand governments, interest groups have had good access to ministers and senior public servants. Other administrations, notably that of the fourth Labour government (1984–90), have been more resistant to bargaining and the granting of concessions to groups and their leaders.[14] The perceived indifference of Labour and National governments to the needs of those affected by free-market policies was a factor in the build-up of anger among electors and the vote for MMP in the two referendums.[15] MMP was widely reported as being more likely to give opportunities for groups to take part in policy-making. For some, that was a reason to *oppose* MMP – the gains of single-minded adherence to principle would be compromised by the special pleading of groups with their own agendas to pursue. Others saw all this as a positive feature, a chance to open up the policy-making process and bring about a more consultative, democratic style: more compassionate and more caring.

Those taking part in this survey expected MMP to break down some of the barriers between policy-makers and those affected by their decisions. A 'greater role in the policy-making process' for interest groups was foreseen by 72 percent. A wide range of groups are expected to benefit from MMP, including those concerned about the environment and social issues. Others are expected to lose influence. Interestingly, some thought that the access of the Business Roundtable to decision-makers might decline, while others predicted the opposite.

One of the results of opening up the policy process to more participants, of course, is that those at present perceived to be in control are expected to surrender some of their power. During the 1980s and 1990s, in particular, and during earlier periods of governance as well, the Treasury, the Reserve Bank, and associated consultants were resented for their control by those unhappy with the direction of government policy. Some survey participants (26 percent) expected that MMP would see 'senior public servants' with 'a lesser role in the policy-making process'. However, 33 percent thought that their role would increase, while 31 percent envisaged little change. Opinions were far less divided on whether 'non-departmental political advisers' were likely to have their role in the policy-making process enlarged under MMP: fully 60 percent thought this likely to happen. If this indeed proves the case, it will represent an extension of recent trends which have seen governments by-pass the public service in favour of overtly political appointees.

Policy outcomes under MMP

How MMP will affect the policy-making process itself may also be regarded as in some sense the object of the entire electoral reform exercise. The purpose of a new electoral system, for many, was not to 'reform' an abstract set of rules about how people vote, or even to refashion Parliament for its own sake. Rather, it was to have new voting procedures, and a new type of Parliament, *in order to* bring about new government policies. Is this likely to be the result? Or is MMP, in the end, likely to change very little?

While it was impossible to survey expectations towards *all* policies, several policy areas have gained greater attention – or notoriety – in recent years. Many of these arise out of a particular free-market ideological persuasion which sees the role of the state declining and the marketplace itself providing the best means for redistributive and expansionary policies. In this view, New Zealand's identity is more libertarian than communitarian or corporatist; the legitimacy of laws and regulations which circumscribe individual opportunity and discretion is questioned, and the responsibility for the expansive use of state power in New Zealand in the past is attributed in part to excessive opportunities for participation in policy-making by individuals and sector groups. All of these major themes of politics can be glimpsed in the several questions about policy outcomes under MMP.

Most survey participants envisaged an MMP environment in which sector groups and smaller parties succeed in reversing some of the policies implemented by market liberals under National and Labour, especially between 1984 and 1993. For instance, the size of the state was expected to grow, not shrink – 58 percent expected 'a higher level of public expenditure as a percentage of GDP'.

Where the funds for increased public spending were to come from under MMP seems less clear. 'Higher top marginal tax rates' – a policy preference associated most closely with the Alliance, a possible participant in post-MMP coalition agreements – were expected by 34 percent of survey respondents. But 36 percent expected 'no change', while 7 percent thought that 'lower top marginal tax rates' were possible under MMP.

As for the cornerstone of National's labour market policy, the Employment Contracts Act, the status quo was not expected to survive MMP unscathed. Only 16 percent thought 'the introduction of MMP will result in no changes' to the Act. Likewise, a comparably sized group (12 percent) anticipated 'major changes'. The majority (56 percent), however, expected only 'minor changes'. The centrepiece of successive governments' anti-inflation policy, the Reserve Bank Act, was seen as more secure: 40 percent expected 'no changes' to the Act (in fact the inflation target of two percent can be adjusted without amending the legislation), while 35 percent predicted 'minor changes'. The Fiscal Responsibility Act, the final contribution to the statute books of former finance minister Ruth Richardson, was also not seen as under threat. The measure, which commits New Zealand governments to debt repayment and a balanced budget, was generally not expected to be changed (42 percent), other than perhaps in 'minor' ways (31 percent).

What, 'on balance', the implications of MMP are likely to be for overall policy stability proved difficult to assess, however. Slightly more opinion leaders (28 percent) thought that MMP would actually *increase* 'policy stability' than expected it to have relatively no effect (27 percent), while 34 percent expected 'less policy stability'.

Constitutional and other issues

The FPP system endured (with some modifications) for most of New Zealand's political history. There have been many other changes: to the role of the state, and its place in providing for individual welfare needs; to the party system; to the franchise; to the relationship between Maori and non-Maori. The electoral system also acquired new features: Maori seats; the secret ballot; women's suffrage; the independent Representation Commission; the 'entrenched' position for some aspects of electoral legislation. Such a history suggests that the most likely future for MMP is for it to be subject to revision, to modification, to the tinkering to which New Zealand law-makers have long been accustomed. Indeed, it is notable that the MMP Act – i.e. the 1993 Electoral Act – has already been subject to not insignificant amendments, the most substantial of which was altering the ballot paper to move the electorate vote from its position above the party-list vote.

The electoral system

The legislation establishing MMP commits New Zealand's Parliament (so long as the legislation is not amended) to appoint a select committee to review MMP as soon as possible after April 2000; the committee's report, including any recommendations for change, must be made before June 2002. Given that MMP has, at least in principle, a sunset clause (that is, a built-in date for review and possible termination) – and that much of the publicity about MMP since the 1993 referendum has been negative (relating especially to the accumulation of small parties in Parliament) – whether MMP has much of a future is an appropriate question. Is this a system to which behaviour needs to adapt? Or need it only be patiently endured, and for a relatively short while at that?

Just under half the respondents thought that 'the new MMP system will prove to be relatively durable' – in other words, that 'it will last for several decades or more'. Apart from any negative perceptions of MMP, however, there may be legitimate scepticism about the ability of *any* new political arrangements to endure for so long any more. In any case, 28 percent doubted whether MMP would survive for that long, while 22 percent could not say.

If not MMP, then what? A range of choices formed part of the 1992 indicative referendum (see Chapter 2),[16] and the question of similar alternatives to MMP was considered by the people we surveyed. Of those who don't expect MMP to last, most envisaged a return to FPP, although the Single Transferable Vote (STV) option, which finished in second place in 1992, was thought by nearly as many respondents to be the most likely successor. Indeed, in response to the question 'what kind of electoral system would be your first choice for New Zealand?', STV (24 percent) was slightly ahead of both MMP (23 percent) and FPP (23 percent).

Whatever their ideal electoral system preference, most respondents (56 percent) thought that MMP 'will enhance the democratic process'. A far smaller group (15 percent) thought that it 'will weaken the democratic process' – a sign that, notwithstanding various misgivings, the participants in this survey of opinion leaders generally regard MMP as consistent with democratic values, indeed enhancing them. It would seem, therefore, that MMP has already acquired considerable legitimacy during the transition period.

The Crown in contention

One of the problematic features of the New Zealand system of government has always been the role of the Crown.[17] This has proved awkward with respect to Treaty of Waitangi issues, almost from the outset, and has been an element in thinking about constitutional change in recent times. Constitutional ambiguity has also surrounded the role of the representative of the Crown – i.e. the Governor-General. It has generally been accepted that a more proportional electoral system *may* lead to more delicate situations in which the Governor-General has to determine whether or not a particular Prime Minister has the confidence of the House. How MMP may already have affected perceptions of the discretionary powers of the Governor-General was also considered in this survey. While 37 percent thought that 'Governors-General are more likely to use their reserve powers (i.e. to act without, or contrary to, the advice of the Prime Minister)', 47 percent rejected that view. Given the infrequency with which New Zealand Governors-General have become involved in the political process, or have made use of such 'reserve powers' as they are believed to hold, even 37 percent is a very high figure. Under FPP, expectations of the Governor-General's using those powers would almost certainly have been close to nil.

An associated issue for New Zealanders interested in constitutional or symbolic topics – apart, of course, from treaty-related matters – has to do with republicanism. Other matters, such as the place of the Privy Council and the honours system in New Zealand, are linked to this debate. Beginning under the then Labor Prime Minister of Australia, Paul Keating, and extended in New Zealand under National's Prime Minister, Jim Bolger, the question of either country becoming a republic has been placed firmly on the agenda. Difficulties for the British Royal family have helped to keep the topic on the table.

The separation of New Zealand from its United Kingdom origins has moved progressively from one category of linkage to the next (see Chapter 1). In *economic* terms, British entry into the European Community in 1973 gave a huge impetus to cutting ties with New Zealand. Guarantees of *military* security collapsed in 1942 with the fall of Singapore. The Statute of Westminster, enacted by Britain in 1931 and adopted by New Zealand in 1947, weakened the formal *political* ties between the two. But psychological and cultural links have remained important. Irrespective of whether New Zealand becomes a republic, these will still be significant. Nevertheless, the topic, bound up with questions of identity and loyalty, oaths of allegiance and national heritage, cannot but be an emotional one for many.

The proposition that New Zealand become a republic was supported by 49 percent of the survey respondents. Those opposed to the change to a republic were by no means negligible (34 percent) and a further 17 percent were unsure or wouldn't say.

How likely is it, then, that New Zealand will actually become a republic? Opinion leaders were evenly split in their predictions: 44 percent thought a New Zealand republic within 10 years was 'likely', while 43 percent thought it 'unlikely' (the rest either couldn't say or didn't know). This was the only constitutional change which a majority (albeit exceptionally slim) considered might happen.

Other scenarios

The introduction of MMP, important as it has already proven to be for so many dimensions of the political system – the party system, Parliament, the public service – does not by itself bring an end to the process of development and change. No single initiative ever does; politics is an ongoing human activity. There are still many unresolved political questions, some of them relating to MMP, others dealing with broader issues. Some of these constitutional topics were canvassed in the survey in two ways: first, through a question asking 'which of the following constitutional changes, if any, do you support?'; and, second, by a question more consistent with the survey generally, focusing on expectations, 'which of the following constitutional changes, if any, do you think likely within the next decade?'

Former Prime Minister Geoffrey Palmer's valedictory speech to the House in 1990 called for a cabinet system more elastic than New Zealand has at present.[18] The retiring former Labour leader recommended giving Prime Ministers the opportunity to go outside Parliament in selecting cabinet ministers, a proposal previously put forward by some political scientists as well.[19] Our sample of opinion leaders rejected that (by 57 to 33 percent) and only 12 percent thought that it was likely to be introduced within 10 years.

The sample was divided (39 percent in favour, 35 percent opposed) about the desirability of 'a clearer separation of the executive and Parliament (e.g. as in Norway, Sweden and the Netherlands, but not as in the United States)'. This was probably the most technical question in the entire survey, and only 19 percent thought such a development likely.

The seemingly perennial topic of the four-year parliamentary term attracted the support of 65 percent of the sample. Not surprisingly, however, given its rejection at two referendums (in 1967 and 1990), most were pessimistic about its being introduced – only 25 percent thought 'a four-year parliamentary term' likely.[20]

New Zealand has had little experience with early elections. National called one in 1951 over its handling of the waterfront dispute and was re-elected with an increased majority.[21] Prime Minister Robert Muldoon's 'snap' election on Bastille Day (14 July) in 1984 proved less happy for him, as it 'liberated' New Zealanders from his government (and the Prime Minister from the burdens of office) and ushered in a six-year term for Labour.[22] A fixed parliamentary term which limited the government's ability to call early elections would represent an important constitutional initiative. Only 27 percent of the sample supported such a restriction on the government's powers, however, and only 13 percent thought such a development 'likely'.

Voting under MMP

The survey was completed by leaders of different sectors of New Zealand society. Their perceptions of MMP – and, more particularly, their assessment of its likely benefits and shortcomings – were by no means uniform. There were some consistent and significant differences in the political perceptions of people in different sectors.[23]

The very last question in the survey asked participants about their voting intentions under MMP: 'which political party would you vote for if a general election were held today?' Naturally, the survey recorded both the party vote and the electorate vote.

The results appear in Table 3.1. Following the trends in recent opinion polls among the public as a whole, National has a commanding lead over Labour and the Alliance. Labour, though, recovers some lost ground in the electorate vote – as is the case in opinion polls generally. However, at a time when New Zealand First was polling around 5 percent throughout the country, it is significant that the party had much more limited appeal in our survey of sector leaders.

When we analyse the partisan preferences of different categories of survey participants – i.e. when we consider the voting intentions of senior public servants as compared with, say, business leaders — we find very different

Table 3.1. *The MMP voting intentions of opinion leaders*

	Party vote %	**Electorate vote** %
National	36	31
Labour	18	22
Alliance	14	11
United	5	5
ACT	4	1
New Zealand First	2	2
All others	4	2
Don't know/Won't say	17	26
(number of respondents)	*(1145)*	*(1145)*

patterns of response, however. For instance, two-thirds of the business leaders polled said they would give their party vote to the National party, as would nearly half the senior public servants. But not one business person said they would vote for the Alliance. Similarly, only two out of 166 senior public servants were willing to give the Alliance their party vote. By contrast, only 14 percent of interest (or pressure) group leaders were inclined to vote National; 32 percent of them favoured Labour and a further 29 percent the Alliance.

While ACT rated 4 percent among the sample as a whole (and at the same time was at 2 percent nationwide),[24] one in eight of our respondents from the business sector said they would vote for the party. Business support for United New Zealand (7 percent) was also more substantial than in opinion polls. Indeed, if *all* New Zealanders took the same view of these parties, both of them would cross the five percent MMP threshold comfortably.

Conclusion

We began this chapter by noting that there were at least two different broad perspectives on New Zealand's new electoral system. The survey findings provide further evidence for this. Most countries do not have questions about their voting system high on the political agenda. Not surprisingly, however, New Zealanders do not yet take their new system, MMP, for granted. There will remain some uncertainty about how it will work in practice at least until the first election is held and the first MMP government takes office. Whether that virtually halts concern or exacerbates existing apprehensions depends, of course, on how those processes are conducted and the outcomes they produce. That will be influenced, in turn, by the nature of the changes which MMP brings to the party system. As we shall see in the next chapter, with the approach of the first MMP election the stability of New Zealand's parties has been disrupted, in some cases dramatically.

Notes

1 For a useful digest of political and editorial opinion about MMP at the time of the first referendum (1992), see A. McRobie (ed.), *Taking It to the People? The New Zealand Electoral Referendum Debate*, Hazard Press, Christchurch, 1993.

2 Questionnaires were sent to 1,605 people; 1,145 responded.

3 All quotations in this chapter in relation to the survey are taken from the instructions, questions and choices in the questionnaire.

4 This notion of policy-making as inevitably something of an experiment is captured in the title of a rare comparative study of political, economic and policy developments in Australia and New Zealand. See F. Castles, R. Gerritsen and J. Vowles (eds), *The Great Experiment: Labour Parties and Public Policy Transformation in Australia and New Zealand*, Auckland University Press, Auckland, 1996.

5 A concise summary of the rise in the number of women in Parliament is given in S. Levine and N. S. Roberts, 'The New Zealand General Election and Electoral Referendum of 1993', *Political Science*, 46, 1, p.61. A guide to each of New Zealand's women MPs is provided in J. McCallum, *Women in the House: Members of Parliament in New Zealand*, Cape Catley, Picton, 1993.

6 Whether increased Maori parliamentary representation under MMP can now satisfy the aspirations of more politically engaged Maori seems questionable. See, for example, H. Melbourne, *Maori Sovereignty: the Maori Perspective*, Hodder Moa Beckett, Auckland, 1996. For Maori reactions to recent National government policies in this area, see W. Gardiner, *Return to Sender: What Really Happened at the Fiscal Envelope Hui*, Reed, Auckland, 1996.

7 There is now a substantial literature on the diverse policies and styles of government of successive New Zealand administrations. For the then Prime Minister's own view, see R. D. Muldoon, *The New Zealand Economy: a Personal View*, Endeavour Press, Auckland, 1985. A critical view is taken in S. Zavos, *The Real Muldoon*, Fourth Estate Books, Wellington, 1978, and in T. Garnier and S. Levine, *Election '81: an End to Muldoonism?*, Methuen, Auckland, 1981. Essays on the first and second terms of the fourth Labour government review its record in various policy sectors: see J. Boston and M. Holland (eds), *The Fourth Labour Government: Radical Politics in New Zealand*, Oxford University Press, Auckland, 1987, and M. Holland and J. Boston, *The Fourth Labour Government: Politics and Policy in New Zealand*, Oxford University Press, Auckland, 1990. The process of change associated with Rogernomics is analysed in J. Boston, J. Martin, J. Pallot and P. Walsh (eds), *Reshaping the State: New Zealand's Bureaucratic Revolution*, Oxford University Press, Auckland, 1991, and in B. Roper and C. Rudd (eds), *State and Economy in New Zealand*, Oxford University Press, Auckland, 1993. National's approach to economic management and the role of the state is discussed forthrightly in R. Richardson, *Making a Difference*, Shoal Bay Press, Christchurch, 1995. A robust critique of Labour and National policies is provided in J. Kelsey, *The New Zealand Experiment: a World Model for Structural Adjustment?*, Auckland University Press/Bridget Williams Books, Auckland, 1995.

8 Specifically, 3 percent of respondents thought that a right-wing government was 'most likely after the first MMP election'; 1 percent considered such a government to be New Zealand's most likely type over the longer term. Left-wing governments were expected by only 1 percent either in 1996 or thereafter.

9 Some of the controversy over Prime Minister Muldoon's use of power is reviewed in the chapter, 'The Muldoon-McLay Era, 1974–86', in B. Gustafson, *The First 50 Years: a History of the New Zealand National Party*, Reed Methuen, Auckland, 1986.

10 The collapse of a viewing platform at Cave Creek in New Zealand's South Island caused the deaths of 14 people. Subsequent controversy surrounded the preparedness of the Department of Conservation and the possible impact of government financial policy on its ability to ensure the safety of such installations. Whether the Minister of

Conservation ought to take responsibility and resign was raised in the media and in parliamentary debate. See SSC, *Review of the Department of Conservation (Under Section 6[b] of the State Sector Act 1988)*, Wellington, December 1995; and Judge Noble, *Report of the Commission of Inquiry into the Collapse of a Viewing Platform at Cave Creek near Punakaiki on the West Coast 1995*, Wellington, 1995.

11 See, for instance, K. Jackson, 'Cabinet and the Prime Minister', in S. Levine (ed.), *Politics in New Zealand: a Reader*, George Allen & Unwin, Auckland, 1978.

12 See G. Palmer, *Unbridled Power? An Interpretation of New Zealand's Constitution and Government*, Oxford University Press, Wellington, 1979, Ch. 6; G. Palmer, *Unbridled Power,* 2nd edn, Oxford University Press, Auckland, 1987, Ch. 8; and G. Palmer, *New Zealand's Constitution in Crisis: Reforming Our Political System*, John McIndoe, Dunedin, 1992, Ch. 5.

13 G. Palmer, *Unbridled Power?*, p.77, and *Unbridled Power*, p.139. The quote comes from a chapter entitled 'The Fastest Law in the West'.

14 For a discussion of the relationship between democracy, interest groups and access to government, see R. Mulgan, *Democracy and Power in New Zealand: a Study of New Zealand Politics*, Oxford University Press, Auckland, 1984, especially Chs. 2–4.

15 See S. Levine and N. S. Roberts, 'The Last Hurrah: the New Zealand General Election of 1993 – What Happened and Why', in J. Vowles and P. Aimer (eds), *Double Decision: the 1993 Election and Referendum in New Zealand*, Victoria University, Wellington, 1994, and J. Vowles et al., *Towards Consensus? The 1993 Election in New Zealand and the Transition to Proportional Representation*, Auckland University Press, Auckland, 1995, Ch. 10.

16 The options put to voters in 1992 were reviewed in some detail in H. Catt, P. Harris and N. S. Roberts, *Voter's Choice: Electoral Change in New Zealand?*, Dunmore, Palmerston North, 1992.

17 The question of what is meant by the term 'the Crown' is the subject of a recent doctoral dissertation: J. Hayward, 'In Search of the Treaty Partner: Who or What Is the Crown?', Department of Politics, Victoria University of Wellington, 1995.

18 *New Zealand Parliamentary Debates* (Hansard), 510, pp.4395–98.

19 See, for instance, P. Aimer, 'Scandinavian Parliaments: Models for New Zealand?' in J. S. Hoadley (ed.), *Improving New Zealand's Democracy,* New Zealand Foundation for Peace Studies, Auckland, 1979, and N. S. Roberts, 'New Models for New Zealand: Three Small Democracies Compared', *New Zealand International Review*, 2, 2, pp.14–17.

20 Public attitudes towards proposals for a four-year parliamentary term are analysed in S. Levine and N. S. Roberts, 'Electoral Reform and Referendums: the Views of Voters in New Zealand in 1987 and 1990', in A. Simpson (ed.), *Referendums: Constitutional and Political Perspectives*, Victoria University, Wellington, 1992.

21 The events leading up to and surrounding that election are discussed in M. Bassett, *Confrontation '51: the 1951 Waterfront Dispute*, Reed, Wellington, 1972.

22 The risky character of that venture is conveyed by the title of a book on the election, *The Gamble: the Campaign Diary of the Challengers*, ANZ Book Company, Auckland, 1984, which was compiled by J. Fyfe and H. Manson for the New Zealand Oral History Archive.

23 These are explored in detail in conference papers (available from the authors) presented to the American Political Science Association (San Francisco, 1996) and the New Zealand Political Studies Association (Auckland, 1996).

24 Colmar Brunton/One Network News poll, November 1995.

CHAPTER 4

The changing party system

The introduction of MMP in New Zealand is likely to mean little or no change for some parts of the political system. Even at the height of the 1992 and 1993 referendum debates, with extravagant claims and counter-claims on both sides, the effects of proportional representation were never going to be as damaging as its detractors feared or as wonderful as its proponents promised. It was obvious from the outset, however, that there would be widespread changes to the number, nature, and structure of the political parties in New Zealand.

Political science, like most of the social sciences, is often accused of being soft, with few laws like those of physics and chemistry. This is undoubtedly true, but one branch of political science with carefully tested and validated propositions (even, one could say, with universally recognised laws) is the study of electoral systems. Indeed, Maurice Duverger's famous 1951 book *Political Parties* contains what is often called 'Duverger's law', which is simply that *'the simple-majority single-ballot system favours the two-party system'.*[1] Sixteen years later, another important work, Douglas Rae's *The Political Consequences of Electoral Laws*, reached a similar conclusion:

> Plurality formulae are always strongly associated with two-party competition except where strong local minority parties exist . . .
>
> Plurality and majority formulae tend to deny representation to larger numbers of small parties than proportional representation formulae.[2]

Labour and National's dominance

It is not surprising, therefore, that there was a strong link – obvious to even the most casual observer of New Zealand politics – between the overwhelming parliamentary strength of the two major parties, Labour and National, and the FPP electoral system. Since the end of the Second World War, these two parties have dominated New Zealand politics. Together, Labour and National won all the seats in the House of Representatives in 11 of the 17 elections held since 1945. On three occasions (1966, 1978, and 1990), the two major parties won all but one of the seats in Parliament; on two other occasions (1981 and 1984), Social Credit won two seats in Parliament; and in 1993 the Alliance and New Zealand First each won two seats, leaving the two major parties with 95 of the 99 seats in the House of Representatives.

Figure 4.1. ***Share of the votes and the seats won by the major parties (i.e. by Labour and National together) in New Zealand general elections from 1946 to 1993***

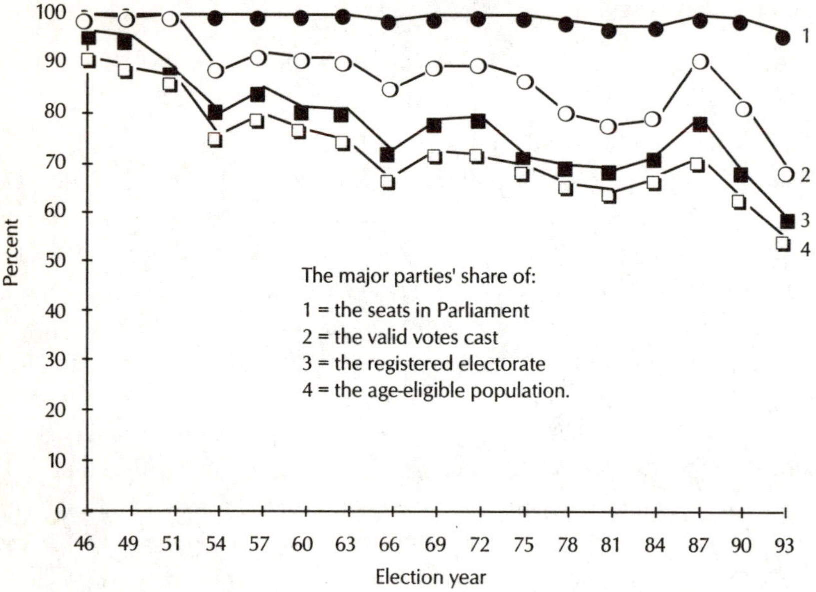

Figure 4.1 puts the strength of the major parties into perspective, however. During the first three elections after the Second World War (1946, 1949, and 1951), Labour and National together won not only all the seats in Parliament, but also almost all the valid votes cast in those elections. When the major parties' votes are measured as a share of the registered electorate or as a proportion of the age-eligible population (that is, taking unenrolled adults into account in addition to people on the electoral rolls), however, they do not appear quite so dominant. In 1946, for example, Labour and National together won the support of only 91 percent of the age-eligible population – admittedly a high figure, but significantly less than the 99.7 percent of the valid votes they won in the election, let alone the 100 percent of the seats they won in Parliament.

The Social Credit Political League (as it was initially known) entered the electoral fray in 1954, and from then on the share of the votes won by the major parties began to decline in a slow but reasonably steady manner (as Figure 4.1 shows). No matter which measure of electoral support is used – be it the share of the valid votes won by Labour and National, or their share of the votes cast by the registered electorate, or their share of support from among the whole age-eligible population – the pattern is both clear and consistent.

The decline in support for the major parties from 1954 to 1966 was followed by a brief recovery in 1969, but there was a marked decline during the period from 1972 to 1981. A small improvement in the position of Labour and National's combined vote in 1984 was succeeded by a significant improvement in 1987 (when all the minor parties and independent candidates together could account jointly for only 8 percent of the valid votes cast in the election). But this was followed immediately by a steep decline in support for the major parties in both 1990 and 1993. At the last general election, for example, Labour and National together won less than 70 percent of the valid votes cast, the support of less than 60 percent of the registered electorate, and the votes of only 55 percent of the country's age-eligible population.

In other words, the overwhelming parliamentary strength of the two major parties – their hegemony, or complete dominance, of the House of Representatives – partially disguises the fact that (as suggested in Chapter 1) New Zealand has become a more diverse, less homogeneous society since the end of the Second World War. Well before New Zealand adopted a system of proportional representation, the country's voters (and its wider electorate) had moved away from a classic model of two-party politics. In the first 45 years after the war, New Zealand society and its electorate had changed considerably even though its electoral system had not. This was highlighted by the results of the 1993 general election (which, it transpired, was the last FPP election). Not only was support (in terms of valid votes cast) for the country's two leading political parties lower than at any time since 1928 (when the Reform and United parties together won only 64.9 percent of the poll), but there were also more parties elected to Parliament than at any time since 1935.[3]

Evolution of the party system

Before trying to assess where the party system is heading, we must review where the parties have come from. The labour movement's early political aspirations were well catered for by Richard Seddon's Liberal government, but by 1905 trades councils throughout the country were pushing for the formation of a separate political party. However, after the Labour party was formed in 1916, its road to power was slow and arduous. Labour regularly won about a quarter of the votes in elections after the First World War, but the party failed to make significantly greater gains until the hardship and misery of the Great Depression resulted in the widespread rejection of the policies and personnel of the United/Reform coalition government, which lost the 1935 election decisively. The anti-Labour parties, which had governed New Zealand for more than 30 years, found themselves on the opposition benches for the first time, and they moved quickly to amalgamate. The National party was formally launched in 1936, its formation the final product of the 1931 coalition between George Forbes's United party and Gordon Coates's Reform party. Given that the United party had been, in effect, the successor to the Liberal party, National's antecedents – like Labour's – can be said to date back to the late 19th century.

After the 1935 general election, New Zealand experienced a period of unparalleled party and parliamentary stability – so much so that the country's political calendar in effect dates from then. The Labour government that was elected in 1935 and held office until 1949 is universally known as the *first* Labour government. Its successor was the *first* National government (1949–57). At the other end of the scale, the Labour government elected in 1984 (the 1984–90 Lange–Palmer–Moore Labour government) was known as the *fourth* Labour government; the administration of Prime Minister Jim Bolger, which succeeded it, is the *fourth* National government.

Following John A. Lee's expulsion from the Labour Party in 1940, the first challenge to the two-party system in New Zealand came from Lee's Democratic Soldier Labour party in the 1943 general election. It was easily rebuffed. Lee's party won 4.3 percent of the votes cast in the election, but no seats. However, in view of the fact that in 1993 Parliament raised the MMP threshold or 'hurdle' from four percent, as recommended by the Royal Commission on the Electoral System, to five percent, it is worth noting that the Democratic Soldier Labour Party's 1943 performance is the only instance in New Zealand since 1935 of a political party winning more than four but less than five percent of the valid votes in an election. Values in 1975 (5.2 percent), the Democrats in 1987 (5.7 percent), and NewLabour in 1990 (also 5.2 percent) would all have cleared a five percent hurdle.

Knocking on the door of the 'two-party club'

The period from 1954 to 1969 saw Social Credit mount the first external challenge to the 'two-party club'. There were no other significant forces chipping away at Labour and National (other parties and candidates never reached a joint total of even 2 percent of the votes during this period), and Social Credit never won less than 7 percent of the poll. In 1966 Social Credit broke the major parties' parliamentary monopoly for the first time, when it won 14.5 percent of the votes and its leader, Vernon Cracknell, won the Hobson electorate. His victory was short-lived: he lost the seat three years later, when Social Credit's overall share of the votes declined by more than 5 percent.

In 1972, another minor party challenged the Labour–National supremacy. Although it stood candidates in only half the country's electorates, the Values Party (which has been referred to as the world's first Green party[4]) won 2 percent of the votes cast. Three years later, it won just over 5 percent, while the share of registered electors that voted for Labour and National again fell below 75 percent (as had occurred in 1966 for the first time). Between 1975 and 1993, the major parties would exceed this degree of support only once, in 1987.

1978 and 1981 saw Social Credit at its peak. The party won almost one in six of all the votes cast in 1978, and more than one in five in 1981. Nevertheless, Social Credit had only a minimal impact on the major parties' hold on Parliament (winning one and two seats in 1978 and 1981 respectively). Moreover, neither Social Credit nor Values were splinter parties. They were genuine third forces in politics, rather than breakaways from the major parties. As such, they represented less of a threat to either of the major parties than would have been the case had they been formed by dissidents from within the two established parties. While the two minor parties clearly attracted support at the polls from people who had previously voted for one or other of the major parties, they drew very few major party activists and organisers into their fold.

Breaking the mould

That changed drastically in 1983, when property developer and millionaire Bob Jones formed the New Zealand party. Many disillusioned National party voters and workers joined Jones's anti-Muldoon crusade. They did not elect any MPs in 1984, but they certainly helped to defeat the third National government decisively.[5] Although there was a move back to the major parties in 1987, an important mould in New Zealand politics had been broken. The fact that the fourth Labour government introduced many of the economic reforms advocated by Jones and the New Zealand party meant that many former National voters were happy to vote in 1987 to keep the Labour government in power.[6] Politics in New Zealand was becoming fluid, even volatile. This was underscored in 1989, when Jim Anderton – a former president of the Labour party – broke away from the party which he represented in Parliament as the MP for Sydenham, and established a new party. Although it was called NewLabour, it articulated traditional Labour policies and values. The party contested all 93 general electorates during the 1990 election. In a sign of things to come, it did not contest the four Maori seats: it had an electoral pact with Mana Motuhake, also formed by a previous Labour

MP, the Minister of Maori Affairs in the third Labour government, Matiu Rata. While the Labour government was decisively defeated at the polls, Anderton had no trouble retaining his own seat. But Anderton's new party was not the star performer among the minor players in 1990. Another new party, the Greens, fielded candidates in 71 seats (22 fewer than NewLabour), won 6.8 percent of the votes cast (1.6 percent more than NewLabour), but captured no seats.[7]

The arguments and divisions which had rent the fourth Labour government asunder were to have their counterparts in the fourth National government. Under the guidance of finance minister Ruth Richardson, the Bolger government quickly implemented economic policies every bit as unpalatable to electors as those adopted under Roger Douglas's Labour regime. Many voters protested, and two MPs – Gilbert Myles (MP for Roskill) and Hamish MacIntyre (MP for Manawatu) – left National and formed the Liberal party. Of considerably more significance was the fact that a member of the National cabinet, Winston Peters, had become increasingly critical of his own government's policies. The Prime Minister dismissed Peters from the cabinet in October 1991, with the inevitable result that Peters was free to be even more outspoken than previously.[8] After the National party executive refused to re-select Peters as its candidate for the Tauranga electorate, he left the party and resigned his seat in Parliament, only to contest it successfully in an April 1993 by-election (in which he was unopposed by the other parties in Parliament, who knew they could not beat him). In July 1993, Peters announced the creation of his new party, New Zealand First. Like Jim Anderton, Winston Peters was now a splinter deeply embedded in the side of his former party.[9]

At the same time, however, Anderton had been busy stitching together a new and potentially powerful force in New Zealand politics. He brought together five minor parties – NewLabour, the Greens, Mana Motuhake, the Democrats (i.e. the renamed Social Credit party), and the Liberals – under a common Alliance banner. Despite frequent predictions to the contrary by the major parties, the Alliance not only held together, but also managed to cut its campaign teeth to good effect in the 1992 indicative electoral referendum and, a few weeks later, the 1992 local body elections (especially in the Auckland area).

Both the Alliance and New Zealand First went on to win two seats each in Parliament in the 1993 general election. Anderton was joined in Parliament by the Alliance's Auckland Central candidate, Sandra Lee (of Mana Motuhake), and Peters was joined by his party's Northern Maori candidate, Tau Henare. It is noteworthy that the two members of the Alliance with seats in the 1993–96 Parliament both represented parties that had broken away from

Labour, while New Zealand First was the direct product of conflict within the National party.[10] Table 4.1 summarises electoral developments over the 1984 to 1993 period.

Table 4.1. ***Election results in New Zealand, 1984 to 1993***

	1984		**1987**		**1990**		**1993**	
	Votes %	Seats	Votes %	Seats	Votes %	Seats	Votes %	Seats
Political parties								
Labour	43.0	56	48.0	57	35.1	29	34.7	45
National	35.9	37	44.0	40	47.8	67	35.0	50
New Zealand	12.3	0	0.3	0	0.1	0	–	–
Social Credit	7.6	2	–	–	0.9	0	–	–
Alliance	–	–	–	–	–	–	18.2	2
Green	–	–	–	–	6.8	0	–	–
NewLabour	–	–	–	–	5.2	1	–	–
Democrat	–	–	5.7	0	1.7	0	–	–
Mana Motuhake	0.3	0	0.5	0	0.6	0	–	–
New Zealand First	–	–	–	–	–	–	8.4	2
Others	0.9	0	1.5	0	1.8	0	3.7	0
Total	100.0	95	100.0	97	100.0	97	100.0	99
Total valid votes	1,929,201		1,831,777		1,824,092		1,922,796	
Registered electors	2,111,651		2,114,656		2,202,157		2,321,664	
Turnout	93.7%		89.1%		85.2%		85.2%	

Giovanni Sartori has listed four 'properties' of two-party political systems. They are: first, that each major party is 'in a position to compete for [an] absolute majority' of parliamentary seats; second, that one of the two major parties wins a parliamentary majority in general elections; third, that 'this party is willing to govern alone'; and, finally, that there is a 'credible expectation' that power will alternate between the two major parties.[11] By these criteria, it is clear that New Zealand was the very model of a modern two-party system from 1935 through to 1993. Indeed, even the composition of the Parliament elected in November 1993 underscores the degree to which New Zealand politics remained a textbook example of a two-party system – 95 of the 99 seats in Parliament were held by the two traditional major parties, Labour and National. The four remaining seats were held by representatives of parties which were splinters from Labour and National.

Changes during the 1993 to 1996 parliamentary session

The results of the November 1993 MMP referendum ensured that further changes to the New Zealand party system would occur. However, some of the changes since the last general election are attributable to factors other than MMP.

First, the result of the 1993 election was exceptionally close. Over and above the fact that Labour and National together garnered an historically low share of the poll, National's 35.1 percent of the valid votes gained the party only 50 of the 99 seats in Parliament. Labour was hard on its heels with 34.7 percent of the votes and 45 seats. As we have seen, the Alliance and New Zealand First won two seats apiece.

Of course, 50 seats is the barest possible majority in a 99-seat Parliament. As a consequence of its minuscule majority, it was inevitable that Bolger's government would be under a great deal of pressure during the 1993–96 Parliament. A caucus with a one-seat majority, and containing 'loose cannons' like Michael Laws and Ross Meurant, would not have had an easy time even if New Zealand had retained FPP. Right from the start, the National government formed immediately after the 1993 election showed just how fragile it was when it was left with little alternative than to invite Peter Tapsell, a Labour MP, to be Speaker.

A second, and even more powerful, cause of the disorder on the current political scene is the reduction in the number of electorates in the next Parliament. 'Downsizing' is an insidious piece of jargon, usually associated with corporate restructuring. During the past decade the process has caused a lot of pain for literally tens of thousands of people throughout the country, and the downsizing of the number of electorates from 99 to 65 was naturally going to do the same for current MPs. To use the title of an old movie, *Three into Two Won't Go*, it was predictable that the two larger parties in Parliament would feel the squeeze.

Between a RoC and a hard place . . .

It was clear from the start of the redistribution, for example, that Ross Meurant's Hobson electorate was going to disappear (and it did: Whangarei has eaten a slice of it, and Northland has swallowed the rest). So it was hardly surprising that Meurant should jump ship initially to form RoC, the Right-of-Centre party. However, it is important to note that, when he left the National party in September 1994, Meurant stayed on as a member of the government, keeping his position as Under-Secretary for Agriculture and for Fisheries, and thus continuing to be a member of the executive. As we point out in Chapter 6, Meurant's departure from the National party *while remaining a member of the executive* meant that New Zealand, in effect, went from having a single-party majority National government to a coalition National/RoC majority government.

Likewise, after Trevor Rogers's electorate, Howick, was incorporated into the redrawn Pakuranga, Rogers left National and joined RoC. Meurant initially argued that the Right-of-Centre party could win about 15 percent of the votes in the first MMP election, attracting support especially in the country's rural constituencies. When successive opinion polls showed that this was not likely to happen, RoC tried to reposition itself by changing its name to the Conservative party. This had no appreciable effect on its performance, however. After Meurant was dismissed from the government for failing to resign his post as a director of a Russian-owned, Vanuatu-based bank, he left the party he had formed to become an independent MP. Trevor Rogers, the sole surviving Conservative MP, became the party's leader. In the absence of distinctive policies, a strong geographical base, and a persuasive leader, the party has little chance of winning seats in Parliament in 1996.

Christian hopes and prospects

Another MP left National to start his own political party. Graeme Lee had been Minister of Internal Affairs (but not in cabinet) during the first term of the Bolger administration, but he was not reappointed after the 1993 election. Disappointed at his treatment, Lee was another obvious source of discontent among members of National's caucus, and observers of the political scene correctly judged that it was only a matter of time before he too struck out on his own. As a prominent member of the conservative Christian community, Lee was seen as a possible leader of the Christian Heritage party, which had contested the 1990 and 1993 general elections.[12] However, relations between the leader of the Christian Heritage party, Graham Capill, and Graeme Lee were somewhat strained, not least because Lee regarded the Christian Heritage philosophy and appeal as too narrow. Lee preferred a party that was not too closely identified with the Reformed churches, that had a greater capacity to win votes from conservative Catholics and Pacific Islanders. As a result, he established the Christian Democrats party in May 1995. Like Meurant's RoC, Lee's Christian Democrats fared poorly in public opinion polls, consistently failing to make a significant impact or establish a viable public profile. It was not surprising, therefore, that in early 1996 the Christian Democrats and Christian Heritage held exploratory talks about a possible merger. Shortly before Easter 1996, they reached a working accommodation as the Christian Coalition, preserving their separate identities but not competing directly with each other at the polls. Even so, it seems unlikely that the two parties – either separately or as a unity ticket – will cross the five percent threshold and qualify for list representation in Parliament in 1996. It is almost as unlikely that any candidate from either party, including Graeme Lee himself, will win a seat in Parliament in 1996 as an electorate MP (and thus qualify for party-list seats despite failing to clear the five percent hurdle).

In the longer term, though, if the Christian Democrats and Christian Heritage were able to amalgamate effectively, and if they managed to attract a capable, charismatic leader, they could win seats in New Zealand's new PR Parliament. In Sweden, for example, where there is a four percent electoral threshold (just 1 percent lower than New Zealand's), the Christian Democratic party struggled for years to clear the hurdle. The party won one seat on a joint Centre/Christian Democratic ticket in 1985, but lost it three years later. In 1991, however, after an effective election campaign and in the midst of a large overall swing to the right, the party broke through the electoral barrier with ease, with 7 percent of the poll. Three years later, the party narrowly survived the major move back to the Social Democratic party and just kept its place in Parliament. The performance and position of the Christian Democrats in Sweden, a country with many similarities to New Zealand, offers some succour to Christian parties on the other side of the world. It is worth remembering, though, that the Christian parties which have flourished in Europe are in countries with large Catholic populations and have been regarded as the main conservative party there.

United they stand – or fall?

On the other side of the House and at the other end of the country, the reduction in the number of electorates also meant unavoidable problems for Labour in Dunedin, long a three-seat citadel for the party. With three active, high-profile MPs – none of whom is ripe for retirement – representing the city, the downsizing of Dunedin to two seats (now known simply as Dunedin North and Dunedin South) was always going to be painful for Labour. This was proved in late June 1995, when Dr Clive Matthewson, a former Labour cabinet minister, broke from the party he had represented in Parliament for 11 years to become leader of the United New Zealand group. He was accompanied by six other MPs – two from Labour (Margaret Austin and Peter Dunne, the latter having come via Future New Zealand), and four from National (cabinet minister Bruce Cliffe, and backbenchers Pauline Gardiner, Peter Hilt, and John Robertson).[13]

The formation of the United party was the clearest illustration of the quest by politicians for a new, distinct place on the political spectrum from which they could pitch their specific appeal to voters under MMP. The cross-party grouping claimed that it occupied the middle ground in New Zealand politics and declared itself ready to work with any future government, be it led by Labour or National. United was slow to develop either a set of principles or a range of policies, however, and for the first nine months of its existence it had little public impact. The party languished at 1 percent or less in the opinion polls. At the beginning of 1996, with an election at most 10 or

11 months away, the National party was becoming increasingly worried about its long-term prospects for forming a government. In late February, National and United clinched an important deal. The National government agreed to form a coalition with United – which included one seat for United in a joint 20-strong National/United cabinet, and the National party agreed not to field a candidate against Peter Dunne in his Ohariu–Belmont electorate. The formal coalition, with a public document as the basis of the agreement (see Appendix 4), was another step on New Zealand's road towards a fully functional PR polity. The consequences of this move are examined further in Chapter 6. Politically, however, it was an astute arrangement. United could gain from a new profile and increased media exposure, while National was able to acquire – almost to invent – a possible long-term coalition partner.

Strategically, the decision not to stand a National candidate against Dunne appears to make sense. In Germany, Christian Democrat (i.e. CDU/CSU) voters have had to make some hard decisions in recent years. In the 1994 federal elections, for example, it appeared as though the Christian Democrats' coalition partner, the German Free Democrats (the FDP, sometimes known as the German Liberals), was in danger of failing to clear Germany's five percent electoral threshold. Such a result would have cost the FDP its parliamentary representation and, more important from the CDU/CSU perspective, would have deprived the Christian Democrats of their natural coalition partner (leaving the government with no close allies in Parliament). The Free Democrats had failed to clear the five percent hurdle in one state election after another, and many Christian Democratic voters feared that lack of support for the Free Democrats could bring down Chancellor Helmut Kohl's government. As a result, considerable numbers of CDU/CSU voters did not give their party-list vote to the Christian Democrats, but instead opted to give their 'zweistimme' – their 'second' but all-important party vote – to the Free Democrats. This saved them: there is clear evidence to show that 55 percent[14] of FDP voters were CDU/CSU supporters casting a strategic vote for the Free Democrats in order to retain the CDU/CSU/FDP coalition. Without the support of this crucial group of voters, the FDP would have failed to clear the five percent hurdle and thus have failed to win parliamentary representation. Voting strategically like this is not an easy decision for electors to make. For a start, the ruse may fail. There is no guarantee that enough like-minded voters will behave in a similar manner; if they do not, then one's strategic vote can end up simply as a wasted vote for a party that fails to clear the five percent threshold.

By agreeing not to oppose Peter Dunne in the new Ohariu–Belmont electorate, the National party has possibly avoided a situation whereby some of its supporters could be forced to decide whether or not to cast their party votes strategically and give them to United New Zealand. As explained in Chapter 2, the 'escape clause' in the Electoral Act establishing MMP means that parties which fail to clear the five percent threshold are still entitled to a share of parliamentary seats based on the number of party votes they receive if one of their candidates wins an electorate seat in Parliament. In Ohariu–Belmont, National supporters can vote for Dunne to be their electorate MP while, at the same time (like National supporters elsewhere), voting National with their party votes. If Dunne is elected, and if United gets only, say, 2.7 percent of the votes cast in the election, then the party will still qualify for additional seats from its party list. While United's chances of surviving the 1996 election and retaining seats in Parliament may have been boosted by the agreements between National and United, ultimately the success of this strategy will depend on whether Ohariu–Belmont's electors are impressed or repelled by Dunne's political peregrinations.[15]

Laws unto himself

Michael Laws had been Winston Peters' research assistant prior to being elected to Parliament in 1990 as MP for Hawkes Bay. An individualist from the outset, he soon began criticising his colleagues publicly. When Peters resigned his seat in Parliament and successfully contested the subsequent Tauranga by-election, Michael Laws was on hand to congratulate him on his victory. However, Laws did not follow Peters and join New Zealand First. Instead, in the 1993 general election he stood for National in Hawkes Bay again, generated a small swing against the tide, and increased his majority (a not inconsiderable achievement in view of the fact that National lost 19 seats). Laws' second term in the House was unhappier than the first. He stopped attending caucus meetings in 1995 and at the same time announced that he would not be standing for National in 1996. In March 1996 Laws resigned from National and joined New Zealand First – increasing the party's complement to three MPs. In late April Laws resigned his seat in Parliament and his membership of the Napier city council following publicity about an opinion poll for the council conducted by a company partly owned by his wife.

Michael Laws was the New Zealand First MP for Hawkes Bay for 55 days; the surprise is that it took him so long – three years – to join Peters' party. The delay was due, in part, to Mike Moore, the former leader of the Labour party. After the 1993 general election, the new Labour caucus was immediately plunged into an intense leadership battle when Helen Clark, deputy leader of the party, stood for the position of leader. Moore was elected Prime Minister in August 1990 to try to minimise the extent of Labour's defeat. His performance as Leader of the Opposition during the first term of the Bolger government was patchy, and he ran a highly personal, poorly thought out, often embarrassing election campaign in 1993. On election night, Moore gave an ill-timed and ill-judged speech claiming victory. The truth was very different: in 1993 the Labour party won an even lower share of the poll than it had obtained when it was overwhelmingly defeated in National's 1990 landslide. Moore and a small band of intensely loyal supporters were very bitter, and he became a remote figure on the Labour benches, declining all offers of a front-bench post and devoting much of 1994 and 1995 to criticising his own party. Many people thought that Moore would launch a new political party, and two National MPs – Michael Laws and Peter McCardle – appeared to be waiting for him to do so. At the beginning of March 1996, Moore seems to have decided not to form a new, centrist political party and, instead, to stay with Labour. Within days of this becoming apparent, McCardle confirmed that he would be seeking National's nomination for the new Rimutaka electorate. A month later McCardle abandoned National and moved across to Peters and New Zealand First. So too did Labour MP Jack Elder, who was unhappy with his low placement on the party list.[16]

The major parties

The fact that Mike Moore did not leave the Labour party – and his own personal popularity in the country means that he could do enormous damage to Labour's cause – ironically underlines the success that Helen Clark has had as parliamentary leader of the Labour party. Her standing in the opinion polls has been extremely low, and yet she has largely succeeded in keeping Labour's caucus together. The Labour party began the 1993–96 parliamentary term with 45 MPs. By April 1996 it had lost only four (the three who formed the United party, and Elder) and had 41 MPs – as many as National, which had begun its reign in November 1993 with 50. On the road to the first MMP election, National has lost nine MPs to Labour's four.

Helen Clark has a clear model for the future of the Labour party in a PR environment. She wants her party to emulate the Norwegian Labour party, and she is an admirer of Gro Harlem Brundtland, Norway's first and very successful female Prime Minister. Clark and her supporters in the Labour party have made it clear that they would like the Norwegian political model to work in New Zealand, emphasising that, for much of the past decade, there has been a minority Labour government in power in Oslo. The problem with this scenario, however, is that, in the last three elections in Norway, the Norwegian Labour party has received an average of more than 37 percent of all the votes cast, whereas the New Zealand Labour party is currently hard-pressed to achieve an average of only 20 percent in opinion polls. Furthermore, Labour is the biggest party by far in the Norwegian Parliament and the 'bourgeois' opposition to its right is fragmented into four separate parties (the largest of which, the Conservative party, averaged only 23 percent of the poll in the last three elections). In New Zealand, however, Labour is markedly weaker than the National party (which, by contrast, had an average of 46 percent support in opinion polls in late 1995 and early 1996),[17] and few people foresee the Labour party winning more seats than National at elections in the near future.

Indeed, the minority administration in Norway is a model that the National party in New Zealand may care to examine. Just as Norway's Prime Minister is a popular and respected figure, widely seen as a fit leader for her country, so can Jim Bolger lay some claim to a similar role. The Prime Minister has relished the challenge of the transition to PR in New Zealand, basking in his role as the 'Great Helmsman'. His party is exceptionally well poised to capture at least 40 percent of the votes, and in these circumstances it is National, not Labour, which may well be able to form a minority government after the first MMP election.

The outsiders

The advent of MMP has also created a scramble to form new political parties outside the House. The 1993 Electoral Act permits only registered political parties to contest the party vote and thus be eligible to win list seats in Parliament. To be registered by the Electoral Commission, a party must have 500 members. By the end of April 1996, 20 parties had been registered by the commission (see Appendix 3). All the parties in Parliament – both those which existed at the time of the 1993 election (National, Labour, the Alliance, and New Zealand First) and those formed since by dissident MPs (the Conservative party, the Christian Democrats, and United New Zealand) – had registered with the commission before the end of 1995. It is worth noting that the Alliance registered as a party in its own right, but three of the Alliance's five constituent parties (NewLabour, Mana Motuhake, and the Liberals) were not registered. Although the Democrats and the Greens chose to register their individual identities with the commission, there is little likelihood that they will field separate lists in 1996.

Few of the political parties registered with the Electoral Commission that do not already have seats in Parliament appear to stand much chance of being elected in the first MMP election. ACT New Zealand began life as a pressure group, the Association of Consumers and Taxpayers, founded by former Labour finance minister Roger Douglas and former National cabinet minister Derek Quigley, as a means of promoting Douglas's continuing proposals – his 'unfinished business'[18] – for restructuring New Zealand society. Despite enthusiastic backing from sections of the business and finance communities, the party consistently failed to engender significant support in the opinion polls. Throughout 1995 and the first quarter of 1996, the party never once reached the five percent threshold. However, Douglas stepped down as leader of the party and was replaced by another former Labour cabinet minister, Richard Prebble, at the end of March 1996. Prebble is a far more ebullient, argumentative figure than the dry (even dour) Douglas, and his undoubted abilities could make an important difference to the party's fortunes.[19] ACT quickly acquired a notably higher standing in opinion polls than United. The party also has a clearer policy message – a flat tax (it had originally proposed an end to income tax altogether) and a compulsory superannuation scheme – whereas United has been criticised for its absence of policies, political philosophy, and personality. If polls show Ohariu–Belmont voters rejecting Dunne, National strategists may need to look instead to ACT (whose hopes for parliamentary representation rest primarily on the party-list vote) for support in the next Parliament.

The formation of the Progressive Green party led to a flurry of interest in yet another potential coalition partner for National. Although the party has a few well-known figures among its ranks (including Wellington city councillor Stephen Rainbow, Guy Salmon of the Maruia Society, and Gary Taylor, who has previously served on both the Waitemata city council and the Auckland area health board), it has also failed to capture the public imagination and appears to stand little or no chance of winning seats in the 1996 general election.

A note of light relief in recent elections has been provided by the McGillicuddy Serious party. In 1993, the party – led by its laird and with members dressed in tartan kilts – even qualified for free broadcasting time. McGillicuddy Serious has formally registered as a political party with the Electoral Commission and, not surprisingly, has indicated that it will contest the 1996 elections. The problem for electors wishing to cast a vote – whether in jest or in protest – for McGillicuddy Serious is that unlike the previous FPP system, in which electors could vote for such a party confident that their candidates would not be elected, MMP means that an individual's vote is now a far more potent weapon. Under PR, voting for McGillicuddy Serious as a joke could conceivably mean that the jokers end up in the House. If that sounds far-fetched, it is salient to bear in mind that a Danish comedian, Jacob Haugaard, stood for Parliament at the last Danish general election. His platform included a promise of tail winds for cyclists, an idea that would have considerable appeal to Wellington electors! He was elected easily and now sits in the Danish Folketing.

The Aotearoa Legalise Cannabis party (in the process of registering with the Electoral Commission) also stands some chance of attracting a not inconsiderable protest vote. The alienated, the disenchanted, the unemployed, and the young may find the legalisation of marijuana a focus for their discontent or an opportunity for some amusement at the expense of the powers-that-be (a 'smoke-in' has already been held outside Parliament during 1996). In the long run, many of the new political parties which have registered with the Electoral Commission will find defeat a bitter pill. Their unrealistic expectations will inevitably lead to a loss of enthusiasm, and many of them will wither and die after the 1996 election. This will not necessarily occur, though, with a single-minded, single-issue group like the Aotearoa Legalise Cannabis party. Electoral setbacks serve only to convince some people that there is a conspiracy of power and hypocrisy against them, and they will redouble their efforts in the field. In this respect, the phrase 'grass-roots political activity' may acquire new meaning under MMP.

Different ideological dimensions

Throughout the world, political parties arise from – and base their appeal to voters on – a seemingly bewildering variety of ideas. However, after comparing parties and party systems in a large cross-section of countries, Arend Lijphart distinguished only seven 'durable ideological dimensions' (as distinct from 'more or less programmatic differences that may emerge in one election and fade away soon afterward') by which parties could be classified. The seven dimensions are: socio-economic, religious, cultural–ethnic factors, urban–rural differences, regime support, foreign policy, and postmaterialism.[20] These are displayed in Table 4.2, with our assessment of the more important parties contesting the 1996 election. Lijphart concluded that New Zealand (along with the US and the UK) had 'only a single interparty ideological dimension' – namely, the socio-economic dimension, which he also noted was 'the most important of the ideological dimensions . . . present in all of the democratic party systems'.[21] Significantly, the parties likely to hold the bulk of the seats in the next Parliament (and accounting for 91 of the 99 seats at present) still derive their distinctiveness primarily from socio-economic and related issues.

Party systems overseas often include parties stemming from ideological dimensions other than the socio-economic (some examples are given in Table 4.2). Australia, for instance, has a party system in which other cleavages – in particular, the religious and the urban–rural dimensions – have been significant, accounting for the formation, respectively, of the Democratic Labor party (the DLP) and the National party (formerly known as the Country party, a better indication of its rural roots).[22] In Norway, to take another example, three dimensions in addition to the socio-economic affect the stance of political parties. There are also salient religious factors (the Christian People's party is particularly well entrenched in the southwest), urban–rural cleavages (the Conservatives are an overwhelmingly urban, Oslo-centred party), and postmaterialist issues (the Centre party has strongly repositioned itself as a Green party).

Table 4.2. *Political parties and their principal ideological dimensions*

Ideological dimension	**Overseas examples**	**New Zealand political parties, 1996**
Socio-economic	Social Democratic party, Sweden	ACT, Alliance, Labour, National, United*
Religious	National Religious party, Israel	Christian Democrats Christian Heritage (Christian Coalition)
Cultural-ethnic	Scottish National party, Britain	Mana Motuhake New Zealand First
Urban-rural	National (i.e. Country) party, Australia	RoC/Conservative**
Regime support	Monarchist party, Italy	
Foreign policy	Radical Liberal party, Denmark	
Postmaterialism	Green Party, Germany	Aotearoa Legalise Cannabis party Greens Progressive Greens

* There can, of course, be significant differences of outlook between parties within a given ideological dimension. There may also be policy differences on other topics (e.g. foreign policy) less central to the party's rationale.

** This classification is based on RoC's original plans for strengthening rural and provincial advocacy in Parliament. Since Ross Meurant's departure from the party and the choice of Trevor Rogers (an MP from urban Auckland) as leader, the guiding aims and overall direction of the Conservative party have been more difficult to discern.

The socio-economic dimension dominated New Zealand politics under FPP. Issues such as public versus private ownership, the role of the state in economic planning, the redistribution of wealth, and the expansion or diminution of social welfare programmes are the hallmark of the socio-economic dimension. They have been the well-spring of party debates in New Zealand and, as a result, this country was categorised as having a one-dimensional party system. Figure 4.2 thus charts the changes and developments in the party system during the past 50 years on the basis of a left–right spectrum. A position on the lefthand side of the figure indicates a greater willingness by political parties to intervene in the organisation, production and distribution of wealth and welfare; the further parties are to the right, the less willing they are to intervene in the economy. The figure of necessity simplifies developments, and there is room for debate about the position of different parties on the spectrum, but it is a useful summary of how political parties have arisen and altered as New Zealand faces its first PR election.

Figure 4.2. ***The development of the New Zealand party system from 1946 to 1996***

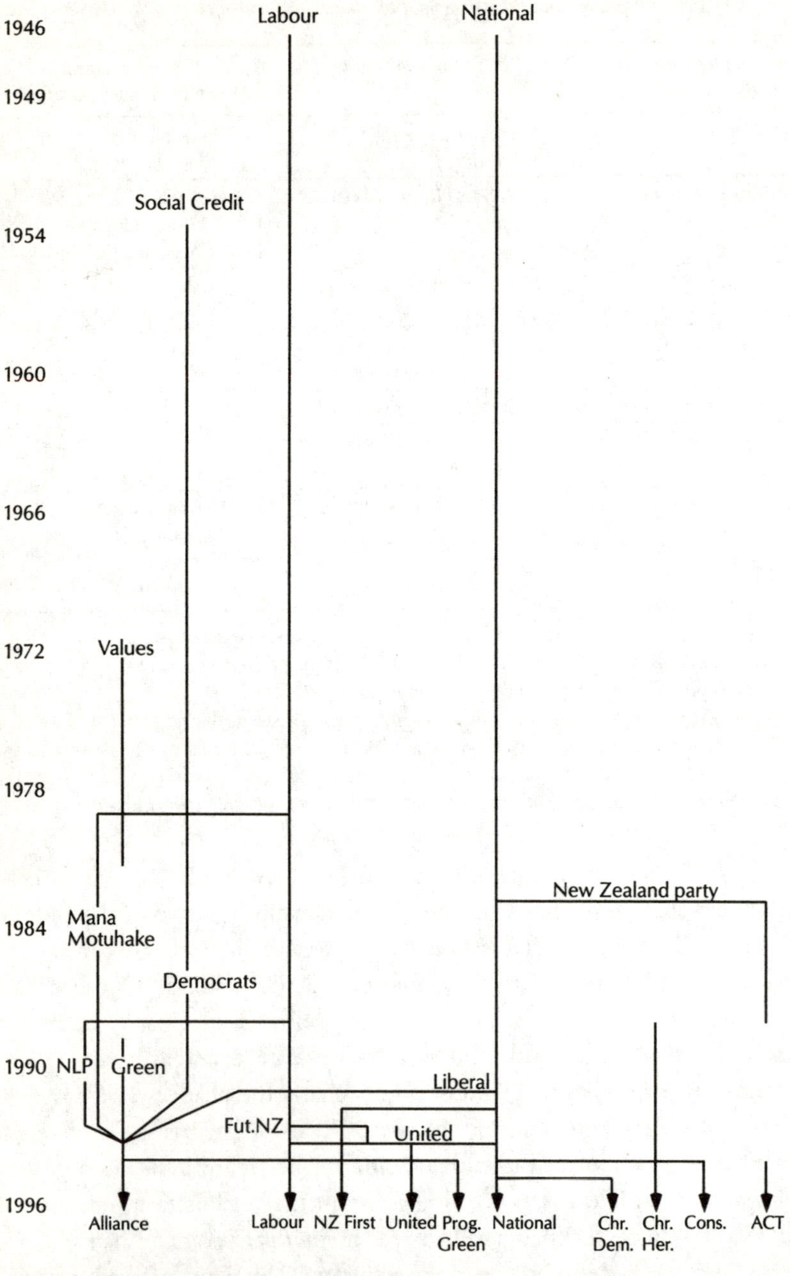

Note: This figure arranges the parties on a nominal left–right continuum according to their general attitudes to the role of the state in the economy.

Back to the future?

How might New Zealand's party system develop in the future? Once the first MMP election has been held, what will the shape of the party system be? As New Zealand moves out of the current transition *to* proportional representation and into a probable period of transition *within* proportional representation, what will the country's party system look like? And what of the long term – 10 or even 20 years from now?

The question of how many parties are likely under MMP has recently been explored. Jack Nagel concluded that a 'realistic estimate of New Zealand's institutional carrying capacity is about seven or eight parties' and added that his personal 'assessment of issue dimensions suggests that at present there are only five dimensions capable of supporting parties'.[23] This is in reasonably close accord with an estimate based on a formula developed by two leading electoral system analysts, Rein Taagepera and Bernard Grofman, which 'yields a societal limit of six parties, [which] should . . . be the predicted upper limit of the number of parliamentary parties in New Zealand under MMP in the medium-term future'.[24] There is, in other words, a limit in any society to the number of viable political parties which can effectively compete for votes in view of the electoral rules, the size of Parliament, and the number of politically salient divisions among the electorate. Consequently, New Zealand – with a relatively high PR threshold, a fairly small single-chamber Parliament, and a narrow (though nonetheless important) range of durable ideologically-charged issues – will only ever be likely to have a few parties prominently represented in its legislature.

Overseas examples

What is the situation in countries similar to New Zealand in size and/or political structures? How many political parties are there in their parliaments? Norway has a population of about four and a half million, it has a PR electoral system and a threshold of four percent for qualifying for compensatory seats in its Parliament, the Storting. There are currently eight parties in the Storting, although two of them won less than four percent of the votes in the country as a whole and have only one seat apiece. Sharing a long common land border with Norway is Sweden, which has a population of eight million (more than double New Zealand's). Sweden has an electoral system similar to Norway's, with a four percent hurdle as well. In September 1994, seven parties won seats in the Swedish Riksdag. The Swedish Parliament is very large by New Zealand standards – with 349 members it is nearly three times the size of New Zealand's new MMP House of Representatives – and the fact that the *smallest* party in the Swedish Parliament (the Christian Democrats) has 14 seats should be seen in this light. By way of contrast, the Social Democrats are the largest party in the Riksdag, with 162 seats. Denmark has a population of about five and a half million, but in area it is far smaller than Norway, Sweden and New Zealand, and the threshold for qualifying for parliamentary representation is much smaller too: only two percent. Not surprisingly, therefore, eight parties and an independent (the comedian Jacob Haugaard, who was elected in one of the country's large multi-member constituencies) currently sit in Denmark's Folketing. It is worth noting, though, that three of the parties in the Danish Parliament won fewer than five percent of the votes in the last general election, and only five parties would have cleared the New Zealand threshold.

Germany, in many ways a very different country from New Zealand – with a population of over 80 million, it is the largest in western Europe – is a federal system. Each state or *land* has its own Parliament in addition to the federal Parliament, the Bundestag (which is currently sited in Bonn but will be moving back to Berlin). Nevertheless, as explained in Chapter 2, New Zealand's MMP electoral system resembles the German system of PR more closely than it does any other electoral system. It is worth noting, therefore, that five parties won seats in the Bundestag in the last federal general elections (in October 1994). The Party of Democratic Socialism failed to clear Germany's five percent electoral threshold but, nevertheless, qualified for seats in Parliament under the system's 'escape clause', which allocates parties that win at least three electorates a share of the party-list seats in Parliament (see Chapter 2).

Significantly, all these actual examples support the calculations made by Nagel: the Danish, German, Norwegian, and Swedish Parliaments each have from five to eight parties in them. It should also be noted that in two cases, Germany and Sweden, the number of parties in Parliament was extremely stable for many years: for roughly 30 years, there were only three parties in the Bundestag (the Social Democrats, the Free Democrats, and the Christian Democrats[25]), while the Riksdag had five parties in it (the Left Communists, the Social Democrats, the Centre Party, the Liberals, and the Conservatives). It was only in the 1980s that new parties – initially the Greens – won seats in the German and Swedish Parliaments.

The first MMP election

Returning to New Zealand, then, this chapter has argued that four parties will definitely secure seats in the first MMP Parliament – and they are the same parties which won seats in the last FPP Parliament. To that extent, MMP will see little change in the party system as it has developed to date. However, the number of MPs each party will win (their share of the seats in the House) will be very different from what New Zealand has seen before. Whereas the four seats won by the Alliance and New Zealand First were the most seats won by parties other than Labour or National since 1935, in the future parties other than Labour and National are likely to win at least a quarter of the seats in Parliament. As Appendix 2 shows, if the political parties were to win the same number of votes in an MMP election as they won in 1993, then National would have 44 seats in a 120-member House, Labour 43, the Alliance 23, and New Zealand First 10 seats. The performance of these four parties in opinion polls at the end of 1995 would have resulted in a House of Representatives composed of: National 59, Labour 26, Alliance 29, New Zealand First 6 seats. The improvements in the New Zealand First poll ratings that began in March 1996 were mainly at the expense of the Alliance, and a consequent distribution of seats in Parliament could therefore be: National 55, Labour 22, Alliance 21, New Zealand First 22. These figures are purely speculative. Former British Prime Minister Harold Wilson's famous aphorism, 'A week is a long time in politics', needs to be stressed, as does the fact that a great deal can happen to change the relative standing and popularity of the political parties in the *months* leading up to the 1996 general election. For example, one phenomenon that usually occurs in New Zealand elections is that the main opposition party improves its public standing during the official election campaign period. In our view, if Mike Moore does not leave the Labour party and form a new centrist splinter party a few months before the election (a possibility that still cannot be ruled out), then it is likely that Labour will improve its performance and image both before and particularly during the election campaign.

If any other parties win seats in the first MMP Parliament, the most likely ones are United and ACT. No other parties have anything more than an outside chance. In the short term, therefore, there are likely to be four to six parties in New Zealand's first MMP Parliament.[26] This view is reinforced by the expectation that many voters will 'err on the side of caution' when casting their votes. A vote under the new MMP system is a powerful weapon. All votes for political parties that qualify for seats in Parliament are equal. Under MMP, a Labour vote in Pahiatua is worth only as much – and just as much – as a Labour vote in Porirua. If voters cast their party-list votes for parties which win parliamentary representation, their votes will be counted and they will have a direct effect on the election results. If, on the other hand, they vote for parties that do not qualify for seats in Parliament, their votes will be wasted: the Sainte Laguë formula (see Appendix 2) is applied only to votes that are cast for parties that actually qualify for parliamentary representation. This, plus the fact that 1996 will be New Zealand's first PR election and many electors will thus be slightly uneasy about the outcome (particularly about possible fragmentation of the political system), makes it likely that electors will choose to vote for a smaller range of political parties than they might have otherwise.

After 1996 . . .

What happens after the first MMP election will depend, at least in part, on the results of the election and on which party or parties form a government (this question is examined in Chapter 6). Many of the small parties outside Parliament won't live to fight another day – let alone another election. Within Parliament, there will still be intense pressures on the various factions within the Labour party. Some within Labour would tolerate co-operation with the Alliance; others are adamantly opposed. Similarly, pressure on the various parties within the Alliance to separate and go their own way, once they have achieved parliamentary representation and, ironically, experienced the powerlessness of Parliament, cannot be discounted. Predictions of the demise of the Alliance have been rife since the five-party grouping was formed. However, the strains on its constituent parts once it acquires a considerable number of seats will be more obvious and more difficult to contain.

Nor will the National party be immune from internal conflicts after the next general election. MMP may heighten some of the contrasts between National's urban and rural sectors. Its list members are likely to be predominantly city MPs, while caucus members from rural constituencies will be kept exceptionally busy servicing very large electorates. The possibility of a disgruntled National MP offering his or her services to another party cannot be discounted. Some National MPs considered using this tactic during 1995; they may do so again.

It is certain, then, that New Zealand's period of political transition will not be over after the first MMP election. It will merely enter a new phase. If the first MMP government disappoints people by either its actions or its inaction, then pressure will inevitably build for new parties to enter Parliament to try to rectify the situation. Just as has occurred in Scandinavia and in Germany, in the long run it is probable that the number of parties in an MMP Parliament will grow – possibly not dramatically, and probably in fits and starts. The Christian Coalition and ACT could eventually enter Parliament in this way (if they don't in 1996). Looking to the future, it is possible that there will be at least five parties in Parliament after the 1999 election, and in the longer term – the first and second decades of the 21st century – there may well be an average of six parties in the New Zealand Parliament. Occasionally seven or even eight parties may win seats, but this will be unusual. The five percent hurdle is high, and many parties will fail to clear it – both in 1996 and thereafter.

Conclusion

The New Zealand electorate has displayed a large measure of conservatism and caution since the end of the Second World War. The reluctance to elect, and then the speed with which it rejects, Labour governments is one example. However, New Zealand's increasing heterogeneity is one of the reasons the country adopted MMP. It will also ensure that the country will probably never return to a simple two-party system. Indeed, the rules governing the conduct of Parliament and parliamentarians (examined in the next chapter) have already been extensively revised to reflect the emergence of a multi-party system. The genie has very definitely been let out of the bottle.

Notes

1 M. Duverger, *Political Parties: Their Organisation and Activity in the Modern State*, Methuen, London, 1951, p.217 (italics in original).

2 D. W. Rae, *The Political Consequences of Electoral Laws*, Yale University Press, New Haven, 1967, p.152.

3 In both the 1931 and 1935 general elections, representatives of four parties as well as four independents were elected to the House of Representatives.

4 S. Rainbow, *Green Politics*, Oxford University Press, Auckland, 1993.

5 For an analysis of the 1984 election, see S. Levine and N. S. Roberts, 'Parties, Policies, and Personalities: a Study of Two Electorates in the 1984 General Election in New Zealand', *Political Science*, 39, 1, 1987, pp.1–16.

6 For further details of the 1987 New Zealand general election, see M. Clark (ed.), *The 1987 General Election: What Happened?*, Social Sciences Research Fund Committee, Wellington, 1987; and S. Levine and N. S. Roberts, 'Parties, Leaders, and Issues in the 1987 Election', in H. Gold (ed.), *New Zealand Politics in Perspective*, Longman Paul, Auckland, 2nd edn, 1989, pp.423–45.

7 Further information on and other perspectives about the 1990 election are contained in C. James and A. McRobie, *Changes? The 1990 Election*, Allen & Unwin, Wellington, 1990; S. Levine and N. S. Roberts, 'The New Zealand General Election of 1990', *Political Science*, 43, 1, 1991, pp.1–19; E. McLeay (ed.), *The 1990 General Election: Perspectives on Political Change in New Zealand*, Department of Politics, Victoria University of Wellington, Occasional Publication No. 3, Wellington, 1991; and J. Vowles and P. Aimer, *Voters' Vengeance: the 1990 Election in New Zealand and the Fate of the Fourth Labour Government*, Auckland University Press, Auckland, 1993.

8 See R. Miller and H. Catt, *Season of Discontent: By-elections and the Bolger Government*, Dunmore Press, Palmerston North, 1993, pp.25–26.

9 For a critical view of Peters, see M. Hames, *Winston First: the Unauthorised Account of Winston Peters' Career*, Random House, Auckland, 1995.

10 Detailed analyses of the voting behaviour in the 1993 general election are contained in J. Vowles and P. Aimer (eds), *Double Decision: the 1993 Election and Referendum in New Zealand*, Department of Politics, Victoria University of Wellington, Occasional Publication No. 6, Wellington, 1994; and in J. Vowles, P. Aimer, H. Catt, J. Lamare and R. Miller, *Towards Consensus? The 1993 Election in New Zealand and the Transition to Proportional Representation*, Auckland University Press, Auckland, 1995. The overall results are analysed in S. Levine and N. S. Roberts, 'The New Zealand General Election and Electoral Referendum of 1993', *Political Science*, 46, 1, 1994, pp.40–69.

11 G. Sartori, *Parties and Party Systems: a Framework for Analysis*, Cambridge University Press, Cambridge, 1976, p.188.

12 In 1990 the party had fielded only 18 candidates, but in 1993 it contested 98 electorates and secured 2 percent of the votes cast.

13 In April 1996 Bruce Cliffe announced that he would not be seeking re-election to Parliament.

14 See Forschungsgruppe Wahlen, *Bundestagswahl 1994. Eine Analyze der Wahl zum 13. Deutschen Bundestag am 16. Oktober 1994*, Berichte der Forschungsgruppe Wahlen, Nr. 76, Mannheim, 1994, p.16.

15 Since the 1993 general election, Dunne has been a Labour MP, an independent MP, the founder and leader of Future New Zealand, a United New Zealand MP; he is now, of course, a member of a predominantly National party cabinet.

16 At position no. 40, he was ranked below 16 people who had never served in Parliament.

17 Based on the One Network News/Colmar Brunton poll results from September 1995 to February 1996.

18 See R. Douglas and L. Callan, *Unfinished Business*, Random House, Auckland, 1993, for a detailed exposition of his views.

19 One indication is that Prebble's book, *I've Been Thinking*, Seaview Publishing, Auckland, first published in February 1996, became an immediate best-seller. In late April Prebble decided to contest the Wellington Central electorate for ACT.

20 A. Lijphart, 'Political Parties: Ideologies and Programs', in D. Butler, H. R. Penniman and A. Ranney (eds), *Democracy at the Polls: a Comparative Study of Competitive National Elections*, AEI, Washington DC, 1981, pp.28–29.

21 Ibid, pp.42 and 31.

22 In addition, the Australian Democrats, which hold the balance of power in the Senate, in many ways reflect Lijphart's postmaterialist dimension.

23 J. Nagel, 'How Many Parties Will New Zealand Have Under MMP?', *Political Science*, 46, 2, 1994, p.154.

24 Ibid. See also R. Taagepera and B. Grofman, 'Rethinking Duverger's Law', *European Journal of Political Research*, 13, 1985, pp.341–52.

25 The Christian Social Union (CSU) in Germany is, in effect, the Bavarian wing of the Christian Democratic Union (CDU). As Lijphart has noted, 'the Bavarian CSU . . . has formed a joint caucus with the CDU in the German Bundestag' (Lijphart, 'Political Parties: Ideologies and Programs', p.38). The two divisions are also treated as one party in J. E. Lane and S. O. Ersson, *Politics and Society in Western Europe*, Sage Publications, 2nd edn, London, 1991, pp.149, 394, 400.

26 This is not to discount the possibility that some MPs will defect from their parties after the 1996 election (though any post-election exodus will probably be smaller than that during 1994–96) and that the Alliance could break up into two or more separate parties. Another mooted scenario has John Banks joining the Christian Coalition shortly before the 1996 election, winning Whangarei, and bringing other Christian Coalition MPs into Parliament even if the grouping fails to clear the five percent threshold.

CHAPTER 5

Parliament: changing the rules of the game

> The new MMP electoral system requires a complete rethink of the way Parliament conducts its affairs. The . . . new Standing Orders are a major step forward for good government and represent the most radical rewrite of Parliament's rules ever.
>
> *Michael Cullen (Labour MP)*[1]

In many ways voters who favoured the adoption of MMP had the reform and restructuring of Parliament in mind. MMP had its beginnings, not in a move to change the electoral system for its own sake, but in a growing dissatisfaction with the institution of Parliament – not only among the public, but among the members themselves.[2]

MMP inevitably involves a focus on Parliament. What is MMP, after all, other than first and foremost a change to the rules and procedures used for electing members to one institution, Parliament? All of the various manifestations of change within New Zealand resulting from the adoption of MMP have their beginnings in a determination to seek a new approach to selecting New Zealand's legislators. Thus all of the changes to the New Zealand political system arising out of MMP are in some way linked to Parliament. On one side are New Zealand's political parties, interest groups and the voters themselves; on the other side are governments, bureaucracies, the policy process, and the policies and regulations produced by the New Zealand state.

Apart from the voting process itself – the new ballot papers, the opportunity to cast two votes rather than one, the competition among the various political parties – the changes within Parliament are the most visible results of New Zealand's vote for MMP. These began virtually as soon as it was clear that MMP had won. On election night 1993 Prime Minister Jim Bolger declared that there was going to be a new style of governance – more inclusive, based on consensus and dialogue rather than the disciplined march of a parliamentary majority – and not long after he was reported as welcoming, even encouraging, the formation of new parties, potential coalition partners for his fragile (and soon to be shrinking) National government.

MMP and parliamentary change

As National's parliamentary caucus began to lose members, the rise of a multi-party Parliament began to present new challenges to parliamentary management. It was relatively easy to sort out members' research and office entitlements when there were only two parties; marginally more difficult when there were three; and just a bit more complicated when there were four. How was this to be done when there were five, then six, then seven? What was the 'opposition'? Indeed, what was the 'government'? Was it one party? Or did it include a one-member self-declared 'party', pledged to support the government, and possessing a virtually nil rating in the opinion polls?

The granting of 'pairs' – matching up the votes of members absent from the House – was sometimes contentious, yet generally straightforward, under two-party politics. It became somewhat more complicated when the Alliance, and then New Zealand First, came on the scene. How were 'pairs' to be sorted out when seven parties were represented in Parliament? For those working in Parliament, MMP was not an abstract idea, a form of protest, or a slogan – instead, beginning in 1994 with the transition period under way, it was a reality which required a lot of time and effort and thought to adapt long-standing practices and conventions.

A new Parliament?

The move to MMP coincides with a physical move – the return of MPs to the exquisitely restored parliamentary buildings. Members and parties will be adapting to their new physical environment at more or less the same time as they adapt to changes in the procedures and operations of Parliament. In a way these various changes, all occurring more or less simultaneously, make matters easier rather than more difficult: one opportunity begat another. All this means a new 'atmosphere' to parliamentary life. There are new offices and new social divisions; some parties are left across the road, in Bowen House, while others adapt to the new layout of the refurbished buildings. As analysts noted with the Beehive, where the separation of ministers from backbench colleagues (and from one another) has had implications for policy management and political relationships, the new structure of party and MPs' offices will inevitably have consequences both unintended and unavoidable.

Relationships among MPs within and between parties change in any case over time. During some periods MPs have interacted more freely than at others, when hostilities between and within parties have been a greater barrier. 'Consensus' and 'consultation' become more meaningful (less prone to use as 'soundbites' and slogans) when MPs of different parties and factions socialise together, more or less regularly. Will the new arrangements at Parliament encourage this to happen? Or will it remain somewhat unusual for MPs to cross party lines socially, thus making more difficult the process of communication and consultation, of working together across party lines on policy-related topics?

MMP also involves a new structure of relationships between MPs and the media. One of the consequences of moving the executive into the Beehive was that a television studio, the Beehive Theatrette, was available on the premises for ministers and MPs generally. The 'new' parliamentary buildings leave a place for the press gallery – no mean feat, as there have been robust suggestions in the past that the media had no such entitlement – but that place, in the Parliamentary Library, is remote from the parliamentary chamber and from the offices of MPs. As with all physical redeployments, this represents another change to parliamentary life to which both MPs eager to 'use' the media and the journalists themselves will need to adjust.[3]

In general, the effects of MMP on Parliament fall into two categories: one is the impact of MMP on the institution of Parliament itself, and the other is the consequences of MMP – the different structure of power, the changes in political and working relationships, the adaptations to established habits and conventions – for the MPs themselves.

Any consideration of the effects of MMP on Parliament must note the changes apparent in the political influence of Parliament *vis-à-vis* the executive. It is possible that New Zealand's legislature will alter from an essentially *arena* type of Parliament to a more *transformative* assembly in which committees, and MPs, have greater autonomy to make, revise and reject policy.[4] As a result of MMP-inspired (or MMP-initiated) developments, a government-dominated Parliament may become one in which the balance of power between the executive and the legislature is more equal. Already, in the transition phase, the National party could no longer guarantee itself a majority on many of Parliament's committees – an unheard-of situation for a government since at least the 1930s.

As for the MPs themselves, it is possible that an MMP Parliament may attract different types of people.[5] In the run-up to MMP, several MPs announced their decision not to stand at the next election, with some of them (including former Prime Minister David Lange) offering acerbic and witty observations describing their unwillingness to serve in an MMP Parliament as their rationale for retirement. Some present MPs, therefore, do not relish the sort of working environment Parliament may become after the first MMP election. Outside Parliament, however, there seems to be no shortage of would-be MPs. An MMP Parliament will possibly be different, not only because of new rules but because some of the people eager to become members will have a different style of politics once they arrive there. It is also possible that veteran MPs, freed from the old adversarial two-party system sustained by FPP elections, may behave differently. Parliamentary behaviour, often deplored by commentators, may therefore improve. What responsibilities 'list' MPs receive will no doubt be a major focus of public and media attention – and of concern to sometimes overworked constituency MPs as well.

MMP, Maori and the Maori seats

The strong support given to MMP by Maori voters in the 1993 referendum may also have implications for MMP-era Parliaments. The first MMP Parliament will already be historic for having five MPs elected off the Maori rolls. In certain circumstances, these MPs may be able to exert a greater influence than was possible in the past (although the five MPs, out of 120, represent roughly the same proportion of the total as the four MPs did when there were between 80 and 99 MPs). There may also be more Maori MPs, as well as Pacific Island and Asian MPs, in Parliament as a result of their selection for party lists. How Maori MPs, and representatives of other groups of New Zealanders, use their influence in Parliament will be of interest to those hoping for less party discipline, and more independence and initiative from MPs, for whom membership of a party caucus may be only one of several identifications they make.

The reactions among certain 'recognised' spokespeople after the MMP referendum contemplated a range of initiatives to enlarge Maori political power. Some looked towards Maori self-determination, even involving United Nations intervention; others spoke of establishing separate Maori political institutions, including a Maori Parliament, as well as new Maori political parties. Whether initiatives of this sort go much further may depend on how well Maori MPs can advance Maori interests in an MMP Parliament. This, in turn, is apt to be influenced by how much the Maori MPs are needed by the government – as well as by how closely they identify with one another as Maori, irrespective of party or type of MP (constituency or list).

For nearly 60 years the Maori seats were held by Labour. The 1993 election and its aftermath revealed that dynamic processes were under way within Maoridom which had gone largely unperceived by the New Zealand media and other observers. Labour's loss of one of the Maori seats and the popularity of New Zealand First (and in particular its leader) among Maori generally suggested that Maori voters were preparing to set out in new directions. The largely unfavourable response of Maori MPs to Helen Clark's election as Labour leader was another sign that at least some Maori might be seeking different results from politics than might have been expected. A politics of ethnicity was also apparent in the favourable reaction among Maori to the selection in December 1993 of Peter Tapsell as Speaker, as well as in the extremely awkward sequence of events in which veteran Labour MP Whetu Tirikatene-Sullivan was passed over for election as a committee chairperson ('chairman' under the old Standing Orders) at the start of the parliamentary session.

In the transition to MMP there seemed already to be political changes among Maori, not only outside Parliament but also within the House. Ultimately, in seeking to understand Maori political relationships, what may be of greatest importance is whether an MMP Parliament, with Maori entering the Chamber in different ways – through a range of political parties; as constituency or list MPs; via the Maori or general electoral roll – will see a rise in the authority of the elected parliamentary leadership of the Maori people *vis-à-vis* Maori and non-Maori (including government) alike.

In any case, an enhanced position for Maori MPs would be consistent with a further increase in the numbers of Maori seeking to be on the Maori roll. A new 'Maori option', conducted after MMP is in place and involving a more extensive attempt to inform all Maori of the consequences of enrolling on the Maori roll (as opposed to being unenrolled or remaining on the general roll), is likely to see more Maori opt for the Maori roll, and possibly in sufficient numbers to cause a further rise in the number of Maori seats.

MMP and Parliament's new Standing Orders

While the first changes to the institution of Parliament were the result of MPs leaving the parties to which they were elected – as we saw in Chapter 4, nine left National to form smaller parties, and four left Labour – the most far-reaching changes have focused on the rules of Parliament itself. In December 1993 the Standing Orders Committee was appointed with the following terms of reference:

- 'examining and reporting on the procedures of the House;
- keeping under review the work carried out by all other select committees; and
- if it considered it necessary, issuing guidelines to the committees relating to their general procedures.'

During 1994 and 1995 the committee held 31 meetings, totalling around 60 hours, as it considered what changes, if any, were needed to Parliament's rules of procedure. What was agreed to in the report of the committee (approved by

Parliament in December 1995, and coming into effect on 20 February 1996) is nothing short of remarkable: a series of changes which enlarge the power of Parliament relative to the executive, increase the autonomy of individual MPs, and widen the scope for action by smaller parties. Many of the changes to Standing Orders were widely recognised as overdue; some political scientists had been calling for them for decades.[6]

Like the changes in New Zealand's parties during the lead-up to MMP, the new parliamentary rules represent a (year-long) period of innovation and experimentation before the first MMP election. The hope is that incumbent MPs and parliamentary staff will be able to accommodate themselves to the new rules and practices – which will become the new 'status quo' – before the entry into Parliament of a large group of first-term MPs (possibly more than 50), many from political parties unused to substantial parliamentary representation.

The thorough review and rearrangement of Parliament's Standing Orders was prompted by the impending enlargement of parliamentary membership and the commencement of an MMP electoral system. Many of the changes made, however, were not strictly speaking required by MMP; thus the approval of MMP opened up opportunities for parliamentary reform – a welcome though perhaps ironic development, as anti-MMP campaigners during the 1993 referendum sometimes argued that what was needed was not a new electoral system but the reform of Parliament (for which they promised to work if FPP were retained). In the event, it appears that New Zealanders will be getting both: a much-heralded new electoral system and, with less fanfare, a potentially revitalised New Zealand Parliament.

The changes to Parliament's rules fall into several categories:

- the parliamentary calendar;
- the role of the Speaker and other presiding officers;
- the status of opposition parties;
- the reporting of parliamentary proceedings;
- the behaviour of MPs;
- voting procedures;
- the select committee system;
- legislative procedures;
- parliamentary privilege;
- financial procedures.

The parliamentary calendar

The length and timing of parliamentary sessions were changed in 1985 under the influence of the then Deputy Prime Minister, Geoffrey Palmer.[7] The previous Prime Minister, Sir Robert Muldoon, had a habit of governing for months at a time without calling Parliament into session, a practice which the opposition Labour party found unacceptable. Labour regarded as especially irksome Muldoon's preference for having Parliament at last begin meeting around the time of Labour party conferences. Palmer's rearrangement of the parliamentary schedule saw Parliament sitting for most of the year, to the displeasure of some MPs (especially, but not only, farmers), with the intention of making Parliament a more 'professional' body and, at the same time, redistributing the workload throughout the year so as to prevent a build-up of legislation towards the end of the session. As with so many of Labour's 'reforms', things did not quite work out as intended: in Parkinsonian fashion, work expanded to fill the time available for it, and late-night sessions and the effective suspension of some of Parliament's rules through the declaration of 'urgency' went on, if not exactly as before, then with embarrassing frequency nonetheless.

The new Standing Orders do not dispense with the idea of Parliament sitting more or less the entire year. However, the rhythm of the parliamentary calendar has been altered in some interesting ways.

Each year in the three-year parliamentary cycle is to begin with a statement from the government about its intended legislative programme. Furthermore, 'the greater complexity in party arrangement in an MMP Parliament and the desirability of introducing more forward planning into the House's proceedings'[8] led the committee to recommend, and the House to approve, the setting-up of a new Business Committee. This committee is to 'be seen as the House's executive responsible for directing the flow of work'; its specific tasks are:

- 'to determine the order of the business to be transacted and the times to be spent on it in the coming week's sittings;
- to recommend to the House a programme of sittings for each calendar year;
- to operate as a committee of selection in respect of recommending the personnel to serve on select committees.'[9]

The membership of this committee, chaired by the Speaker and meeting in the Speaker's office, would include one person from 'every party with six members [or more]' and, for parties with fewer than six members, one person to represent them.[10] While in some respects the broad purpose of the reforms to Standing Orders (like MMP itself) has been to redirect attention towards Parliament, and so reduce the dominance of an executive generally formed from one party, the decision-making process of the Business Commitee should permit the government to maintain control over the flow of legislative business, notwithstanding the level of representation on the committee given to opposition parties. The Business Committee strives to reach agreement by 'consensus (or unanimity)' or, if this cannot be done, then by 'near-unanimity'.[11]

Some of the stress on MPs, and much of the criticism of their performance (criticism not limited to the public, but heard from MPs themselves), centres on the lengthy evening sittings of Parliament – necessary, it seems, for Parliament to complete its business, even though some overseas legislatures with substantial responsibilities manage to do so exclusively within daylight hours. There would be grounds for feeling that the problem of Parliament's sitting hours – which have implications for the outlook and conduct of members as well as the morale and efficiency of parliamentary and departmental staff – will become more serious under MMP, given that the number of MPs increases by 21 (just over 20 percent). Of course, limitations on speaking times are one way in which a greater number of MPs can take part in parliamentary business without extending the sitting hours of Parliament.

The new MMP Parliament, however, like the MMP system as a whole, will be to some extent on trial from the moment it comes into existence. Its ability to survive will depend on whether it improves the status and stature of Parliament. In turn, the legitimacy of MMP will hinge very much on how MPs behave; on how Parliament conducts its affairs; on the quality of representation and discourse provided by MPs who would not be in the House at all were it not for the party list and the need to gain only five out of every 100 party-list votes (i.e. cross over the five percent threshold).

The Standing Orders Committee rightly perceived that electors voted not so much for a change to the electoral system – that was only the means, the instrument, the procedural tool, for a quite different end – but for a change to Parliament, and policy-making, and the character of New Zealand's parties. We examine some of these topics elsewhere (see Chapters 4 and 9). With respect to the quality of parliamentary decision-making, the committee referred to submissions it received from people 'who advocated no evening sittings', on the grounds that 'working long days could not be conducive to good decision making'. But most MPs do not live in Wellington; their families, their domestic lives, are away from the capital. In the absence of evening meetings of Parliament, it is argued, they would be working on parliamentary or party business in any case.

But perceptions of Parliament depend to some degree on what is broadcast over the radio, and not on the work being done in select or caucus committees or on party work. Ultimately, the Standing Orders Committee decided to recommend a 'normal' sitting week in which the House met on:

- Tuesdays from 2.00 to 6.00;

- Wednesdays from 2.00 to 6.00 and from 7.30 to 10.00; and
- Thursdays from 10.00 to 1.00 and from 2.00 to 6.00.

In effect these arrangements give further recognition to the primacy of party in modern parliamentary politics: Tuesday mornings are unavailable for meetings of Parliament because 'party caucus meetings would be held'[12] at that time (a shift from Thursday mornings). In addition, Wednesday mornings are set aside for select committee meetings.

The role of the Speaker

The committee expected that 'the Speaker's role will be enhanced in an MMP Parliament'.[13] It was agreed that there would be two Assistant Speakers, and the committee – in keeping with the MMP philosophy of consensus and co-operation between parties – expressed the hope that 'a convention [would] develop whereby one will be appointed from the Government side and one from the Opposition side of the House'.[14]

Recognition of parties in parliamentary procedure

Many countries with vigorous party systems give little attention to parties in constitutional documents, formal rules or legislation. The previous Standing Orders of the House of Representatives did not give explicit recognition to political parties, but both formal rules and conventions (some of them found in Speakers' rulings) recognised the existence of a governing and an opposition party. Obviously, a multi-party Parliament complicates such arrangements. In addition, given that the MMP ballot papers explicitly call upon electors to cast a party vote, maintaining a silence about parties in Parliament's own rules would seem to be both increasingly awkward and constitutionally inappropriate.

The Standing Orders Committee acknowledged that Standing Orders and the administration of the House and its committees would need to 'take account of parties and their sizes'.[15] This will affect the allocation of speaking time, the order of speaking, representation on committees, and so on. In general a principle of proportionality is to be followed with respect to debates, asking of questions, and other matters, with the time allocated reflecting parties' relative strength in the House.

The role of Leader of the Opposition

The position of Leader of the Opposition has been part of the parliamentary scene since 1889, with statutory recognition first occurring in 1933.[16] How the position is to be defined – and whether it is to exist at all – was considered by the committee, given expectations of a multi-party Parliament under MMP. Although there is something of a fiction in describing the leader of the largest opposition party as Leader of *the* Opposition, the committee decided that 'the position is still appropriate and should be retained'.[17]

Reporting parliamentary proceedings

Although there has been an official report (known as Hansard) since 1867, the verbatim transcription of parliamentary proceedings has never covered the very important and detailed debate on bills during the 'committee of the whole House' stage of consideration. The new Standing Orders remedy this gap in the parliamentary record, thus enhancing parliamentary accountability, and hence the democratic process, in a direct and straightforward manner.

Quorum requirements and members' behaviour in the House

The committee took a realistic view of the influence on MPs of most formal parliamentary discussion and debate. 'Members are elected on a party platform and . . . spending time in the Chamber listening to debate on the issues is unlikely to make significant changes to their attitudes. . . . The debate in the House is an opportunity for parties to state their views on particular matters which, primarily, the Government is proposing. It is not normally a means of changing members' opinions.'[18]

As a result of this surprisingly frank though entirely accurate statement, the committee recommended that the quorum requirement should be abolished altogether (except for a division, at which 20 members must be present). Although in some ways the votes for MMP in 1992 and 1993 were expressions of disenchantment with party control – and the behaviour and popularity of dissident MPs, claiming to represent either their own conscience or their constituents rather than espousing the views of their caucus, show that the public preferred MPs who took a view independent of their party – the committee noted, rightly, that 'an MMP-elected system, which is based on party votes, is going to reinforce the party decisions taken outside the House'.[19] The pretence that parliamentary debate actually matters to MPs (in terms of their votes on legislative proposals) is thus dispensed with; so too is the need for MPs to sit in the Chamber, where, ostensibly listening, their enforced presence leads to behaviour which lowers the reputation of Parliament and may even convey a misleading impression about the actual workload of MPs.

Concern about 'the public's perception of members' behaviour in the Chamber'[20] was expressed by the Standing Orders Committee. It was right to do so. Already, under the new rules, unruly behaviour by MPs has been held up as precisely the sort of thing which MMP – and the new Standing Orders – was intended to curb. There is, of course, an almost instinctive readiness on the part of the public and the media, and among MPs themselves, to proclaim that 'nothing has changed' or indeed *can* change. But there is a desire for change in Parliament and this Standing Orders Committee – unlike some previous reviews, which, notwithstanding public dissatisfaction with Parliament, saw little need for Parliament to do much that was different[21] – supported that view and sought to advance it. 'The committee is aware that many people are critical of behaviour in the Chamber and accepts that some of that criticism is valid.'[22] The remedies were to increase the authority of the Speaker; for 'presiding officers to take a firm stance'[23]; for presiding officers to take 'firm action' against MPs who raise 'irrelevant and lengthy points of order which waste the time of the House'.

Some parliamentary customs themselves were responsible for Parliament's low esteem. Like the judicial changes introduced in 1996, which saw counsel and judges dispense with the wearing of wigs, so too Parliament has modernised some of its practices. Since 1988 wigs have generally been worn by the Speaker and the Clerk only on formal state occasions and during the formal part of each day's parliamentary business (although the present Speaker prefers to wear a wig at all times when presiding in the House). The new Standing Orders also address the rules governing how members may refer to one another. 'The present rules do not allow members to refer to each other by name in the House, and members are normally referred to by their electorate or by their portfolio title. This will not be able to be maintained in an MMP Parliament as there is no suitable form of address for list members.'[24] Of course the key word here is 'suitable'; MPs, with a gift for abuse and invective peculiar to their profession, would surely be able to discover ways of referring to members elected on party lists. No doubt such descriptions as, for example, 'the number 5 member for the Peters party' would be invented without much delay, and these could be expected to proliferate. Indeed, media comment on the very first day in which Parliament operated under the new Standing Orders focused principally on the much more familiar approach being taken by MPs to one another, with Winston Peters apparently being the first MP to refer to another MP by his first name in the manner now permitted by Standing Orders.[25]

Voting procedures

The committee recognised the waste of time – and, again, the effect on public perceptions of Parliament – due to the then existing methods of voting, with the ringing of bells and members filing through doors marked 'Ayes' and 'Noes'. Instead, the committee recommended a three-tiered system of voting in Parliament. In the first instance, questions will be decided on a voice vote. However, requests may be made for what is known as a 'party vote', allowing for a formal recording of MPs' preferences. As further recognition of the central place of parties in modern parliaments, this takes the form of 'a member from each party in the House . . . [stating] the number of votes that the party is casting'.[26] An independent member may then state his or her vote, followed by any members not voting with their party (and thus 'effectively crossing the floor').[27]

Members may also request a 'personal vote'. This is expected to occur on conscience issues, and also when the Speaker determines that the decision on the party vote 'is so close that a personal vote may make a material difference to the result'.[28]

The committee rejected the use of electronic voting, as found in some overseas parliaments. The committee indicated that it would keep Parliament's voting system 'under review' during the pre-MMP transition period, however, and there is still the possibility of Parliament deciding to move to a wholly new system if this seems appropriate.

Two other innovations were introduced into Parliament's voting rules by the new Standing Orders. As New Zealanders have been given greater voting choice with MMP – two votes to cast, and many new parties from which to choose – so too MPs have been given greater discretion and flexibility. In addition to the types of vote noted above, MPs have now been given the option of casting a vote of abstention and having that vote formally recorded. Previously, MPs not wishing to vote for or against a measure had to remain outside the locked doors of the Chamber while the vote was being taken. They were thus not shown as being present, rather than choosing to abstain. This option could have important implications on sensitive issues and even on confidence measures, with one or more MPs effectively saving (or sinking) the government by opting to abstain. Whether New Zealand's voters will regard this sort of behaviour as acceptable remains to be seen. It is possible that an abstention will be caricatured as a vote not to vote, as an evasive tactic, as a 'weasel' ploy to avoid taking a stand one way or the other. MPs whose abstention on key issues causes a government to fall, or allows one to survive, are certain to be subjected to a strong examination of their intentions from the media, at the very least.

The second important innovation allows for proxy voting. This replaces the system of pairing, which has come under increasing stress as a result of both narrow government majorities – a 'pair' for an absent government member has sometimes been criticised as allowing the government to escape defeat in the House – and the more complicated MMP environment (with many parties with whom absences of MPs may be linked through 'pairing'). Given that most absent MPs would vote with their party were they present, pairing was an important and even necessary legislative device which preserved the actual political balance in Parliament while allowing government and non-government MPs alike discretion to be away from the Chamber on other duties. This has been especially important for cabinet ministers, who need to be absent from the Chamber – and even from New Zealand, at times for lengthy periods – in order to carry out government business.

The new rules preserve the consequences of pairing but do away with the procedure. Members will be able to give authority for a proxy vote to be cast in their name. However, there are limitations on the use of proxy votes: parties will not be able to cast proxy votes for more than 25 percent of their MPs (except that there is a minimum of one proxy for each party, thus allowing small parties to cast a proxy vote).

The Speaker has been given a deliberative vote – a change from previous practice, where the Speaker cast a vote only in the case of a tie – so that a party will not 'lose' a vote when one of its members takes up the position. 'The committee considers that under an MMP election it may be critical to the formation of a government that the balance of the party representation in the House is not disturbed because the Speaker does not have a deliberative vote.'[29] Thus, in considering 'that a majority of the House should be required to decide a question',[30] it was decided in effect that the vote of the Speaker will be part of that majority.

The new select committee system

The new select committee system was also shaped by the onset of MMP and the enlarged parliamentary membership. The committees are the pride of Parliament, the engine room where much of the detailed legislative work is carried out, and they are invariably pointed to (sometimes defensively) by MPs concerned about criticism of the image of Parliament arising from what they regard as an undue focus on the debating Chamber. Certainly the committees, professionally staffed and deliberating beyond the public gaze (and hearing), are where multi-party, non-partisan co-operation among MPs and staff can take place in an effort to remedy flaws in proposed legislation.[31]

The Standing Orders Committee recognised that the mathematics of an enlarged Parliament appeared to require some committee restructuring. 'In a Parliament of 120 members, around 96 members may be available to serve on select committees. This assumes an executive of some 20 members and the presiding officers sitting only on special purpose or *ad hoc* committees . . .'[32] As a result, the review recommended that 12 subject select committees be established, each of them to have a membership of eight MPs. Ministers would be expected to brief committees and attend when relevant Estimates were being examined. Committee reports were to be taken more seriously: 'the House needs to give more attention to debating committee reports, which should identify matters for consideration by the House'.[33] Some committee reports may now present 'the range of members' views on matters of significance'. Although separate 'minority reports' were not envisaged, 'there could be greater desire in an MMP Parliament for dissenting views to be known' and indeed full agreement on all issues before a committee was 'not to be expected'. The Standing Orders Committee distinguished between cabinet conventions and committee procedure: 'There is no convention of collective responsibility attaching to committees . . .'[34]

Committees are also to be more appropriately serviced, with greater access to independent advice. This may, in time, enable committees to develop a greater expertise, which would be separate from the resources available through the executive (i.e. departmental officials) and on which committees have tended to rely. It is also expected that committees will provide 'a record of the proceedings',[35] thus bringing committee practice into line with what takes place in the much-disparaged (yet very well-documented) debating Chamber.

Legislative procedures

The new Standing Orders modify some long-standing legislative practices. The amalgamation of legislative changes into omnibus bills has been criticised in part for the difficulties faced by individuals and groups seeking to make submissions on the matters being covered. The new rules restrict the use of omnibus bills to:

- finance or confirmation bills, which are to be used 'only for the validation of illegal actions and for authorisation of actions that would otherwise be illegal';[36]
- local legislation bills;
- Maori purposes bills;
- reserves and other lands disposals bills;
- statutes amendment bills;
- law reform bills, when they amend Acts which deal with an interrelated topic.

The rules for statutes amendment bills stipulate that *any* MP objecting to any clause in the bill during the committee of the whole House stage will succeed in having that clause struck out of the bill. This 'veto', formalising a previous convention, nevertheless reflects the MMP ethos; it is designed to 'ensure that consultation with all parties represented in the House takes place before such a bill is introduced'.[37]

Recognising that 'the process of passing legislation is the House's primary function', the Standing Orders Committee sought (in part through a study of procedures in European parliaments) to discover or develop more expeditious procedures. As a first step, the committee recommended the end to first-reading debates on bills presented to the House. The first debate on a bill will instead take place when it is proposed that the measure be read a second time. The committee proposed having more extensive explanatory notes at the front of bills, identifying not only the principles behind the bill but 'the policy the Minister or member in charge is intending to implement through the legislation and matters it is intended to remedy'.[38] The approach suggests a greater attempt at rationality, and accountability, but whether as a result the public will sense much of an improvement in Parliament is perhaps doubtful.

Critics of Parliament will be pleased to see a reduction in the use of supplementary order papers by governments. These items contain at times important amendments to legislation, and they are tabled in the House during a bill's committee stage. Over the years they have had the effect of reducing opportunities for the public and interested groups to make their views known, and these late amendments also bypass the much-vaunted select committee process. About this, the Standing Orders Committee was forthright: 'This is not a practice that should continue'.[39] Government amendments that are outside what was contemplated during the committee process are to be referred back to a select committee for further public hearings. Here too a change to the rules is designed to raise the stature of Parliament and MPs relative to the government; how it works in practice will depend on the outlook and conduct of the MPs themselves. These modifications to parliamentary procedure, which restrict the power of government, are, however, compatible with a more vigorous Parliament in which more than two parties compete for influence – with an MMP Parliament, in short, rather than a two-party Chamber in which the opposition must always lose.

Parliamentary privilege and civil liberties

The expansive powers of Parliament have at times been of concern to civil libertarians, with some recent incidents calling into question the long and important tradition of parliamentary privilege. The new Standing Orders do not curb the freedom of speech of MPs. At the same time, new rules endeavour to adhere more closely to principles of 'natural justice' than before. For instance, Standing Order [SO] 391 stipulates that 'a member who makes an allegation of breach of privilege or of contempt may not serve on an inquiry into that allegation'.

In the face of criticisms that 'breaches of privilege' may be offences against rules too vague to provide 'fair warning' in advance to the person charged with the breach, attempts have been made to give greater specificity to matters of privilege. SO 386 requires that allegations 'of breach of privilege or of contempt must be formulated as precisely as possible so as to give any person against whom it is made a full opportunity to respond to it' – a perhaps obvious requirement, but one included in the new Standing Orders only after a recommendation to the committee by constitutional expert Professor Philip Joseph (who was commissioned to report to the committee on 'issues of natural justice').

SO 393 gives 18 separate examples of contempts, some of them restricted to MPs – 'as a member, accepting fees for professional services rendered by the member in connection with proceedings in the House or at a committee'[40] – and others applicable to anyone in New Zealand (though often written with the news media in mind: e.g. 'publishing a false or misleading account of proceedings before the House or a committee').

SO 394 defines as 'a contempt of the House' an absence of more than seven consecutive sitting days 'without obtaining leave of absence'. SO 395 extends 'contempt' to any 'member who, before participating in the consideration of any item of business, fails to declare any pecuniary interest which the member has in that business'.

The new Standing Orders also respond to concerns about the rules of 'natural justice' and their place in the parliamentary environment. People may exercise their right to counsel when called to give evidence to select committees. Rejecting proposals (as in a private member's bill from Labour MP David Caygill) that MPs 'intending to make an allegation against an individual' should give prior notice to the Speaker and proceed only with the Speaker's concurrence, the committee wrote into the new Standing Orders a quasi-right of reply: 'It is a right to apply to the Speaker for a response to be incorporated in the record'.[41] The request to the Speaker must take place within three months and 'the Speaker's role is simply to determine whether, in all the circumstances, a response should be put on the parliamentary record'.[42] While these new procedures in the area of privilege should meet some previous public concerns, in fact very few cases of privilege generally arise in the life of a Parliament – affecting either MPs or the public.

Parliament, taxation and expenditure

Of perhaps greatest importance to the actual work of Parliament are the new Standing Orders dealing with the scrutiny of government finances.[43] Previous Standing Orders prevented MPs from moving any proposal that might involve even the slightest expenditure of public monies unless the government agreed to it. The new rules permit MPs 'to initiate proposals involving expenditure or taxation', subject to a government 'financial veto'. This could be exercised only if such proposals 'would have more than a minor impact' on:

- 'the Crown's total operating expenses;

- the Crown's total operating revenues;
- the balance between the Crown's total operating expenses and the Crown's total operating revenues;
- the level of the Crown's total debt; or
- the level of the Crown's net worth.'[44]

The new rules give MPs, at least in principle, an enhanced power with respect to government policy-making. As virtually *every* proposal has *some* financial cost or implication, the previous long-standing rules vested great power in the executive and stripped Parliament of much of its capacity for independent action. However, the opportunity now to move legislative proposals, notwithstanding their financial implications, gives opposition and backbench MPs greater incentive to take the legislative business of the House (and their own role in it) more seriously.

Most parliamentary reforms come up against 'the predominance of party politics', however.[45] Will party politics subvert this change to Standing Orders, so that few MPs endeavour to make use of it? It is also accepted that the government remains accountable for 'the Crown's financial performance and position' and that it therefore needs to maintain 'control over the fiscal aggregates that determine that performance and position'. But the language of the relevant Standing Orders does not make that 'control' as axiomatic as it has been in the past. For instance, SO 312 (1) states that:

> A certification by the Government not concurring in a bill, amendment or motion on the ground that, in its view, the bill, amendment or motion would have more than a minor impact on the Government's fiscal aggregates must state with some particularity the nature of the impact on the fiscal aggregate or aggregates concerned and the reason why the Government does not concur in the bill, amendment or motion.

How this requirement is interpreted in practice will be an important element in determining whether this latest effort to raise the stature of the House *vis-à-vis* the executive succeeds. Another will be the attitude taken by MPs and by parties towards the exercise of their still modest but nonetheless enhanced position.

In any case, new procedures have been circulated to ministers, parliamentary under-secretaries, chief executives, parliamentary staff and the Speaker describing in some detail the Crown financial veto procedure contained in the new Standing Orders adopted by the House. These provide guidelines for departments and ministers, so that they will have processes in place 'for monitoring developments in the House and select committees affecting their minister's portfolio or Vote and for identifying initiatives which may have an impact on the Government's fiscal aggregates or the composition of a Vote'.[46]

It would be surprising if, at least at the outset, there were any significant disruptions to a government's spending programme as a result of the new capacity of MPs to persevere with proposals that have some financial consequences associated with them.

A summary of some of the differences between the previous Standing Orders and the new rules is given in Table 5.1. Note that many of the changes made were not, strictly speaking, required by MMP. As noted earlier, many of them have long been favoured by students of Parliament and by many MPs themselves. What the introduction of MMP has done is create an opportunity for MPs to restructure the rules of Parliament – to overhaul and modernise them – under circumstances which permitted the normal institutional inertia and leadership opposition to procedural changes to be overcome. Thus the column headed 'New Standing Orders' includes procedural changes which could have been introduced under FPP; however, they were not, and it is no coincidence that the Standing Orders Committee, authorised to review parliamentary procedure, interpreted its mandate broadly and with confidence: 'As the next Parliament would be elected by the mixed member proportional (MMP) system, the committee decided to treat its order of reference as requiring it to carry out a complete review of the Standing Orders to ensure that the House of Representatives and its committees were prepared to operate in the new environment.'[47]

Table 5.1. *New Zealand parliamentary procedures under different Standing Orders*

	Old Standing Orders	**New Standing Orders**
Parliamentary calendar	Parliament sits over entire year; regular evening sittings and provisions for parliamentary business to be considered under 'urgency'.	Parliament sits over entire year; evening sittings Wednesday only. 'Urgency' sitting hours commence on the day following agreement to the motion for urgency; 'extraordinary urgency' (which permits the House to meet through the night) may be claimed only if the Speaker agrees that the business to be considered justifies it. Each year begins with statement from the government about its intended legislative programme. Business Committee established to direct the flow of work in the House.

	Old Standing Orders	New Standing Orders
Role of the Speaker and other presiding officers	The Speaker remains a member of his or her party after election to the chair.	The authority of the Speaker is enhanced; party membership remains. Speaker chairs the Business Committee. A Deputy and two Assistant Speakers to be elected. Presiding officers to take firmer action against MPs who waste the time of the House.
Status of opposition parties	Standing Orders do not give explicit recognition to parties. Leader of the Opposition position recognised since 1933.	Standing Orders take account of parties and their size. Leader of the Opposition position retained for reference to leader of largest opposition party.
Reporting of parliamentary proceedings	No reporting of parliamentary proceedings in the committee of the whole House.	There will be a report of the committee of the whole House proceedings; meetings of select committees can be recorded where a committee resolves to do so, subject to resources.
Behaviour of MPs	Quorum requirement in the House is 15. MPs are referred to by their electorate or portfolio title.	Quorum requirement in the House is abolished. MPs may be referred to by name.
Voting procedures	The bells are rung and members file through doors marked 'Ayes' and 'Noes' to record a division. Speaker (or chairperson in committee) has casting vote in the event of a tie.	Requests may be made for party and proxy voting. MPs can cast a vote of abstention and have it formally recorded. Speaker does not have casting vote if the division is a tie but does have deliberative vote. Speaker is assumed to vote with his or her party and not the government.
Select committee system	Present structure adopted in 1985, with 13 subject select committees plus ad hoc committees, each having a membership of five and quorum of three. They have combination of legislative and scrutiny functions.	After 1996 election, 12 subject select committees established plus ad hoc committees, each having a membership of eight MPs and quorum of four.* Ministers can brief committees, hear evidence, and answer for

* This was reduced to three by leave of the House for the period leading up to the first MMP election in 1996.

	Old Standing Orders	New Standing Orders
Select committee system *(continued)*	Abstention votes not recorded. Chairperson has casting vote.	policy, but do not have voting powers. Committee reports take on new significance, and may give differing (or 'minority') views of committee members. Greater access to independent advice. Abstention votes recorded. Chairperson has no casting vote.
Legislative procedures	Debate in the House follows introduction of bill. No bill is introduced during an adjournment unless it is a local bill (if the House is not sitting within the next 14 days). No limit on select committees for time taken to consider a bill. After consideration, bill is reported to the House with recommendations for change. A debate of up to one hour ensues and the bill is set down for second reading. The second reading debate is followed by a stage where the committee of the whole House	No debate in the House following introduction of bill. Bills may be introduced during an adjournment if the Business Committee agrees in the case of government and members' bills. Main debate takes place at second reading, after which bill is referred to select committee. Limit of six months for consideration of bill; committees can now divide a bill. Debate on the consideration of the report from select committees. Committee of the whole House considers bill clause by clause and bill is enacted after the third reading. The four types of bills are called: government bills, members' bills, private bills and local bills.
Financial procedures	Appropriation rule in place which prevents members from moving any proposal that involves even smallest amount of expenditure requiring an appropriation unless government agrees.	Financial veto procedure which gives members the right to propose expenditure or taxation but gives the government of the day the right to veto proposal if it thinks it will have more than a minor impact on a range of fiscal aggregates.
Parliamentary privilege	Natural justice procedures and Bill of Rights Act requirements not fully observed.	Principles and procedures of natural justice to be observed; members of public given limited right of reply to allegations made about them in the House.

MPs' salaries and allowances: two rates of pay?

Other changes to Parliament have been instituted quite apart from the formal changes made to Standing Orders. These include decisions about the allocation of resources to parties and MPs and, partly as a result, changes to the research units which service MPs and parties represented in the House. The success of MMP will depend on appropriate resources being made available to the larger number of MPs and parties represented in the House.

Some of the changes originate from other sources: for instance, pursuant to section 16 of the Civil List Act 1979 and the Higher Salaries Commission Act 1977, the Higher Salaries Commission issued the Parliamentary Salaries and Allowances Determination 1996, altering the salary levels and allowances of MPs from the Prime Minister to the most junior backbencher. In late 1995, the Higher Salaries Commission announced the salaries of the Speaker, Deputy Speaker and each Assistant Speaker, noting in an explanatory memorandum that this was necessary 'to reflect the new Standing Orders of the House of Representatives' under which the positions of Chairman and Deputy Chairman of Committees had been abolished, with the positions of Assistant Speaker being newly created.[48]

The 1996 determination of new allowances was necessary to establish the salaries and allowances for 'members taking office in the first House of Representatives to be elected under the MMP voting system'. It was important, according to the commission, that 'both constituency candidates and list candidates should be made aware in advance what the salaries and allowances payable after the election will be'. It is also noteworthy that the commission gave explicit consideration to the way in which it expected MMP to operate once the election was over (i.e. how MMP would affect the running of Parliament): 'The Commission has to direct its mind not so much to the new voting system as to the way in which the House and its members, once elected, will operate thereafter.' But there were too many uncertainties: 'there are questions still unanswered in that regard, and only time will answer them. It will not be surprising if the Commission finds it necessary, as the picture unfolds, to amend the post-election provisions of this determination.'

Consistent with the Standing Orders Committee's report, the commission continued its recognition of the status of Leader of the Opposition, describing the person holding that title as in effect 'a Prime Minister-in-waiting'. As a result, it decided to persevere with the practice of equating the salary of the Leader of the Opposition with that of a cabinet minister, although, like the committee, it recognised the added complexities of this determination in a multi-party House.

The commission described its 'most difficult' question as whether to pay constituency and list MPs the same salary. It noted, perhaps tartly: 'On the basis that the Commission's task is to fix a rate for a job, it would be helpful to know with reasonable certainty what the job specifications of constituency members and of list members respectively will be.' The commission knew what constituency MPs do: they take part in the work of Parliament and they service 'the needs and demands of the constituency in the member's electorate'.

As for list MPs, however, 'the position is much less clear', since they have no electorate to service. Furthermore, with fewer constituency members, it seemed to the commission that there would be '65 constituency members trying to do the constituency work now done by 99'. This was likely to prove an onerous burden. While the royal commission had contemplated that list MPs would have some constituency responsibilities, the Higher Salaries Commission stated that it had 'communicated with each of the 20 political parties which have so far registered under the Electoral Act 1993 in the hope of ascertaining what expectations the parties have of their list members; but with little result'.

In the end, although clearly tempted to do so, the commission decided not to distinguish between the two types of MP on the basis of speculations about their comparative workloads. This would have disrupted the introduction of MMP, as the commission would have divided constituency and list members, 'for salary purposes, into first and second class members'. However, the commission did decide to differentiate between them in their allowances. There is a basic expenses allowance which takes into account that MPs have demands made upon them as a result of their accountability to a specific geographical electorate. The basic expenses allowance given to constituency MPs was set at a rate higher than for list MPs ($7,000 per annum as against $4,000) and constituency MPs were given a 'constituency allowance', with the commission undertaking to 're-visit the question of some corresponding allowance to list members if appropriate'.[49]

Conclusion

If the Higher Salaries Commission is unsure what list MPs will do, and the political parties selecting candidates for party lists are unable or unwilling to tell them, little wonder there are wider uncertainties throughout the community. Our survey of opinion leaders included members of Parliament themselves. Although MPs have become generally unwilling to fill out questionnaires, a high proportion (67 out of 99) completed our survey.

Perhaps most relevant is what the MPs thought the impact of MMP would be on their working environment, i.e. Parliament. Most (79 percent) thought that cabinet would have 'less control over Parliament'; that select committees would have a greater role over legislation (75 percent) and over the executive (70 percent); and that the legislative process would be 'slower than in the past' (79 percent). Most (75 percent) thought that there would be more Maori MPs in the next Parliament and 61 percent expected there would be more women MPs too.

What we did not ask MPs, however, was whether they were looking forward to MMP. There is little doubt that this final year of New Zealand's last FPP Parliament is already proving to be interesting for MPs. It is characterised by a government whose majority (when it has one) keeps changing, a multi-party environment in which the number of parties, and their members, continues to fluctuate, and a new regime of Standing Orders offering greater opportunities for legislative influence to those non-executive MPs interested in taking advantage of them. This may be the beginning of a Parliament in which there will be 'a higher degree of public consultation and discussion than has been common in the past',[50] a vision to be fulfilled in its entirety when the members of the first MMP Parliament take their seats. If it is not, then the changes to the electoral and parliamentary rules of the 1990s will have been largely in vain, and there will be much work to be done exploring what went wrong, and why.

Notes

1 *Dominion*, 14 December 1995, p.10.

2 For instance, a 1982 survey of MPs found that (of those taking part) 74 percent of National MPs and 79 percent of Labour MPs agreed that Parliament's Standing Orders 'should be revised'. This was one of the few matters on which Labour and National MPs were in agreement, and they proposed a fairly extensive list of changes. See S. Daniell, 'Reform of the New Zealand Political System: How Likely Is It? A Survey of the Attitudes of Members of the New Zealand Parliament to Reform Proposals', *Political Science*, 35, 2, 1983, pp.151–89.

3 Generally speaking, the media are likely to remain more interested in matters outside the House – particularly the activities of ministers and the manoeuvrings of parties – especially if the 1996 election produces a coalition government.

4 A 'transformative' legislature possesses an 'independent capacity, frequently exercised, to mold and transform proposals from whatever source into laws'. An 'arena' type of legislature serves as a setting for 'the interplay of significant political forces in the life of a political system', where parties and MPs can put their rhetorical and representative skills on display. See N. Polsby, 'Legislatures', in F. I. Greenstein and N. Polsby, *Handbook of Political Science*, Volume 5, Addison-Wesley, Reading, Mass., 1975. For a discussion of the type of Parliament (and government) which we have traditionally had in New Zealand, see R. M. Alley, 'Parliamentary Parties in Office: Government –Backbench Relations', in S. Levine (ed.), *Politics in New Zealand: a Reader*, George Allen & Unwin, Sydney, 1978, pp. 96–112.

5 The political science literature on leadership and representation includes a number of typologies which seek to categorise political leaders and/or representatives and predict their behaviour. See, e.g., J. D. Barber, *The Lawmakers: Recruitment and Adaptation to Political Life*, Yale University Press, New Haven, 1965; I. Diamond, *Sex Roles in the State House*, Yale University Press, New Haven, 1977; and J. J. Kirkpatrick, *Political Woman*, Basic Books, New York, 1974.

6 See, e.g., K. Jackson, *New Zealand: Politics of Change*, Reed, Wellington, 1973, Ch. 9; S. Levine, *The New Zealand Political System*, George Allen & Unwin, Sydney, 1979, Ch. 3; various essays in Sir John Marshall (ed.), *The Reform of Parliament: Contributions by Dr Alan Robinson and Papers Presented in His Memory Concerning the New Zealand Parliament*, New Zealand Institute of Public Administration, Wellington, 1978.

7 A review of these developments, which in some ways set the stage for the more far-reaching changes brought about by the latest Standing Orders review, is found in G. Skene, 'Parliamentary Reform', in J. Boston and M. Holland (eds), *The Fourth Labour Government: Radical Politics in New Zealand*, Oxford University Press, Auckland, 1987, pp.72–88. See also G. Palmer, *New Zealand's Constitution in Crisis*, John McIndoe, Dunedin, 1992, especially pp.110–18.

8 *Report of the Standing Orders Committee on the Review of Standing Orders*, House of Representatives, Wellington, 1995, p.20.

9 Ibid, pp.20–21.

10 Ibid, p.21. SO 76 provides that 'parties with fewer than six members which are in a Government coalition are entitled to choose one member between them to represent them on the committee. Other parties with fewer than six members and independent members are entitled to choose one member between them to represent them on the committee'.

11 Ibid, p.21. See SO 77.

12 Ibid, p.19.

13 Ibid, p.13.

14 Ibid, p.15.

15 Ibid, p.16.

16 Ibid.

17 Ibid.

18 Ibid, p.23. Note that the formal debate in the House would be irrelevant to MPs' voting behaviour whether MPs were considering themselves to be representing their party's view or the outlook (however determined) of their electorate. Only MPs who were using their own best judgement, and were accountable at election time for the way in which they had used their intellectual and moral faculties in making up their minds on issues, would presumably be open to having their vote changed as a result of speeches given in the House.

19 Ibid.

20 Ibid, p.24.

21 While earlier reviews did not successfully address all of the issues surrounding public unhappiness with the performance of Parliament or the behaviour of MPs (ultimately a matter for the MPs themselves, their parties' approach to parliamentary politics, and the 'culture' of parliamentary life), significant changes were introduced from time to time: particularly in 1985, with the revisions to the select committee system, and in 1991, with the development of a new set of procedures for considering financial matters (see *Report of the Standing Orders Committee on a New Financial Procedure for the House of Representatives*, House of Representatives, Wellington, 1991).

22 *Report of the Standing Orders Committee*, p. 24.

23 Ibid.

24 Ibid, p.26.

25 The old Standing Orders provided that 'No member shall refer to any other member by name' (SO 162). MPs are still not permitted to refer to one another *only* by their first name.

26 *Report of the Standing Orders Committee*, p.28.

27 Ibid.

28 Ibid.

29 Ibid, p.30.

30 Ibid.

31 Select committees are open to the public during the hearing of submissions. They are closed when MPs are deliberating over the contents of legislation and working through proposed revisions.

32 *Report of the Standing Orders Committee*, p.32.

33 Ibid, p.42.

34 Ibid, p.44.

35 Ibid.

36 Ibid, p.50.

37 Ibid, p.51.

38 Ibid, p.54.

39 Ibid, p.56.

40 Note that this would make 'a contempt' the asking of questions in the House in return for payment, as has occurred (with subsequent outcry) in the House of Commons.

41 *Report of the Standing Orders Committee*, p.81.

42 Ibid.

43 An authoritative account of the relationship between Parliament and questions of public finance (appropriations, financial scrutiny, taxation) is given by the Clerk of the House, D. McGee, in his *Parliamentary Practice in New Zealand*, 2nd edn, GP Publications, Wellington, 1994, Chs. 30–34.

44 *Report of the Standing Orders Committee*, pp.61–62.

45 K. Jackson, *The Dilemma of Parliament*, Allen & Unwin/Port Nicholson Press, Wellington, 1987, p.178. One of the themes of Jackson's study is that efforts to change (or 'reform') Parliament have often come to nothing as a result of the party system. Whether we now have the 'electoral reform coupled with a good parliamentary committee system' which Jackson saw as the 'far more promising approach to reform' will be tested by New Zealand's experience once the first MMP Parliament has been sworn in.

46 Cabinet Office Circular (96) 2, 16 February 1996, p.1.

47 *Report of the Standing Orders Committee*, p.10.

48 *The Parliamentary Salaries and Allowances Determination 1995, Amendment No. 1*, New Zealand Government, Wellington, 1996.

49 All quotes are from 'Explanatory Memorandum' appended to *The Parliamentary Salaries and Allowances Determination 1996*, New Zealand Government, Wellington, 1996.

50 R. Mulgan, 'The Democratic Failure of Single-Party Government: the New Zealand Experience', *Australian Journal of Political Science*, 30, special issue on 'Party Systems, Representation and Policy Making', 1995, p.94.

CHAPTER 6

Who is going to govern? Forming and changing governments under MMP

> . . . my Government has moved – over a period of just 24 months – from a single party majority, to a coalition majority, to a coalition minority . . . We now expect to return to a coalition majority.
>
> *Jim Bolger*[1]

Previous chapters have considered the implications of MMP for the party system and the role of Parliament. It is now time to explore how the new electoral system will affect the processes of forming and changing governments. This chapter begins by distinguishing between four different types of government and examining which of these is the most likely outcome under MMP, in both the near future and the longer term. Next, the constitutional conventions surrounding the dissolution of Parliament and the formation of governments are considered, paying particular attention to the role of the Governor-General. Finally, the chapter outlines the powers of, and limitations on, caretaker governments.

Types of government

A common way of categorising governments is according to whether they hold a majority or a minority of seats in Parliament and whether they comprise a single party or more than one party (i.e. a coalition of parties). The term 'coalition' in this regard refers to a government in which at least two parties are represented in the political executive, or more specifically the cabinet. Based on these distinctions, four types of government are possible:

- single-party majority government;
- multi-party majority government;
- multi-party minority government; and

- single-party minority government.

For examples, see Table 6.1.

In classifying kinds of government, many other distinctions can be made. The academic literature on coalition governments, for instance, distinguishes between coalitions according to their size, ideological cohesiveness, and the number of parties involved.[2] Hence, distinctions are made between minimum winning coalitions (i.e. those with the minimum number of parties necessary to secure a parliamentary majority), minimum connected winning coalitions (i.e. those which are not merely the smallest necessary to control Parliament but are also relatively cohesive ideologically), oversized coalitions (i.e. those which contain more parties than are necessary to secure a parliamentary majority), grand coalitions (i.e. those which contain all the major parties), and all-party coalitions. Minority governments can also be subdivided according to various criteria, such as the nature and degree of the support they receive from non-government parties.[3]

Table 6.1. ***Different kinds of government, with overseas examples***

	Minority (i.e. less than half the seats held by the government)	**Majority** (i.e. more than half the seats held by the government)
Single party	Labour government, Norway (1990–) Social-Democratic government, Sweden (1994–)	Conservative government, Britain (1979–) Labor government, Australia (1983–96)
Multi-party (i.e. coalition)	Centre-Right government, Sweden (1991–94) Centre-Left government, Denmark (1994–)	CDU/CSU/FDP government, Germany (1982–) Liberal-National government, Australia (1996–)

Parties frequently co-operate with one another without entering into formal coalition arrangements. For instance, a party may offer to help maintain another party (or parties) in government (e.g. by voting with it – or at least abstaining – on motions of no confidence) yet not make this support conditional on securing seats in the cabinet. Such parties are sometimes referred to as 'supporting' parties.[4] From time to time they may sign formal agreements with the Prime Minister specifying the matters upon which they will vote with the government and noting any conditions that may apply. Supporting parties can be distinguished from: (a) those parties which consistently oppose the government (i.e. the 'opposition' parties); and (b) those parties which adopt a more equivocal stance (especially with respect to motions of no confidence and issues of supply). Table 6.2 summarises the various positions taken by the parties in the 1993–96 Parliament (i.e. as coalition partners, supporting parties, opposition parties, and equivocators).

Remarkably enough (as Table 6.2 shows) all four types of government have occurred in New Zealand since the 1993 general election. In fact, by early March 1996 there had been no fewer than six different governing combinations over the preceding two years. Some of these have been relatively unusual by international standards. For instance, in the case of the arrangement between National and RoC between September 1994 and August 1995, Ross Meurant – RoC's leader and initially its only MP – was his party's sole office-holder in the so-called 'coalition'. Moreover, he retained his position as a parliamentary under-secretary rather than being elevated to membership of the cabinet – as would be normal in coalitions overseas.[5] For this reason, the National/RoC arrangement was on the very margins of being a genuine coalition. By contrast, the deal between National and United in February 1996 involved both United's Peter Dunne becoming a full member of the cabinet and the negotiation of a formal (albeit brief) two-party agreement. Yet even this coalition was unusual. First, despite having seven MPs to National's 43, United secured only one cabinet post (out of 20). Second, the cabinet post went not to United's leader or deputy leader but to a more junior MP. The fact that there were good political reasons for these decisions does not detract from their novelty.

A cursory glance at Table 6.2 and Appendix 1 might suggest that New Zealand entered a period of considerable governmental instability after the 1993 election. This, however, was not the case. Although there was much political turbulence, this does not equate with instability. The National party

Table 6.2. ***Different kinds of government in New Zealand, 1993–96***

Minority government	Majority government
	National (50 MPs) 29 November 1993–11 September 1994 Supporters: none Opposition: Labour & NZ First (47 MPs) Equivocal: the Alliance (2 MPs)*
	National and Right-of-Centre (50 MPs) 11 September 1994–9 May 1995 Supporters: Future NZ (from 16 November 1994) (1 MP) Opposition: Labour & NZ First (47 MPs, then 46 from 12 October 1994) Equivocal: the Alliance (2 MPs)

Minority government	Majority government
National and Right-of-Centre (49 MPs until 28 June 1995, then 45) 9 May 1995–28 August 1995 Supporters: Christian Democrats (1 MP from 9 May), and United (7 MPs from 28 June) Opposition: Labour, NZ First & the Alliance (from 8 June) (46 MPs until 8 June, 48 until 28 June, then 46) Equivocal: the Alliance (until 8 June) (2 MPs)	
National (43 MPs) 28 August 1995–28 February 1996 Supporters: United, Right-of-Centre (Conservatives) & Christian Democrats (10 MPs in total) Opposition: Labour, the Alliance & NZ First (46 MPs)	
	National and United (50 MPs) 28 February 1996–6 March 1996 Supporters: Christian Democrats (1 MP) Opposition: Labour, the Alliance & NZ First (46 MPs) Equivocal: Trevor Rogers (Conservatives) & Ross Meurant (independent) (2 MPs)
National and United (49 MPs) 6 March 1996–3 April 1996 Supporters: Christian Democrats (1 MP) Opposition: Labour, the Alliance & NZ First (47 MPs) Equivocal: Trevor Rogers (Conservatives) & Ross Meurant (independent) (2 MPs) **National and United** (48 MPs) 3 April 1996– Supporters: Christian Democrats (1 MP) Opposition: Labour, the Alliance & NZ First (48 MPs) Equivocal: Trevor Rogers (Conservatives) & Ross Meurant (independent) (2 MPs)	

* The Alliance's support for National before June 1995 was highly conditional. Indeed, as early as March 1994 the leader of the Alliance, Jim Anderton, indicated that the Alliance would not necessarily support the government on a motion of no confidence.

remained in government throughout the period, the membership of the cabinet altered relatively little, and there were only a few significant changes in the allocation of portfolios. Most policy settings also remained relatively stable. Hence, although in a formal sense there were many changes in the *kind* of government between 1994 and 1996, their political significance was not as great as might initially be suspected. The main reason was that throughout this period the majority of MPs favoured a National-led government and opposed an early election.

Nevertheless, as Table 6.2 indicates, the various parties represented in the 1993–96 Parliament adopted very different stances towards the government. In the period immediately after election night – when it seemed that there might be a hung Parliament – the Alliance initially adopted a stance of conditional support on confidence matters, at least until arrangements were in place for an MMP election. The party subsequently moved to a position of firm opposition and in early June 1995 introduced a motion of no confidence in the government. Labour and New Zealand First, by contrast, adopted a consistent policy of opposition from the 1993 election (i.e. they remained committed to voting against the government on all motions relating to confidence and supply). Meanwhile, several of the new splinter parties – particularly the Christian Democrats and United – gave firm assurances to support the government on issues of confidence and supply. Lastly, the Right-of-Centre/Conservative party began life as National's coalition partner in late 1994 but by early 1996 had moved to a much more equivocal stance. Of course, even those parties which offered full support on matters of confidence reserved their right to oppose the government on specific measures.

Historically, three of the four kinds of government depicted in Table 6.1 have been relatively rare in New Zealand, certainly during the twentieth century. Single-party minority governments have occurred only once since the Great Depression (the National government between mid-1995 and late February 1996). Multi-party minority governments were unknown until May 1995. And multi-party majority governments have been uncommon (the exceptions being wartime, the Great Depression, and the transition to MMP). Instead, New Zealand has had mainly *single-party majority* governments (although some have had very slender majorities). By international standards this is unusual (see Table 6.3). In many European countries, for instance, coalition governments have been the norm rather than the exception. Since the Second World War about a third of all governments in democratic countries have been minority governments.[6] As Table 6.3 indicates, minority government (whether single party or multi-party) has been particularly common in Scandinavia. In the main, single-party majority governments have been limited, with a few notable exceptions like Ireland

and Japan, to countries with FPP electoral systems (e.g. Britain, Canada, India, and New Zealand).

Table 6.3. *Majority and minority governments, 1945–87*

Country	Total number of governments	Number of majority governments	Number of minority governments	Percentage of minority governments
Belgium	31	27	4	13
Canada	17	9	8	47
Denmark	25	3	22	88
Finland	32	21	11	28
Germany	14	14	0	0
Ireland	17	10	7	41
Israel	29	26	3	10
Italy	48	28	20	42
Netherlands	19	16	3	16
New Zealand	18	18	0	0
Norway	21	9	12	57
Spain	5	2	3	60
Sweden	21	9	12	57
United Kingdom	18	16	2	11

Notes

a. For the purposes of this table, the definition of change of government includes a change in the parties represented in the cabinet, a change of Prime Minister, and the reconstitution of the (same) government after a general election.

b. Finland has had seven non-partisan governments in addition to the 32 mentioned above.

Source: K. Strom, *Minority Government and Majority Rule*, Cambridge University Press, Cambridge, 1990, p.58. Revised by authors.

Types of government under MMP

Under MMP a party need not necessarily win 50 percent of the party vote in order to obtain a majority of the seats in Parliament. This is because some parties are unlikely to win constituency seats or secure sufficient party votes to cross the five percent threshold. Hence, a proportion of votes are likely to be 'wasted' – judging by recent opinion polls, between 5 and 10 percent in the first MMP election. In this event, a party would be able to secure a majority of seats with around 45–47 percent of the party vote. In New Zealand, it has not been uncommon for parties to win such high levels of electoral support under FPP, but no party has won more than 50 percent of the vote since 1951.[7] In view of this, single-party majority governments under MMP cannot be ruled out. Indeed, given National's high opinion-poll ratings since early 1995 – with public support in excess of 45 percent in some polls – there is certainly a chance that it might win an overall majority at the 1996 general election.

While single-party majority government is a possibility, it is arguably the least likely *long-term* outcome under MMP. Which of the remaining three types of government, then, is most likely? The survey conducted in late 1995 (see Chapter 3) indicates that a majority of respondents expect New Zealand to have a majority coalition government. Around 56 percent thought this was the most likely outcome in the short term, while 76 percent expected majority coalitions to be the norm over the longer term. By contrast, some kind of minority government was considered most likely in the short term by 27 percent of respondents and over the longer term by less than 15 percent. Within the 'policy community' in New Zealand (see Chapter 9), therefore, there is a strong expectation that majority governments will predominate.

How does this conclusion fit with the academic literature on the subject? Specialists in comparative government contend that the type of government which occurs under proportional representation systems is influenced by a range of factors.[8] Three of these are particularly important: first, as suggested in our opening chapters, the country's political culture, history and traditions, especially views about the desirability or otherwise of majority governments; second, the constitutional rules and conventions relating to the formation of governments and the dissolution of Parliament; and third, the nature and configuration of the parties in Parliament.[9] Let us explore how each of these factors may affect the kind of government which eventuates under MMP.

Political culture and the expectation of majority governments

Because of New Zealand's long history of majority governments, both the political elites and the public at large expect that majority governments will, and ought to, be formed if at all possible. In the short term, at least, their expectations may encourage parties to look for coalition partners more seriously than is necessary to form an effective and stable government. Expectations aside, having a relatively stable parliamentary majority, even a small one, gives a government substantial political advantages. The outcome of votes on key legislation can be virtually guaranteed. Consultation with opposition parties need not be so extensive or burdensome. And a government with a firm majority can – at least in principle – determine the date of the next election. It thus has the potential to seize the opportunity afforded by favourable opinion-poll ratings to secure an electoral advantage over its major political rivals. Hence, there will be strong pressures for parties to seek to form a majority government.

Yet, while the political elites may prefer majority governments, New Zealand does not have a 'coalition culture' like Belgium, Germany or the

Netherlands. Similarly, the recent experience of minority government has demonstrated that stable and relatively effective government does not require a formal parliamentary majority. Coalitions also may have significant disadvantages. The benefits of office must be shared among a larger group of MPs. There are also the ongoing difficulties of reconciling the competing interests of the various parties which make up the coalition. Moreover, in New Zealand, unlike Australia and Britain, there is no well-established tradition of prime ministers calling early elections, and voters may react negatively to a government which sought to exploit a favourable political situation by going to the polls early. In practice, therefore, the capacity of a majority government to dissolve Parliament early may afford little or no electoral advantage.

Constitutional rules and conventions

If New Zealand's political culture is currently ambivalent about, if not ill disposed to, minority governments, its constitutional conventions relating to government formation and the dissolution of Parliament can be expected to facilitate – though not necessarily encourage – minority governments. Three institutional rules are important here.

First, and most obvious, there is no constitutional requirement for the government to hold a majority of the seats in Parliament. Indeed, there are no constitutional provisions precluding governments below a certain size. In theory, therefore, a relatively small party, having, say, fewer than 20 seats, could – if the political circumstances dictated – form a government.

Second, New Zealand's rules concerning government formation are expressed in negative rather than positive terms.[10] That is, an incumbent government does not require Parliament's explicit endorsement after an election in order to remain in office; rather, it can continue until it loses a vote of confidence. And, for one reason or another, the opposition parties may choose not to move such a motion immediately after an election, preferring to wait until the political circumstances are more opportune. Similarly, there is no formal constitutional requirement for a *new* government to submit to a vote of confidence or win a vote of investiture in Parliament before it can assume power (or before the Prime Minister and other ministers are sworn in by the Governor-General). A new government, once formed, simply retains power until it loses a vote of confidence. In practice, of course, no Governor-General will wish to swear a government into office unless it represents that grouping of MPs which either obviously commands, or is more likely than any other grouping to command, the support of Parliament (see below). Nevertheless, the hallmark of 'negative parliamentarism' is that, while

Parliament retains the power to unseat a government, there is no constitutional requirement for a government to receive a confirming vote in Parliament before taking office. Under 'positive parliamentarism', by contrast, the head of state cannot act without an explicit direction from Parliament (via a formal vote) on whom to appoint as Prime Minister.[11]

Overall, the empirical evidence strongly suggests that negative parliamentarism is more conducive to minority government than positive parliamentarism. Countries with PR and negative parliamentarism (e.g. Denmark, Finland, Norway and Sweden[12]) have significantly more minority governments than countries with PR and positive parliamentarism (e.g. Belgium and Germany).[13] Negative parliamentarism is also associated with small minority governments (i.e. governments with less than 40 percent of the seats in Parliament) and relatively short government formation processes (e.g. one to two weeks).[14] Precisely why 'negative' formation rules encourage minority government is open to debate. Plainly, however, the answer lies in the way the particular 'rules of the game' interact with and influence the strategies of political parties, thereby affecting the relative political advantages of particular governing options.[15]

The third rule is that a government does not require an *absolute* parliamentary majority in order to win a vote of confidence. All that is required is a simple (or relative) majority. Hence, if a party (or parties) sympathetic to the government is prepared to abstain in such a vote – as is now an option under Parliament's new Standing Orders (see Chapter 5) – it is perfectly possible for a minority government to survive opposition censure.

Against this, under New Zealand's current constitutional conventions, the leaders of minority governments are potentially in a weaker position than those of majority governments over calling early elections. This is because the Governor-General may, in rare circumstances, refuse a Prime Minister's request for a dissolution (unlike the situation in, for instance, Denmark). This could arise, for example, if there is doubt over whether the existing Prime Minister commands the support of the House and if another person may be able to form a government instead.[16] This point is developed later in the chapter.

The configuration of the party system

The future configuration of the country's party system will also have a major impact on the type of government which is most common. The nature of the party system has implications for the level of political certainty, the willingness of the parties to bargain with one another, and their willingness to entertain short-term or long-term alliances. Key features of the party system which will be important under MMP are the number, size, stability, and ideological orientation of parties represented in Parliament.[17] Drawing on the analysis in Chapter 4, the following brief observations can be made about the composition of Parliament under MMP.

First, in the short term there is only one party – National – which can realistically expect to secure significantly more than a third of the party vote. Hence, under MMP there may be only one major party rather than two relatively evenly balanced major parties (as was the case for most of the post-war era, and remains the case in a few countries with PR, such as Austria and Germany).

Second, unlike the situation in some other jurisdictions, there is little prospect of an extremist or anti-system party securing seats in Parliament. Anti-democratic or illiberal political movements have never secured much popular support in New Zealand, and the five percent threshold imposes a major barrier for extremist parties seeking parliamentary representation. Accordingly, all the parties which secure seats in the future are likely to be acceptable as potential coalition partners.

Third, a large question mark hangs over whether the political landscape under MMP will be characterised by a 'two-bloc' or a 'balancing-centre' approach. With the two-bloc approach, there is a relatively clear political divide in Parliament, with the minor parties remaining aligned more or less permanently with one or other of the bigger parties. In this scenario, governments change when one bloc of parties gains sufficient electoral support to oust the opposing bloc. With the balancing-centre approach, a party (or parties) in the centre of the political spectrum oscillates from time to time between supporting parties of the centre-left and parties of the centre-right. In this scenario, changes in government depend to a significant degree on the decisions of the centre party (or parties).

The pattern which emerges under MMP will depend on which (if any) centre parties secure representation in Parliament, and whether such parties align themselves more or less permanently with another party (e.g. National or Labour) or remain open to a range of coalition partners. At the time of writing, only New Zealand First (of the current parties positioned near the centre of the political spectrum) stood a high chance of securing over five percent of the party vote at the first MMP election, and thereby winning at least six seats. United's Peter Dunne can reasonably be expected to win his Ohariu–Belmont seat in Wellington (because of National's agreement not to stand a candidate). But, unless United's overall popularity improves, it will at best win only sufficient party votes to entitle it to a single list seat.[18] The prospects for the other minor parties currently represented in Parliament – the Christian Democrats and the Conservatives – winning seats at the first MMP election are not nearly so good. Likewise, of the parties currently unrepresented in Parliament, only ACT stands a realistic chance of winning seats.

Accordingly, a potentially critical issue in determining who governs after the 1996 general election will be how New Zealand First and United choose to align themselves. United's stance is reasonably certain: as National's current coalition partner it can be expected to side with National rather than Labour. Of course, if it has only a few MPs its capacity to affect the shape of the first MMP government may be strictly limited (i.e. unless National and any supporting parties, like ACT, secure at least 57 or 58 seats). Much, then, could depend on New Zealand First. As it stands, New Zealand First's policy position, together with the disposition of its leadership, make it more likely to align with Labour than National. If this situation remains unchanged and if New Zealand First retains its parliamentary representation in the longer term, then the political landscape in the early years of MMP will be characterised by a two-bloc rather than a balancing-centre approach. That is, there will be two opposing blocs of parties: the Alliance (in some form), Labour (in some form) and New Zealand First versus National and United (and any other allies, such as ACT and/or the Christian Coalition).

Fourth, under such a regime, the critical matter determining whether the government is of the centre-left or the centre-right is which bloc secures more parliamentary seats. Hence, if National and United fail to secure a majority of seats, they will be able to remain in office only in the following circumstances:

- if a party on the right, such as ACT, wins sufficient seats to give the centre-right bloc an overall parliamentary majority;
- if a centre or centre-right party, such as the Christian Coalition, chooses to support National/United and wins sufficient seats to give the centre-right bloc an overall parliamentary majority;
- if a number of MPs on the right of the Labour party, fearful of Labour being held to ransom by the Alliance or New Zealand First, defect to one of the existing centre-right parties (or form their own party); or
- if, despite having a clear majority of seats, members of the centre-left bloc (e.g. the Alliance, Labour and New Zealand First) are unable to co-operate sufficiently to form a stable government. In this event, National (or National and an allied centre or centre-right party) would continue in office, but may have major difficulties enacting its legislative programme.

Plainly, there are many potential governmental outcomes beyond 1996, depending on the particular combination and relative strength of the parties securing representation at the first MMP election. It is not sensible to sketch each possible scenario here. Let us therefore consider just a few of the more likely outcomes and consider their implications for the kind of government which might eventuate.

Suppose, for the sake of argument, that there are five parties in the first MMP Parliament: the Alliance, Labour, National, New Zealand First and United. Suppose further that National and United fail to secure an overall majority; the same applies to the combined strength of the Alliance and Labour. This means that New Zealand First holds the balance of power. Furthermore, suppose that no party is prepared to join the National/United coalition, that a minority Alliance government would be unacceptable to the other parties (even if the Alliance secures more seats than Labour), and that a minority Alliance–New Zealand First government would be unacceptable to Labour and National. In these circumstances, the following outcomes are theoretically possible:

(i) the continuation of a minority National/United government;
(ii) a minority National government;
(iii) a minority Labour government with declared support on matters of confidence, including supply, from both the Alliance and New Zealand First;
(iv) a minority coalition government comprising the Alliance and Labour;
(v) a minority coalition government comprising Labour and New Zealand First; or
(vi) a majority coalition government comprising the Alliance, Labour and New Zealand First.

Assessing which of these options is most likely poses difficulties. However, political realities suggest that options (iv) and (vi) are unlikely, largely because the Alliance would probably consider it contrary to its longer-term political interests to be part of a coalition government in the immediate aftermath of the first MMP election. For one thing, the Alliance will have only two MPs with parliamentary experience (Jim Anderton and Sandra Lee). For another, joining with Labour in government would require significant policy compromises, which might cause disaffection, resulting in a loss of electoral support at the second MMP election. By contrast, if the Alliance remains outside the government, it will still be able to exercise considerable influence on policy development without being seen by its supporters to have compromised on key policy commitments. The counter-argument, of course, is that many new Alliance MPs may find the potential benefits of ministerial office – greater power, status, resources, and salaries – very attractive. Nevertheless, on balance the Alliance is likely to conclude that its best interests are served by being outside the government.

This leaves options (i), (ii), (iii) and (v). In each case the outcome is a *minority* government. Hence, if the composition of Parliament after the first

MMP election is along the lines sketched above (and of course it may not be), there is a strong likelihood that New Zealand will see a continuation of minority government. While options (i) and (ii) are possible, they are unlikely. The Alliance and New Zealand First would probably prefer a minority Labour government to a minority National/United coalition or a minority National government, because they have greater policy affinities with Labour than with National. Against this, personality clashes may make for an uneasy relationship between the Alliance and Labour. Also, one must not lose sight of the Alliance's strategic objective of replacing Labour as the principal party on the centre-left of the political spectrum.

Arguably, option (v) offers greater advantages to both Labour and New Zealand First than option (iii). Labour secures a larger number of guaranteed votes in Parliament and additional MPs with whom to share the burdens of office. New Zealand First secures posts in the cabinet and more influence over day-to-day policy issues. Against this, there would be the problems of securing a satisfactory coalition agreement and maintaining a semblance of unity between two uneasy bedfellows. On balance, however, the most likely outcome is option (v).

Such a conclusion, of course, depends on Parliament containing the five parties as specified above. If more than five parties are represented in the first MMP Parliament, many other possibilities present themselves, depending on the nature of these parties and their relative parliamentary strength. Were a party sympathetic to National (in addition to United) to secure seats, and were this party willing to join with National and United to form a majority coalition government, that would become a strong possibility. Similarly, if the Labour party were to suffer further serious internal difficulties, with several MPs leaving to join (or form) a centre or centre-right party, then again it might be possible for a majority government to emerge. Minority government, therefore, is by no means the only realistic outcome.

Types of government in the long term

The discussion so far has concentrated on the kind of government most likely in the short term. But what about the medium to longer term? Assuming that PR remains in place for several decades, then, based on the experience of other countries with PR and taking into account the distinctive features of MMP and New Zealand's social structure and political culture, the following rough predictions can be offered.

- New Zealand can expect to have further minority governments, some of which will be coalitions. However, it is doubtful whether minority government will become the norm.
- Coalitions are more likely than single-party governments. These will

typically consist of two parties and are most likely to be minimum winning coalitions. Oversized coalitions, grand coalitions or all-party coalitions will be rare.

- Most coalitions will comprise parties which are relatively close to each other on the ideological continuum (i.e. minimum connected winning coalitions). Nevertheless, coalitions of strange political bedfellows – as have occurred occasionally in Denmark and Ireland – cannot be ruled out.[19]
- Coalition governments will tend to include the party or parties close to the centre of the ideological continuum (or the most central party in a multi-dimensional policy space).[20] Politicians primarily interested in enjoying the fruits of ministerial office will thus have an incentive under MMP to form or join centre parties (unless, of course, such parties have little prospect of securing at least five percent of the party vote or winning a constituency seat).
- There will almost certainly be changes from time to time in the ideological orientation of governments. Nevertheless, it is unclear whether there will be a roughly equal balance of centre-left and centre-right governments or whether New Zealand will enter a period of long-term centre-left or centre-right dominance. Similarly, although a two-bloc approach to parliamentary politics is likely in the short term, the longer-term pattern is much less certain. It is possible, for example, that a balancing-centre pattern (i.e. the German model) could become the norm.

Forming and changing governments: the constitutional framework

Having considered the four types of government that are possible under MMP and the factors that will influence which of these is most likely after the first and subsequent MMP elections, we should now turn to the formal constitutional principles governing the process of government formation, the dissolution of Parliament, the changing of governments between elections, and the powers of caretaker governments.

The mechanics of government formation

Under FPP it has usually been clear on election night, or at least after the final count, which party has the confidence of Parliament and will thus form the next government. The period of caretaker government has therefore been limited to that between election day and the swearing-in of the new government by the Governor-General, generally within two weeks of the election.[21] Likewise, it has been plain which party leader the Governor-General should call on to form the next government (and hence to be Prime Minister). Under MMP, however, it may not be immediately clear after an election which party (or parties) can command the support of Parliament (i.e. on votes of confidence). Forming a government in such circumstances is thus likely to be more complex and time-consuming. As a result, there could well be more extended periods of caretaker government, even if very long periods of caretaker government – as, for instance, have occurred in the Netherlands – are highly unlikely.[22]

Under New Zealand's current constitutional arrangements, Prime Ministers are appointed by the Governor-General under the general power to appoint ministers contained in the Letters Patent.[23] In determining whom to appoint, the Governor-General – currently Sir Michael Hardie-Boys – is expected, by convention, to choose the person most likely to command the confidence of Parliament. If, of course, it is not immediately apparent after an election who this person is, then various issues of the utmost constitutional sensitivity arise. For instance, from whom should the Governor-General seek advice on whom to appoint: the incumbent Prime Minister alone, or all the party leaders? Should he seek consultations with each party leader or should he call on each leader in turn to try to form a government? If adopting the latter approach, whom should he ask first: the leader of the party with the largest number of seats, or the leader of the party who is most likely in the Governor-General's judgement to command majority support (even if this person does not lead the party with the largest number of seats)? In short, when the political situation is unclear, and particularly when it is uncertain who is best able to command the confidence of Parliament, when and how should the Governor-General exercise his 'reserve powers'?[24]

By convention, Governors-General are expected to act as neutral umpires and non-partisan upholders of the constitution. Their role is not to be 'king-makers' but to confirm the verdict of the people via their elected representatives in Parliament. There is a risk of the Governor-General's neutrality being compromised were he to use his independent judgement in appointing (or dismissing) a Prime Minister. This could damage the credibility of the office, as well as undermine the democratic process. Consequently, after an election it would normally be preferable for the party leaders to be left to resolve between themselves who should govern. In almost all circumstances, such inter-party consultation should produce the person who is clearly most likely to command the confidence of Parliament. It will then be possible for a government to be formed and for Parliament to be summoned. (Under Section 19 of the Constitution Act 1986 Parliament must be summoned within six weeks of the return of the writs.)

In the unlikely event that inter-party consultations do not produce within a reasonable time an agreement on who can command the support of Parliament, the Governor-General may have to exercise his constitutional judgement. Two main options would be available. First, he could simply allow the existing 'caretaker' Prime Minister to continue until the question of confidence had been tested in the House. Thus Parliament would be summoned, and appropriate confidence votes would no doubt shortly ensue. In those circumstances, the Governor-General would be able to await the appropriate 'signal' from Parliament and, once satisfied that a particular party, or grouping of parties, had the confidence of the House, act accordingly. Second, he could appoint as Prime Minister the person whom he believes to be more likely than any other to command the confidence of the House. This could, for example, be the existing Prime Minister or the leader of the party with the most seats.[25]

As a general rule, the Governor-General should intervene directly in the process of government formation only when the party leaders are unable to secure agreement on who should govern. In such situations, various principles and precedents (within the Commonwealth and beyond) are available to guide his actions.[26] It is crucially important that the Governor-General avoid actions which might be construed as partisan. To this end, he would be unwise to rely solely on the advice of the incumbent Prime Minister. For one thing, it could be argued that the incumbent's electoral mandate to tender advice had expired; although it might be reconfirmed by Parliament, this could by no means be assured. For another, the incumbent is not a neutral adviser but rather the leader of a political party with a keen interest in who is to govern. Hence, where the parties have failed, despite repeated efforts, to arrive at a political solution within a reasonable time, the appropriate course is likely to be for the Governor-General to consult with each party leader separately and seek a way forward. In certain (rare) circumstances, the political configuration of Parliament may be such that there is no feasible alternative to the Governor-General, on the advice of the incumbent Prime Minister, calling another election. Such a drastic step should not be taken without lengthy consultations between (and within) the respective parties.

Whether situations arise under MMP in which the Governor-General is required to exercise his reserve powers in appointing Prime Ministers remains to be seen. Interestingly, more than a third of the respondents in our survey (see Chapter 3) believe that Governors-General are more likely to use their reserve powers under MMP than FPP. Among MPs the figure was 45 percent. Only time will tell whether these expectations are correct.

Changes of government and the dissolution of Parliament

Changes of government (or of the parties within a government) between elections have been relatively rare in New Zealand. Aside from recent developments, they last occurred in 1912, when the Liberal government was replaced with Reform after four Liberal supporters switched their support, and 1930, when Reform joined United to form a coalition government. Under MMP, changes of government (and in the composition of coalitions) between elections may be more common. Certainly this is the experience in many other countries with PR (see Chapter 7).

Changes of government between elections are most likely to occur in one or other of the following circumstances:

- when a minority government loses the support of its non-government allies within Parliament, thereby enabling another party to form a government;
- when a majority coalition government suffers the defection of a coalition partner;
- when a single-party government with a wafer-thin majority loses a crucial by-election, or a member of the government switches his or her support to an opposition party.

Although changes of government (or in the composition of governments) between elections may be more common in the future, they are unlikely to be frequent. The parties in Parliament will be constrained in switching their formal (and informal) allegiances by various political considerations. For instance, any party which is seen to be acting irresponsibly could be penalised by voters at the next election. Likewise, if a party switches its support in Parliament and backs a party (or parties) with which its policy affinities are tenuous, it runs the risk of dividing its caucus, alienating its activists, and losing support at the next election.

Given that governments under MMP are likely to have greater difficulty securing and then maintaining majority support in Parliament, there may be pressures for more frequent elections. For instance, Prime Ministers may threaten to seek an early dissolution of Parliament as a means of bringing recalcitrant MPs and parties into line. Under current constitutional arrangements, the formal legal power to dissolve Parliament and order an election rests with the Governor-General. In exercising this power, the Governor-General is expected, by convention, to act on the advice of the Prime Minister. However, this convention may not apply if the Prime Minister no longer commands a parliamentary majority and there is good reason to believe that another party leader is capable of forming a viable government. Hence, before agreeing to an early dissolution, the Governor-General would be well advised to seek information from the Prime Minister (and possibly other party leaders). He should ask for details of the political configuration within the House, the position of the leaders of the other parties, and whether another party leader is able to form a new government and wishes to do so. Bear in mind that, if a minor party (or parties) – presumably for political reasons – is strongly opposed to an early election, it may prefer to support a change of government. Equally important is the fact that the term of Parliament in New Zealand is limited to three years (short by international standards), which provides a further disincentive to parties when confronted with a Prime Minister keen to force an early election. Issues of timing may also arise in this context: there are likely to be stronger objections, for instance, to an election being called in the first year or two of a new Parliament than during the first half of the third year. Timing issues of this nature will, of course, be among the considerations to which a Governor-General may need to give attention.

In order to avoid the Governor-General feeling obliged to use his reserve powers (and thus risk political controversy, if not a constitutional crisis), it would be highly desirable for the Prime Minister to refrain from seeking an early dissolution until it is clear that no other government can be formed from within the existing Parliament. In the longer term, it may be appropriate to consider the introduction of a fixed parliamentary term – although our survey in late 1995 revealed relatively little support for this (see Chapter 3).

The question of an early election arose frequently during the transition to MMP. After the close result of the 1993 election, the National government was widely expected not to complete its three-year term. Moreover, speculation about an early election intensified during 1995 with the finalisation of the new electoral boundaries and the reconfiguration of party support in Parliament. It was also expected that the Prime Minister might seek to capitalise on Labour's disarray and National's favourable opinion-poll ratings and request an early dissolution. In the event, it now seems likely that the 1993–96 Parliament will run its full term, or nearly so.

Yet if the Prime Minister, Jim Bolger, had sought a dissolution during 1995 or early 1996, it is questionable whether that would have been granted. This is because the United party – which has more or less held the balance of power in Parliament since its formation in June 1995 – indicated then that it was firmly against an early election (no doubt partly for self-interested reasons). Indeed, its support for National appears to have been contingent, at least until its coalition deal in late February 1996, on Parliament running its full term. In these circumstances, had Bolger requested an early dissolution the Governor-General might reasonably have been expected to discuss with the Prime Minister whether the majority of MPs supported this course of action, and whether another government could be formed (presumably led by Labour) which commanded a parliamentary majority. If it had become apparent that the majority of MPs favoured a change of government rather than an early election, then the Governor-General may have had little alternative but to reject Bolger's advice and ask Helen Clark (or another person) to form a new government. Bolger's capacity to call an early election may therefore have been limited, certainly if United and at least one other party had been prepared to support the formation of an alternative (Labour) government.

In the event of an early election in the future, it will be critical to ensure that the outgoing government has sufficient funds to last until a new administration can be sworn in. Adequate supply must be ensured during any period of caretaker government after the election and until the new Parliament can be called. The government's advisers will have to draw to the Prime Minister's attention any budgetary difficulties that could arise as a result of an early election. Arguably, too, the Governor-General should receive an assurance from the Prime Minister that the government has sufficient funds before a dissolution is granted. If it does not, then the dissolution may need to be delayed until Parliament has voted supply. Supply is not just a technical matter; it is an issue of considerable constitutional importance. A central purpose of Parliament under the Westminster system of government is to authorise taxation and expenditure on behalf of the Crown (see Sections 21 and 22 of the Constitution Act 1986).

The powers of a caretaker government

Although the term 'caretaker government' is used in various ways, it is generally applied to the following situations:

- the period between a general election and the formation of a new government; and
- the period between an incumbent government losing the confidence of Parliament and the swearing-in of a new government.

In recent years various conventions and guidelines have been developed and refined to guide the conduct of governments (including the role and powers of cabinet and the role of the public service) during caretaker periods. Underpinning these conventions is the basic principle that, while the business of governing must be able to continue during a period of political uncertainty, no decisions should be taken which 'would inappropriately bind an incoming Government and limit its freedom of action'.[27] More specifically, during a period of caretaker government it is important, to quote the SSC, that:

- 'The Governor-General is not left without responsible advisers [i.e. ministers].
- The day-to-day business of government continues.
- An outgoing Government is still the legitimate executive authority, but does not have a mandate to implement new policies or undertake major decisions such as making significant appointments or entering into major contracts.

- [If there is] an incoming Government [which clearly] has the confidence of the House to govern . . . once that Government has been identified, any significant decisions in the transition period are taken on its advice.
- If the make-up of the new Government is not certain, the caretaker government should if possible defer all significant decisions – if an immediate and final decision is required on a matter of long-term significance, it may consult other parties to see whether a proposed action has the support of the House.'[28]

In New Zealand, relatively few difficulties have arisen during caretaker periods. There are at least three reasons for this: in most cases it has been plain immediately after an election which party would form the next government; few external crises have occurred during a change of government; and the caretaker periods have all been brief. The main exception in recent times occurred in 1984, when the outgoing Prime Minister, Sir Robert Muldoon, initially refused to follow the instructions of the incoming Labour government, on the advice of the Treasury and the Reserve Bank, to devalue the dollar. As it happened, the Prime Minister was eventually prevailed upon by his cabinet colleagues to abide by the instructions of an incoming government (and thereby conform to a convention that, while not explicitly recognised hitherto in New Zealand, was certainly accepted in other Westminster systems).

The conventions surrounding caretaker governments were tested most recently in 1993, when it was not immediately clear on election night whether National would continue to enjoy a parliamentary majority after the counting of special votes. There was thus a period of uncertainty for 10 days, during which various issues arose concerning what the caretaker National government should and should not do. There was also uncertainty over the appropriate conduct of public servants. In order to clarify matters, the cabinet agreed upon the following set of guidelines:

'1. The basic rule is that all significant decisions which do not have to be taken within this period should be deferred.
2. If it is known that a decision will need to be taken shortly after this period, preparatory work should be undertaken so that the issues are able to be presented for decision to the appropriate Minister/Cabinet at the appropriate time.
3. In some situations where urgent decisions are needed it may be appropriate to extend the status quo and/or make temporary, holding arrangements which do not commit the Government in the longer term.
4. If there are issues on which decisions must be taken urgently and where temporary/holding arrangements are not appropriate, they may be taken by Ministers after consultation with Opposition party leaders, provided a

degree of consensus is obtained which plainly reflects support of a majority in the new Parliament. Unless this is obtained, decisions would have to be made by the full Cabinet and it is expected such decisions would be taken only in areas such as those of major constitutional or economic significance.

5. If a Minister wishes to make an approach to Opposition leaders that should be cleared in advance with the Prime Minister or Cabinet.
6. If Ministers are in any doubt or have been asked by their officials about whether a particular issue or proposal for decision can properly be taken, it is suggested that the matter be worked through by the Chief Executive of the Department of Prime Minister and Cabinet, the Secretary of the Cabinet and the State Services Commissioner, with final decisions resting with the Prime Minister.'[29]

With the prospect of more frequent, and in all likelihood longer, periods of caretaker government under MMP, there will doubtless be occasions when the conventions surrounding caretaker government will require further clarification and elaboration. In general, the occurrence of caretaker governments, however frequent or infrequent they may be, is no cause for concern. To date, the existing conventions have proved generally robust, and maverick behaviour – such as that of Sir Robert Muldoon in July 1984 – is most unlikely in the future.[30] The role of public servants during caretaker governments is considered further in Chapter 8.

Conclusion

The nature and composition of the first MMP government will depend on which parties secure representation in the House, the relative size of each party, and the political calculations made about the merits of various potential inter-party alliances, formal or otherwise. Because of the likelihood that no single party will hold a majority of the seats, inter-party bargaining will be a central feature of the new political culture. Also, the period of caretaker government following elections may be significantly longer than has been customary in New Zealand. From time to time, situations may arise in which the Governor-General is called upon to exercise his reserve powers in relation to the appointment and dismissal of Prime Ministers. While there is little prospect of major constitutional crises arising, the move to MMP poses a number of issues to do with the formation of governments and the dissolution of Parliament which deserve further consideration. One is whether a particular individual, such as the Speaker, should be designated as the person responsible for calling the party leaders together to discuss possible governing options. Another issue is whether, as in Denmark and Sweden, the Prime Minister should have a right to call an early election, irrespective of whether the incumbent government has majority support in Parliament. Further, there is the question of whether the Governor-General should have a *publicly* designated group of constitutional advisers to whom he can turn for assistance in the event of there being protracted political uncertainty following an election.[31] Issues of this nature, together with some broader constitutional issues, are discussed briefly in Chapter 10.

Notes

1 *Evening Post*, 2 March 1996, p.2.

2 There is an extensive theoretical and empirical literature on coalition governments. Various theories have been developed to explain, for instance, why coalitions take the form they do (e.g. in terms of size, composition and ideological cohesion), why some parties prefer to remain (or are kept) outside a coalition, and why some coalitions are more stable than others. Some of these issues are covered in Chapter 7.

3 See K. Strom, *Minority Government and Majority Rule*, Cambridge University Press, Cambridge, 1990.

4 See J. Blondel, 'Towards a Systematic Analysis of Government–Party Relationships', *International Political Science Review*, 16, 1995, pp.127–43.

5 Generally, a coalition government is taken to mean that two or more parties have members in the cabinet. However, in some jurisdictions, such as New Zealand, there are positions in the *political executive* aside from cabinet ministers. These include parliamentary under-secretaries and ministers outside the cabinet. When Ross Meurant left the National party in September 1994 to form RoC, he retained his position as Parliamentary Under-Secretary to the Ministers of Agriculture and Fisheries. He thus remained part of the political executive. Accordingly, it is probably legitimate to refer to the ensuing government as a coalition of National and RoC. When Meurant was dismissed from his post by the Prime Minister, Jim Bolger, in August 1995, RoC ceased to have representation in the political executive and the coalition, in a formal sense at least, was thereby terminated. As it happens, RoC continued to refer to itself as being in a coalition with National. This, however, was not correct. Rather, it became a 'supporting' party – like the Christian Democrats and United.

6 Strom, *Minority Government*, p.8, p.58. The precise percentage depends on how 'government' and 'change of government' are defined.

7 C. James and A. McRobie, *Turning Point: the 1993 General Election and Beyond*, Bridget Williams Books, Wellington, 1993.

8 See T. Bergman, 'Constitutional Design and Government Formation: the Expected Consequences of Negative Parliamentarism', *Scandinavian Political Studies*, 16, 4, 1993, pp.285–304; V. Bogdanor (ed.), *Coalition Government in Western Europe*, Heinemann, London, 1983; I. Budge and M. Keman, *Parties and Democracy: Coalition Formation and Government Functioning in Twenty States*, Oxford University Press, Oxford, 1990; P. Harris and E. McLeay, 'The Legislature', in G. Hawke (ed.), *Changing Politics? The Electoral Referendum 1993*, Victoria University Press, Wellington, 1993; P. Pesonen and A. Thomas, 'Coalition Formation in Scandinavia', and B. Sarlvik, 'Coalition Politics and Policy Output in Scandinavia: Sweden, Denmark and Norway', both in V. Bogdanor (ed.), *Coalition Government in Western Europe*; K. Strom, I. Budge and M. Laver, 'Constraints on Cabinet Formation in Parliamentary Democracies', *American Journal of Political Science*, 38, 1994, pp.303–35.

9 It is worth emphasising that there are very few constraints on the kind of government which can be formed in New Zealand. The rules governing the formation and operation of the cabinet, the operation of Parliament (i.e. Standing Orders), and the

activities of parties are conducive to a wide range of governing options (and party combinations). Further, there are no players outside Parliament (or beyond New Zealand) who can effectively veto any particular combination of parties coming together to form (or support) a government.

10 See T. Bergman, 'Constitutional Design and Government Formation', p.287.

11 Ibid.

12 In Sweden a vote is required in the Riksdag before a new government assumes power. However, the government is not required to win this vote, in the sense of winning more votes than those cast against it. Instead, it can assume office unless an absolute majority of all MPs cast their votes against it. Hence, if at least one party chooses to abstain, it is possible for a minority government to 'win' such a vote. Sweden is thus classified under negative rather than positive parliamentarism.

13 See T. Bergman, 'Constitutional Design and Government Formation', pp.287-8.

14 Ibid, p.289.

15 Ibid, p.299.

16 See C. Morris, 'The Governor-General, the Reserve Powers, Parliament and MMP: a New Era', LLB (Hons) research paper, Victoria University, 1994, pp.17–21; C. Morris, 'The Governor-General, the Reserve Powers, Parliament and MMP: a New Era', *Victoria University of Wellington Law Review*, 25, 1995, pp.359–64; P. Harris and E. McLeay, 'The Legislature', in G. Hawke (ed.), *Changing Politics?*, p.111. The last time a Governor refused a Prime Minister's request for a snap election in New Zealand was in 1877 – the individuals in question being Lord Normanby (Governor) and Sir George Grey (Prime Minister).

17 There is an extensive academic literature, drawing particularly on game theory and rational choice theory, which seeks to account for the behaviour of parties and the nature of inter-party bargaining. Some scholars, for instance, assume that parties are interested only in seeking office (i.e. because of the benefits that office-holding confers in power, status and financial rewards). Others, by contrast, maintain that parties are motivated by a much broader range of considerations, in particular the pursuit of policy and ideological objectives. As might be expected, theoretical models which include both policy and office-seeking objectives generally have a much better predictive capacity than those which assume only office-holding objectives.

18 Under MMP, the precise number of seats allocated to each of the political parties in Parliament is determined by the number of votes that the parties win (i.e. not by the precise percentage of the votes they win). Given the number of valid votes cast in previous New Zealand elections, the Sainte Laguë formula (see Appendix 2) means that the 120th quotient in 1996 will be about 8000 to 9000 votes. A party that has won one electorate seat in Parliament will, therefore, have to win three times this many party votes – from 24,000 to 27,000 votes – in order to be entitled to two seats in Parliament. If two million valid votes are cast in the 1996 election and if United gains a total of only 1 percent of the party vote, it will get only 20,000 votes. This would not be enough to secure a second seat in Parliament (i.e. in addition to that of Peter Dunne).

19 See J. Christensen, 'In Search of Unity: Cabinet Committees in Denmark', in T. Mackie and B. Hogwood (eds.), *Unlocking the Cabinet: Cabinet Structures in Comparative Perspective*, Sage, London, 1985; B. Farrell, 'Coalitions and Political Institutions: the Irish Experience', in V. Bogdanor (ed.), *Coalition Government in Western Europe*; B. Sarlvik, 'Coalition Politics and Policy Output in Scandinavia'.

20 I. Budge and M. Laver, 'The Policy Basis of Government Coalitions: a Comparative Investigation', *British Journal of Political Science*, 23, 1993, p.508.

21 As a result of the Constitution Act 1986, it is no longer necessary for the swearing-in of a new government to await the counting of special votes and the return of the writs (unless the outcome of the election is unclear).

22 It generally takes at least two months to form a government in the Netherlands, and

sometimes longer. See T. Bergman, 'Constitutional Design and Government Formation', p.288. In New Zealand there will be pressures from at least three sources to form a new government reasonably quickly. First, there will be public pressure (including pressures from the financial markets) to minimise political uncertainty. Second, the Constitution Act (S.19) requires that Parliament meet within six weeks of the return of the writs following a general election. Given the desirability of a new government being formed by the time the House meets, the political parties will have around two months to determine who is going to govern. Third, under the Constitution Act (S.6) ministers who have lost their seats at the election can serve for only 28 days within a caretaker administration. This provision also will put pressure on party leaders to form a new government quickly (though there is nothing to stop ministers who have retained their seats from being given the portfolio responsibilities of their defeated colleagues).

23 An excellent summary of the existing constitutional provisions for government formation is provided in the State Services Commission's *Working Under Proportional Representation: a Reference for the Public Service*, Wellington, 1995, pp.87–99. See also C. Morris, 'The Governor-General, the Reserve Powers, Parliament and MMP', 1994.

24 The term 'reserve powers' refers to three particular powers which can, under existing conventions, be exercised by the Governor-General *independently* (i.e. in the absence of, or even contrary to, the explicit advice of ministers). They are: the power to refuse a request from the Prime Minister for a dissolution of Parliament before the summoning of Parliament; the power to appoint a Prime Minister; and the power to refuse a request from the Prime Minister for a dissolution of Parliament when Parliament is in session.

25 There are no clear examples from Commonwealth precedent. But in a recent case in the state of Sabah, East Malaysia, a court ruled that, in the absence of a clear majority for any particular party, the leader of the party with the most seats should be appointed as chief minister. See *Mustapha* v *Mohammad and Another* [1987], *Law Reports of the Commonwealth (Const)*, 16.

26 C. Morris, 'The Governor-General, the Reserve Powers, Parliament and MMP', 1994, pp.11–17.

27 State Services Commission, *Working Under Proportional Representation*, p.78.

28 Ibid., p.77.

29 Cabinet Office Circular, 'Decision Making by Cabinet and Ministers in the Immediate Post-Election Period', CO (93) 18, 9 November 1993. The cabinet revised its guidelines on caretaker government in late 1995: see 'Conduct During Periods of Caretaker Government', CO (95) 15, 19 December 1995. The State Services Commissioner also issued guidelines, 'The Public Service During the "Caretaker" Period', to all public service chief executives shortly after the 1993 general election.

30 Problems could arise in the event of extended periods of caretaker government. See State Services Commission, *Working Under Proportional Representation*, pp.83–4.

31 Governors-General have no doubt in the past had occasion to rely on private groups of constitutional experts for assistance. However, the time may have come to make such arrangements more formal and transparent.

CHAPTER 7

Cabinet government in a multi-party Parliament

The previous chapter explored some of the constitutional and political issues surrounding the formation and change of governments in New Zealand under MMP. This chapter considers how the move to proportional representation is likely to affect the composition, organisation, management and stability of the cabinet.[1] It also examines the possible impact of MMP on key constitutional conventions, such as individual ministerial responsibility and collective responsibility. Two main theses are advanced: first, MMP can be expected to alter neither the role of the cabinet nor the conventions under which the cabinet system operates; second, the formation of coalition governments – which, as argued in previous chapters, is much more likely under MMP than FPP – will bring inevitable changes to the process of selecting ministers and allocating portfolios. It will also alter the dynamics and day-to-day workings of the cabinet system.

The cabinet under MMP: general issues

The cabinet in New Zealand is a creature of convention rather than statute. Its composition, structures and processes are governed largely by political considerations, not by legal rules. As a consequence, the cabinet is a relatively flexible institution, more than capable of adapting to the new pressures and constraints that are likely to arise under MMP.

Whatever the changes to the political terrain wrought by the introduction of PR, New Zealand will continue to have a system of cabinet government.[2] In other words, the cabinet will remain the powerhouse of the political system. It will continue to make the key decisions on all important matters of public policy. It will remain responsible for the introduction of government legislation into Parliament, the drafting and passing of regulations, the preparation of the Budget, appointments and honours, and the exercise of all the

Crown's prerogative powers which do not require validation by Parliament (e.g. the negotiation of treaties). At the same time, of course, the cabinet's power will be significantly constrained if the government does not enjoy an overall parliamentary majority – as highlighted by the experience of the National government from mid-1995.

Other continuities can also be expected. Unless the Constitution Act 1986 is amended, cabinet ministers and other members of the executive will continue to be selected solely from within the ranks of parliamentarians. They will also remain as MPs while serving in the executive.[3] In all likelihood most of the cabinet's work will continue to be handled via a series of committees (both standing and ad hoc). These committees will be serviced, as currently, by the staff of the Cabinet Office (within the Department of the Prime Minister and Cabinet) and their decisions will be ratified at weekly meetings of the cabinet. Equally, departmental officials will almost certainly continue to prepare most of the policy papers upon which ministers depend for their advice. This is not to suggest, however, that there will be no changes in the role of public servants (see Chapter 8).

If the broad shape, role and powers of the cabinet will remain largely unaltered by MMP, certain features of the cabinet system, however, can be expected to change. The magnitude of these changes will depend primarily on the kind of government formed (i.e. majority or minority, single party or multi-party). For instance, the relationship between the executive and Parliament will be different under single-party majority government from that under single-party minority government (see Table 7.1). Under the latter, the cabinet will be unable to pursue policies which lack the support of the majority of MPs. It will thus need to do the same kind of inter-party consultation and consensus-building that occurred during part of the transition to MMP. Also, while in most cases a minority government is likely to rely for its parliamentary majorities primarily on parties closest to it on the ideological continuum, from time to time it may seek support for particular legislative initiatives from the main opposition party (or parties). This mustering of support from different combinations of parties is sometimes referred to as 'jumping majorities'.[4] Apart from the need for much more extensive consultation, both overseas and recent domestic experience indicates that the operation of the cabinets of single-party minority governments is little different from that of single-party majority governments (e.g. in the selection of ministers, the nature and allocation of portfolios, the structure of cabinet committees, the rules governing the handling of cabinet business). By contrast, the establishment of a fully-fledged coalition government can be expected to bring more significant changes to the workings of the cabinet system. Such changes will be all the greater when a coalition: (i) holds only a minority of the seats in Parliament, (ii) comprises more than two parties, or (iii) comprises parties with significant policy or ideological differences.

To date, New Zealand's experience of coalition government has been strictly limited. As argued in the previous chapter, the relationship between National and RoC between September 1994 and August 1995 was on the

Table 7.1. ***Cabinet formation and operations under different types of government***

	Majority single-party government*	**Majority coalition**	**Minority single-party government**	**Minority coalition**
Policy agreements	Few formal policy agreements between government and non-government parties.	Formal, detailed coalition agreement; occasional specific policy deals with non-coalition parties.	Formal and informal policy agreements with supporting parties, and occasionally with opposition parties.	Formal, detailed coalition agreement; regular specific policy deals with non-coalition parties.
Choice of Prime Minister	Determined by caucus of governing party.	Determined by negotiations between coalition parties; usually leader of larger coalition party.	Determined by caucus of governing party.	Determined by negotiations between coalition parties; usually leader of larger coalition party.
Selection of cabinet ministers	Determined by the Prime Minister or the governing caucus.	Determined by the leaders of the coalition parties and/or their caucuses; cabinet places are generally allocated on a proportional basis between the coalition parties.	Determined by the Prime Minister or the governing caucus.	Determined by the leaders of the coalition parties and/or their caucuses; cabinet places are generally allocated on a proportional basis between the coalition parties.
Allocation of portfolios	Determined by the Prime Minister.	Determined by negotiations between the leaders of the coalition parties.	Determined by the Prime Minister.	Determined by negotiations between the leaders of the coalition parties.

	Majority single-party government*	**Majority coalition**	**Minority single-party government**	**Minority coalition**
Co-ordinating mechanisms	Regular meetings of the full cabinet; formal cabinet committee structure.	Regular meetings of the full cabinet; formal cabinet committee structure; additional high-level committee of senior party figures usually established to resolve inter-party policy differences.	Regular meetings of the full cabinet; formal cabinet committee structure.	Regular meetings of the full cabinet; formal cabinet committee structure; additional high-level committee of senior party figures usually established to resolve inter-party policy differences.
Individual ministerial responsibility	A central constitutional doctrine; the PM is solely responsible for sacking ministers.	A central constitutional doctrine; the PM may need to consult leaders of other coalition parties before sacking a minister.	A central constitutional doctrine; the PM is solely responsible for sacking ministers.	A central constitutional doctrine; the PM may need to consult leaders of other coalition parties before sacking a minister.
Collective responsibility	A central constitutional doctrine.	A central constitutional doctrine; however, cabinet unity may be more difficult to preserve, especially in the run-up to an election.	A central constitutional doctrine.	A central constitutional doctrine; however, cabinet unity may be more difficult to preserve, especially in the run-up to an election.

* The features of single-party majority government in this table are based on New Zealand practice and do not necessarily accord with those of other parliamentary systems.

very margin of being a genuine coalition. The short-term agreement between National and United signed on 28 February 1996 (see Appendix 4) is also unusual: United has only one minister in a 20-person cabinet; United's parliamentary leadership is not part of the political executive; and National appears to have offered few, if any, policy concessions to secure United's support. Hence, the February agreement should be seen as representing a *first* step towards a more comprehensive, balanced and longer-term coalition pact. It should not be seen as the model upon which future coalitions will be based.

Forming coalition cabinets

The process of forming fully-fledged coalition cabinets is complex.[5] A wide range of issues usually needs to be negotiated between the party leaders, and numerous bargains struck. Among the key questions normally requiring resolution are: the government's broad priorities and strategic objectives; the formulation of common positions on major policy issues (including expenditure priorities); the choice of Prime Minister and Deputy Prime Minister; and the distribution of cabinet seats between the parties, the ranking of ministers, and the allocation of portfolios. Because of the importance, complexity and range of the issues which must be addressed, the process of coalition-building can sometimes prove very time-consuming. Typically, new governments in countries with PR take around two to three weeks to form; occasionally, however, the process may take two to three months.[6] Both the difficulties and the chances of failure will be all the greater when:

- there are more than two parties involved;
- there is a low level of trust between the respective party leaders; and
- there are significant policy differences between the prospective coalition partners.

A multitude of political pressures and constraints will also come into play. For a major party, for instance, a key factor determining its negotiating stance will be whether it believes it will be better off governing alone (as a single-party minority government) – assuming, of course, that this is a viable option – or in coalition with another party or parties. It will need to assess the overall costs and benefits (e.g. in terms of securing its policy objectives and maximising its long-term electoral appeal) of each potential governing option. Minor parties, likewise, will need to make cost–benefit calculations, though some of the issues will be different from those facing a major party. For instance, in deciding whether to join a coalition, a minor party will need to consider whether it is likely to have more influence over the direction of public policy from within the government, whether its allocation of ministerial portfolios fairly reflects its relative parliamentary strength and strategic position in the political arena, whether it can secure those portfolios which are central to its particular policy interests, how direct participation in the government might affect party unity, and whether its longer-term electoral prospects are likely to be enhanced or weakened by aligning formally with another party or parties. In short, the question will be whether the tangible and intangible benefits of ministerial office outweigh the inevitable policy compromises and possible electoral costs.

Coalition agreements on policy

Typically, the process of forming a coalition government begins with negotiations over policies. Other matters, such as the distribution of cabinet posts, are settled later – once agreement has been reached on the central policy issues. It is common in other countries for the parties forming a coalition to negotiate, and publish, not merely a set of broad principles and priorities but also a set of detailed policy positions.[7] Indeed, some coalition agreements are comprehensive and cover most of the issues likely to face the incoming government, at least over the first year. The level of specificity reflects the degree of trust between the parties, the extent of their policy differences and whether the coalition is new or a continuation of a previous arrangement. Sometimes, coalition agreements provide for the coalition partners to take different positions on controversial matters,[8] since a coalition agreement may be impossible unless the parties involved are able to retain their distinctive positions on vital ideological or moral issues.

Where parties have been in a coalition for many years (as in the case of the Christian Democrats, the Christian Social Union and the Free Democrats in Germany), they will already have agreed positions on many matters. They are also likely to have built up a reasonable degree of trust, certainly at senior levels. In Germany, as in most countries with PR, it is not uncommon for two or three opposition parties to indicate that they will collaborate to form a coalition government if able to do so as a result of the forthcoming election. Such declarations of intent, which are usually accompanied by agreements in principle on key policy issues, are designed, among other things, to boost voter support by demonstrating that the parties in question have the ability to govern.

In New Zealand, any coalition formed between National and United after the 1996 election will be able to build on their existing relationship. Any policy agreement they enter into is likely to be significantly longer than the two-page statement issued in February 1996 (see Appendix 4). Any formal coalition involving Labour, the Alliance or New Zealand First will, of course, have to begin from scratch, and may well take longer to negotiate than a further National/United deal.

Over time, the introduction of MMP can be expected to generate pressures for broader, multi-party agreements on various controversial issues (such as the superannuation accord between National, Labour and the Alliance in 1993). As such accommodations are reached, so the number of issues on which there is likely to be significant disagreement will be reduced, thereby making coalition-building easier.

Another likely influence on the nature of any longer-term coalition agreements in New Zealand is the system of strategic management introduced by National in the wake of the 1993 general election.[9] The government developed a series of so-called strategic result areas (SRAs) and key result areas

(KRAs). SRAs specify the government's medium-term strategic objectives and policy priorities, while KRAs endeavour to translate these broader concerns into shorter-term and more concrete policy initiatives in order to focus departmental energies. (KRAs now form a key element in the annual performance agreements of departmental chief executives.) The new strategic management system provides a possible framework for the negotiation and subsequent implementation of a coalition agreement. For instance, were National to continue its coalition arrangement with United after the 1996 election, its current SRAs, along with the party's election manifesto, would almost certainly serve as the basis for negotiating statements of priorities and objectives with prospective coalition partners. Such statements could, in turn, be used to develop a suitably revised set of SRAs, which could then be translated into more specific policy agreements, or KRAs. Plainly, there would be nothing to stop another potential coalition (e.g. Labour and New Zealand First) from adopting (or building on) the new strategic management framework, and using a coalition agreement as the basis for a subsequent list of SRAs and KRAs.

The choice of Prime Minister

Within parliamentary systems of government, the position of Prime Minister invariably has a status and influence exceeding those of any other minister.[10] It is, after all, the Prime Minister who generally chairs the cabinet (and its leading committees), determines the cabinet's agenda, allocates portfolios, and speaks for the government on major policy issues. A key question facing a prospective coalition government, therefore, is which party should hold the prime ministership. Sometimes this matter can be controversial. Indeed, it may prove to be one of the crucial determinants of whether a coalition is formed and, if so, what form it takes.

The usual practice around the world is for the Prime Minister to be the leader of the coalition partner with the largest number of parliamentary seats.[11] This has been the norm, for instance, in Denmark, Germany and Norway. Exceptions are not uncommon, however. In Japan, Tomiichi Murayama (the leader of the Socialist party, the second-largest in the three-party coalition) was Prime Minister for some 19 months in the mid-1990s. He was eventually replaced in January 1996 by Ryutaro Hashimoto, the leader of the Liberal Democratic party (the largest party in the coalition). Similar instances have occurred in various European countries (including Italy and Sweden). Nor is the practice unknown in New Zealand. In the United/Reform coalition government between 1931 and 1935, the Prime Minister was George Forbes, leader of the United party. Yet throughout this period the Reform party had, in effect, more seats than United, and its leader,

Gordon Coates, was widely seen as being head and shoulders above Forbes in intellect, administrative competence, oratory and leadership skills.[12]

There are various reasons why the leader of a party other than the largest in the coalition might hold the prime ministership. Where three or more parties are involved, the leader of the largest party may not be the most acceptable candidate, as a result of personality, electoral or ideological factors. In other situations, the largest party in a coalition may be willing to forgo its claim to the prime ministership in return for other concessions (e.g. additional cabinet posts, key portfolio responsibilities such as Finance, or support for major policy initiatives). Occasionally, where two parties of roughly similar size form a coalition, the fact that one party has slightly more seats (and possibly votes) than the other may not be regarded as the decisive determinant of who should be Prime Minister. In short, therefore, it should never be assumed that the prime ministership will automatically be secured by the largest party in a coalition government. If it does not, however, it is highly likely that the largest party will be rewarded with the position of Deputy Prime Minister and other senior ministerial posts.

The composition of cabinet and the allocation of portfolios

The allocation of ministerial portfolios and the selection (and ranking) of ministers are often matters of intense negotiation between prospective coalition partners. In most situations overseas, ministerial places (as well as more junior positions within the government) in coalition governments are allocated to the various parties on a proportional basis. That is, the number of seats that a party secures at the cabinet table broadly reflects its relative parliamentary strength.[13] In general, the proportionality rule also applies to the allocation of places on cabinet committees, including chairpersonships. Future coalitions in New Zealand under MMP can be expected to conform to international practice.[14]

Proportionality accords with notions of fairness. Any significant deviation from it – certainly on a long-term basis – is likely to be unacceptable to the disadvantaged party (or parties). Nevertheless, the proportionality rule is not always rigidly applied. In a multi-party coalition, for instance, the two largest parties may agree to have the same number of ministers even though their parliamentary representation is unequal.[15] Similarly, where the same combination of parties stays in office after an election, the previous allocation of ministerial positions may remain unchanged, notwithstanding substantial variations in the electoral fortunes of each partner. Any attempt to alter the balance of ministerial posts between the parties could destabilise the coalition. Deviations from the proportionality rule may also occur if a party with a pivotal role in Parliament (typically a party towards the centre of the political continuum) threatens to change sides unless it receives adequate concessions.

It is relatively common for small parties, particularly in two-party coalitions, to receive a disproportionate allocation of cabinet seats. In Germany, for instance, the two smaller parties – the Free Democrats and the Christian Social Union – have consistently received more ministerial seats than warranted by their parliamentary representation.[16] Correspondingly, the two large parties – the Christian Democrats and the Social Democrats – have been under-represented in the cabinet. Such outcomes are not hard to explain. On the one hand, the costs to a large party (in diminished influence or patronage) of conceding a few extra ministerial posts to its coalition partner(s) are likely to be insignificant. On the other, displays of generosity of this nature may contribute to a more cohesive and durable government. Moreover, small parties may find it difficult to participate effectively in government if they have only one or two cabinet ministers. United's experience during 1996 will be interesting to observe in this respect.

The method of allocating particular portfolios, such as Foreign Affairs, Defence, Education and Health, varies between coalitions. There are common practices, however. In general, the distribution of portfolios reflects the policy interests and ideological dispositions of the parties in the coalition. Hence, Agriculture typically goes to the party with a well-established rural or farming interest, Commerce or Industry to the party with a strong business orientation, and Conservation or Environment to the party with a 'green' emphasis.[17] The particular interests of leading party figures may also be a factor. Another general rule of thumb is that the party which holds the prime ministership ought not to be allocated *all* the other influential cabinet positions, such as Finance and Foreign Affairs. Also, it is not uncommon for positions of associate minister or deputy minister to go to a party which does not hold the main portfolio responsibility.[18] Such arrangements can help to resolve inter-party disputes, enhance policy co-ordination, and reduce the number of issues requiring the attention of the whole cabinet. Whether New Zealand coalition governments will adopt such practices in the future remains to be seen, but it is highly likely.

One matter that could well cause tension between prospective coalition partners in New Zealand is the allocation of the Finance portfolio. The Minister of Finance is able to exert considerable influence over the budgetary process, as well as having direct access to the intellectual resources and bureaucratic power of the Treasury. Furthermore, unlike the situation in many other countries, the Treasury has no rival department, such as an economics department or a treasury board.[19] Accordingly, unless the Treasury's responsibilities are divided between two portfolios – which is certainly a possibility – the parties in a coalition may be unwilling to allow the Finance portfolio to be held by the party which holds the prime ministership. At the very least, a minor party is likely to demand the position of Associate (or Deputy) Finance Minister. The allocation of most other portfolios should be less contentious, although some may be regarded as politically unattractive, or alternatively pivotal to a government's electoral prospects. In New Zealand, the Education and Health portfolios are among the latter.

In single-party governments, the decision as to who will hold which portfolio is generally the responsibility of the Prime Minister. Certainly, this has been the case in New Zealand, and will remain so under MMP. By contrast, in multi-party governments, each party is likely to choose which of its MPs will serve in the cabinet, with the actual allocation of portfolios being negotiated between the party leaders rather than decided by the Prime Minister alone.[20] Currently, in New Zealand, the rules for selecting cabinet ministers differ between the parties. National, for instance, gives the party leader sole responsibility. With Labour, ministers are elected by the caucus. The move to MMP may prompt a change in Labour's approach (e.g. to avoid possible difficulties if the caucus selects for cabinet a person who is not acceptable to the other party or parties in the coalition). Such an outcome is not inevitable, but it is likely that the party leaders in a coalition government will use their influence to ensure that the cabinet's overall composition is suitably representative, particularly in terms of gender. There may also be increased pressures under MMP for the inclusion of Maori and perhaps Pacific Island MPs in the cabinet.

Just as Prime Ministers in coalition governments will have less influence than in single-party governments over the cabinet's composition and the allocation of portfolios, so too they will have less freedom to manoeuvre in making cabinet reshuffles or sacking a particular minister. As a result, there is little likelihood of regular cabinet reshuffles under MMP. In fact, they may be even less frequent than has traditionally been the case under single-party governments in New Zealand – and by international standards the composition of New Zealand cabinets has been remarkably stable. Against this, *governments* may be less durable in the future – as is discussed later in the chapter.

The size of the cabinet

For several decades, New Zealand cabinets have had around 19–20 members, along with a number of ministers outside the cabinet and/or several under-secretaries. The overall political executive has thus numbered around 25–26. This is in line with the average across parliamentary democracies.[21] It has been suggested that the advent of coalition government under MMP will generate pressures for larger cabinets, if not an expanded political executive. The argument is that each party in a coalition will want to maximise the number of portfolios it holds, and that party leaders will seek to reward as many of their supporters as possible with cabinet seats. While such pressures may well arise from time to time, it is doubtful whether cabinets will be significantly larger in the future. For one thing, there is no systematic tendency for the cabinets of coalition governments elsewhere to be larger than those of single-party governments. For another, there are good reasons for not increasing the size of the cabinet any further. In terms of political management, larger cabinets are likely to be more unwieldy. Moreover, with the recent reduction in the size of the core public sector and the privatisation of various state-owned enterprises, the range of ministerial responsibilities has been reduced. Another pressure constraining the size of cabinet arises from the broader impact of MMP on Parliament, especially the role of select committees (see Chapter 5). If select committees become more important forums for inter-party deliberations on legislative and policy matters, they will require MPs with the requisite ability and experience. Party leaders, therefore, will not necessarily wish to have all their most gifted MPs in the cabinet.

If cabinets are unlikely to grow under MMP, in certain conditions they could be substantially smaller. Suppose, for the sake of argument, that a single-party minority government took office which had only 25–30 percent of the seats in Parliament (i.e. 30–35 seats). (Such an outcome is improbable, admittedly, but not beyond the bounds of possibility. There are examples elsewhere (e.g. Denmark and Sweden) where single-party governments have been formed with no more than 10–12 percent of the seats.) A government with less than 35–40 seats would find it difficult to keep the executive at its current size while at the same time taking up its full allocation of places on Parliament's 12 subject select committees (see Chapter 5). Note that, in accordance with current parliamentary practice, cabinet ministers may serve on special purpose and *ad hoc* committees but are not normally members of subject committees (though, of course, they do attend on occasion to answer questions and to hear evidence on proposed legislation for which they are responsible). In any case, there would be practical difficulties if ministers served as full members of these committees, since they frequently meet at the same time as cabinet committees. Hence, the cabinet of a minority government with less than 35–40 seats is likely to be smaller than at present, with some senior MPs being allocated to key select committees rather than ministerial responsibilities.

Another possibility – foreshadowed by the Prime Minister, Jim Bolger, at the time of the National/United coalition deal – would be to alter the *structure* of the executive by reducing the size of the cabinet to around 12–14 members while simultaneously increasing the number of ministers outside the cabinet. This would be in keeping with the pattern in some other jurisdictions (e.g.

Australia). It is argued that such a model might improve the efficiency with which the cabinet's business is conducted and enhance cabinet discipline.

The operations of the cabinet

In many respects, the operations and internal dynamics of a coalition cabinet under MMP will be similar to those of a single-party government. Weekly meetings of the full cabinet can be expected to remain the norm – as is the case in most other parliamentary systems. Most issues are likely to be determined by negotiation and consensus rather than votes. The rules governing the preparation, submission and flow of cabinet papers – as set out in the *Cabinet Office Manual* – are bound to remain in place (although amendments can be expected from time to time, as happens at present).[22] Another major continuity will be the heavy reliance on cabinet committees. Almost certainly, as noted earlier, most policy decisions will be taken by committees rather than by the whole cabinet. Similarly, the more important committees are likely to be serviced by a 'shadow' or parallel committee of officials. As at present, the committee structure and relative importance of particular committees will vary according to the changing priorities and concerns of the government. No doubt, too, a great deal of the government's day-to-day business will be conducted via bilateral meetings between ministers, and between ministers and departmental officials.

Despite these continuities, experience elsewhere suggests that various changes in the operations of the cabinet can be expected under coalition arrangements.[23] Indeed, some of these are already evident under the National/United government.

First, coalition governments in other countries often establish a small, high-level committee, comprising the most senior members of each party, to co-ordinate the government's political strategy and resolve inter-party disputes. In Germany, for instance, such a committee meets before the weekly cabinet meeting to discuss politically sensitive issues.[24] In some countries senior party figures other than ministers, such as party presidents, may be invited to participate in committees of this nature. In New Zealand, as part of the National/United deal in February 1996, it was agreed that a Disputes Group comprising the leaders and deputy leaders of each party would be established to consider areas of serious disagreement (other than on matters of confidence). In all likelihood, similar procedures will be instituted under a future coalition government.

Second, Prime Ministers generally have less power in a multi-party government. Consequently, prime ministerial dominance of the kind associated with the Muldoon years is unlikely. Against this, the Prime Minister's role as a mediator, conciliator, and final arbiter of inter-party and intra-party disputes will doubtless be more important. What implications such changes might have for the staffing of the Prime Minister's Office and the Department of the Prime Minister and Cabinet are unclear. Although some commentators have suggested that there will be pressures for the bureaucracy around the Prime Minister to grow under MMP, in most Scandinavian countries (where coalition governments are common) Prime Ministers have traditionally had only modest levels of staff support.[25]

Third, in any future multi-party government, there will be inevitable changes to the composition of cabinet committees. Doubtless, each party in the coalition will want permanent representation on most (if not all) committees, even though none of its ministers has formal responsibility for the issues dealt with by a particular committee. Such pressure may result in larger committees. Senior ministers may also have to sit on more committees than in a single-party government. Against that, many cabinet committees are already quite large (e.g. in March 1996 eight committees had 10 or more members). Moreover, under current cabinet procedures, ministers are able to attend and speak at any committee regardless of whether they are formally a member of it.

Fourth, each coalition party can be expected to organise regular meetings of its own ministers to discuss their party's political strategy and priorities, and to formulate a common position on major policy issues, in addition to each party's regular caucus meetings. In the Netherlands, for instance, the ministers of each government party meet for dinner on a Thursday evening to discuss the agenda for the cabinet meeting the following day.[26]

Fifth, the decisions taken by individual ministers could be subject to greater scrutiny by their colleagues, especially where such decisions have not been referred to the cabinet for consideration. Likewise, where the coalition partners are mistrustful of each other, various devices may be introduced to ensure that individual ministers do not take decisions which are contrary to the wishes of the other coalition partners. For instance, in Denmark a system of pairing was adopted in the late 1970s to help prevent major conflicts. According to Jørgen Christensen, the system operated as follows:

> In 1978–9 only a minimum of trust was present between the Social Democrats and their Liberal partners. Under these circumstances an elaborate system of so-called contact ministers was added to existing cabinet committees. Each minister was paired with a minister from the other party. The Social Democratic prime minister had the Liberal leader and Minister of Foreign Affairs as his counterpart. To take another example, the Liberal Minister of Industry had the Social Democratic Minister of Environmental Protection as his contact minister and vice versa. The implication was the creation of a procedure where a minister from one party was not allowed to make a decision on an issue falling clearly within the jurisdiction of his or her department without

> the prior consent of his or her contact minister. If consent was not given, a negotiation had to take place between them. If they were still not able to reach agreement on a decision, the issue would be referred first to the relevant cabinet committee and in case of further disagreement to the planning committee of the cabinet. This committee thus became the final clearing house for many issues which had been blocked by the veto of the contact minister.[27]

Procedural arrangements of this nature are invariably burdensome, and are bound to cause delays in government policy-making. Against this, of course, they may be essential to the government's political survival.

Finally, where a coalition does not enjoy a parliamentary majority, further changes in the procedures of cabinet government will be necessary (as also with a single-party minority government). Ministers will need to consult more frequently with senior members of parties outside the government, especially on controversial legislative proposals where the government cannot be certain of a parliamentary majority.[28] This will have implications for the role of Parliament, not to mention other participants in the policy community (public servants, lobbyists, interest groups and so forth). Among other things, minority government is likely to contribute to greater openness in policy-making and more extensive public debate on major policy issues.

Government stability

Under FPP, governments in New Zealand have been remarkably stable, many surviving for more than two terms, and some for more than three (i.e. more than nine years). Is such stability likely to continue under MMP? Several problems arise in trying to answer this question. First, there is considerable disagreement among scholars about what constitutes a 'change of government'.[29] Second, the relationship between government type and stability is not fully understood, and there are many competing theories about the causes of government instability.

Most commentators accept that a change of government occurs whenever there is a change in the *party composition* of the cabinet. However, while some argue that this is the only relevant criterion, others maintain that a change of government also occurs when certain other conditions are met (e.g. a change of Prime Minister, the reconstitution of the same coalition after an election, a government's gaining or losing its majority as a result of an election).[30] Clearly, measures of government durability or stability are sensitive to the way 'change of government' is defined: the more criteria considered relevant, the more frequently 'governments' will change, and the greater the appearance of instability. Without delving further into this definitional debate here, it is perhaps useful, as Lawrence Dodd argues, to distinguish between three main forms of government durability: *partisan* durability (which refers to the length of time particular parties remain in office), *coalition* durability (which refers to the length of time a particular grouping of parties remains in office), and *leadership* durability (which refers to the length of time Prime Ministers remain in office).[31]

The empirical evidence for the relationship between government type and cabinet durability is unambiguous: single-party majority governments are much more stable than the other three types of government. In an analysis of 342 democratic governments during the post-war period, Kaare Strom found that single-party majority governments survived an average of 30 months.[32] By contrast, majority coalitions survived on average less than 18 months. According to Strom, minority governments (whether single or multi-party) are even less durable, surviving an average of only 13-14 months.

At first sight, this evidence appears to have unequivocal implications for New Zealand: if single-party majority governments are rare under MMP (as seems likely), the durability of governments can be expected to decline, especially if minority governments become the norm. This means, in turn, the likelihood of a more rapid turnover of ministers, including Prime Ministers. Yet such outcomes are not inevitable. Some countries with PR, such as Austria, Germany and Sweden, have had relatively stable governments – certainly as judged by the criterion of party composition – for much of the post-war period. In New Zealand, any reduction in government stability is likely to depend on the extent to which the party system fragments and/or polarises under MMP (see Chapter 4). The larger the number of parties which secure parliamentary representation and the greater their ideological and policy differences, the greater the complexity of the bargaining environment, and hence the harder it will be to form durable governments. The five percent threshold, together with the relative absence of politically salient social, moral, regional or cultural cleavages, will significantly limit the fragmentation of New Zealand's party system under MMP. Consequently, there is little prospect of New Zealand witnessing the level of government instability experienced in countries like Italy.

Of course, even if governments are less durable, the consequences may not be very great. For instance, while *coalition* and *leadership* durability may decline, *partisan* durability may remain relatively high. The same party might remain in office for a long time, sometimes governing on its own and sometimes in coalition with another party (or parties). In these circumstances, any increase in government instability will not necessarily result in greater policy instability, let alone regime instability. In fact, comparative studies indicate that policies may, on the whole, be more stable under proportional representation (see Chapter 9).

In New Zealand in the past, election outcomes have been the chief determinant of whether a government stays or falls. Few governments have changed between elections, and snap elections have been rare. Under MMP, the evidence from other countries with PR indicates that elections are likely to remain the most frequent cause of government termination.[33] However, other factors are almost certain to become more important, with the result that governments may change from time to time between elections.

Bo Särlvik argues that coalition governments, as distinct from governments in general (see Chapter 6), generally collapse for one of three reasons:

- policy disputes of an essentially ideological nature;
- policy disputes that have little to do with traditional left-right distinctions (e.g. the merits of nuclear power); and
- the effect of the existing coalition on the parties' perceptions of their likely prospects at the next election.[34]

On the last point, one of the problems confronting a party in a coalition is that it becomes identified with a range of policy positions and government decisions, some of which may be opposed by the party's core supporters. There may be pressures on the leadership to leave the coalition prior to an election in order to distance the party from the coalition's policies. This occurred in Sweden before the 1982 election, when the Moderates (i.e. the Conservative party) left the three-party coalition as a result of a deal between its coalition partners (the Centre party and the Liberal party) and the opposition Social Democrats over tax policy.[35]

Ministerial responsibility

Various commentators have suggested that the move to MMP may undermine, or at least weaken, the conventions of collective responsibility and individual ministerial responsibility. The results of our survey are interesting in this respect: while the majority (59 percent) of respondents thought that the doctrine of individual ministerial responsibility would either be strengthened or remain unchanged under MMP, a similar majority (62 percent) thought that the doctrine of collective responsibility would be weakened. Such an outcome would be serious, since it would reduce the political accountability of ministers, and hence of governments. As it happens, the evidence from other parliamentary systems suggests that neither convention is likely to be significantly affected by the move to MMP.[36]

Collective responsibility (i.e. the convention that ministers must take joint responsibility in Parliament for all cabinet decisions) remains a central doctrine in all systems of cabinet government, irrespective of the electoral system or the precise composition of the government. This is hardly surprising. After all, there are powerful political incentives for a government to present a united face to the country, and equally strong incentives for ministers to defend the government's record when it is under opposition attack. Nevertheless, with coalition cabinets policy disagreements may well be aired more often in public than occurs with single-party governments. Also, Prime Ministers in coalition cabinets are more likely to tolerate a higher level of dissent, at least where the parties have irreconcilable differences. Such dissent can be expected to increase in the period leading up to an election as each party seeks to differentiate its policies and philosophy from that of its partner(s). New Zealand may well have a taste of this at the forthcoming election.

In accordance with the doctrine of individual ministerial responsibility, ministers are responsible to Parliament and the public for all that happens within their portfolios (especially their own decisions and those of their officials). In New Zealand this doctrine has been under siege for many decades, with ministers tending to hide behind the doctrine of collective responsibility or blame others for administrative errors. Despite such behaviour, ministers are still required to answer parliamentary questions about their portfolios and there are political penalties for those who appear to be shirking their responsibilities. In principle, the move to MMP – and, in particular, the greater likelihood of coalition government – should make little difference to the willingness or otherwise of ministers to take responsibility for their own actions and those of their officials.

Conclusion

Cabinet government will remain a central feature of New Zealand's constitutional arrangements under MMP. Whether and to what extent the composition, size, operations and durability of the cabinet change will depend largely on the kind of government which emerges (i.e. majority or minority, single party or coalition). In the improbable event of a single-party majority government, no significant changes from the general post-war pattern are likely. Similarly, in the event of a single-party minority government, the composition and procedures of the cabinet can be expected to remain largely unchanged. Against this, ministers in such a government will need to do a good deal of consultation and negotiations with other parliamentary parties (as was evident between mid-1995 and early 1996 when National no longer enjoyed a parliamentary majority). Also, single-party minority governments are likely to be less durable than single-party majority ones.

Coalition government, by contrast, will have more significant implications for the operations of the cabinet. The National/United coalition provides a foretaste of this – particularly in the heightened degree of inter-party consultation and co-operation. But the current coalition represents only a beginning. Under a fully-fledged multi-party government there is likely to be a more comprehensive agreement on policy issues, a fairer allocation of cabinet positions between the coalition partners, and greater constraints on the powers of the Prime Minister in relation to cabinet appointments (and dismissals), rankings and portfolio allocations.

Notes

1 The material in this chapter draws heavily on an article by J. Boston, 'Electoral Reform in New Zealand: the Implications for the Formation, Organization and Operations of the Cabinet', *Australian Quarterly*, 66, 1994, pp.67–90, and a chapter by P. Harris and E. McLeay, 'The Legislature', in G. Hawke (ed.), *Changing Politics? The Electoral Referendum 1993*, Victoria University Press, Wellington, 1993. Other useful analyses of the likely implications of MMP for cabinet government can be found in Marie Shroff, 'The Operation of Central Government Under Proportional Representation Electoral Systems', Cabinet Office, Wellington, September 1994; State Services Commission, *Working Under Proportional Representation: a Reference for the Public Service*, Wellington, 1995, esp. pp.11–20, 101–28; and 'Proceedings of the Public Service Senior Management Conference', State Services Commission, Wellington, 1994.

2 The most comprehensive and up-to-date account of cabinet government in New Zealand is E. McLeay's *The Cabinet and Political Power in New Zealand*, Oxford University Press, Auckland, 1995. Other useful accounts can be found in J. Boston, 'The Cabinet and Policy Making under the Fourth Labour Government', in M. Holland and J. Boston (eds), *The Fourth Labour Government: Politics and Policy in New Zealand*, Oxford University Press, Auckland, 1990, pp.62–82; G. Palmer, *Unbridled Power* (2nd edn), Oxford University Press, Auckland, 1987, pp.34–69; E. McLeay, 'Selection Versus Election: Choosing Cabinets in New Zealand', in H. Clarke and M. Czudnowski (eds), *Political Elites in Anglo-American Democracies: Changes in Stable Regimes*, Northern Illinois University Press, DeKalb, 1987, pp.279–306; R. Mulgan, *Politics in New Zealand*, Auckland University Press, Auckland, 1994, pp.69–92; and M. Palmer, 'Collective Cabinet Decision Making in New Zealand', in M. Laver and K. Shepsle (eds), *Cabinet Ministers and Parliamentary Government*, Cambridge University Press, New York, 1994, pp.226–50.

3 In many other countries there is nothing to prevent a Prime Minister from recruiting cabinet ministers from outside Parliament, and in many cases they do so. Also, in some European countries (e.g. Norway and Sweden) MPs who are appointed to the cabinet have their positions in Parliament taken by 'alternates'.

4 V. Bogdanor, 'Introduction', in V. Bogdanor (ed.), *Coalition Government in Western Europe*, Heinemann, London, 1983, p.6.

5 There is an extensive theoretical and empirical literature on the issues surrounding the formation, composition and durability of coalitions. The theoretical literature, which has been strongly influenced by rational choice approaches, has sought to explain and predict a range of matters, including which parties are most likely to join the government, how ministerial portfolios are allocated, what policy choices and compromises are most probable, and how durable particular kinds of coalitions are likely to be. For a useful introduction to, and survey of, this literature, see: J. Blondel and F. Muller-Rommel (eds), *Cabinets in Western Europe*, Macmillan, London, 1988; V. Bogdanor (ed.), *Coalition Government in Western Europe*; E. Browne and J. Dreijamnis (eds), *Government Coalitions in Western Democracies*, Longman, London, 1982; I. Budge and M. Keman, *Parties and Democracy: Coalition Formation and Government Functioning in Twenty States*, Oxford University Press, Oxford, 1990; I. Budge and M. Laver, 'The Policy Basis of Government Coalitions: a Comparative Investigation', *British Journal of Political Science*, 23, 1993, pp.499–519; L. Dodd, *Coalitions in Parliamentary Government*, Princeton

University Press, Princeton, 1976; M. Laver and K. Shepsle, 'Government Coalitions and Intraparty Politics', *British Journal of Political Science*, 20, 1990, pp.489–507; G. Luebbert, 'Coalition Theory and Government Formation in Multiparty Democracies', *Comparative Politics*, 15, 1983, pp. 235–49; W. Riker, *The Theory of Political Coalitions*, Yale University Press, New Haven, 1962; N. Schofield and M. Laver, 'Bargaining Theory and Portfolio Payoffs in European Coalition Governments 1945–83', *British Journal of Political Science*, 15, 1985, pp.143–64; and P. van Roozendaal, *Cabinets in Multi-Party Democracies*, Thesis Publishers, Amsterdam, 1992.

6 See T. Bergman, 'Constitutional Design and Government Formation: the Expected Consequences of Negative Parliamentarism', *Scandinavian Political Studies*, 16, 1993, pp.285–304.

7 In some cases, these agreements are renegotiated every year. A useful account of the negotiation of coalition programmes in Germany, the Netherlands, Sweden and Ireland is provided in the State Services Commission, *Working Under Proportional Representation*, pp.101–28.

8 H. Rommetvedt, 'Norwegian Coalition Governments and the Management of Party Relations', *Scandinavian Political Studies*, 17, 1994, pp.244–45.

9 See J. Boston and J. Pallot, 'Linking Strategy and Performance: Developments in the New Zealand Public Sector', unpublished paper, Victoria University of Wellington, 1996.

10 See P. Weller, *First Among Equals: Prime Ministers in Westminster Systems*, Allen & Unwin, Sydney, 1985.

11 Party leaders are usually elected by their party caucus. However, in some parties (e.g. the British Labour party) the leadership is determined by the party conference.

12 See M. Bassett, *Coates of Kaipara*, Auckland University Press, Auckland, 1995, pp.174–75. One reason for this outcome was the fact that Forbes was the incumbent Prime Minister, and he skilfully used his position to his party's (and his personal) advantage.

13 See I. Budge and M. Keman, *Parties and Democracy*, pp.89–131; E. Browne and M. Franklin, 'Aspects of Coalition Payoffs in European Parliamentary Democracies', *American Political Science Review*, 76, 1973, pp.453–69; E. Browne and J. Frendreis, 'Allocating Coalition Payoffs by Conventional Norm: an Assessment of the Evidence from Cabinet Coalition Situations', *American Journal of Political Science*, 24, 1980, pp.753–68.

14 This would be consistent with recent changes to Parliament's Standing Orders, as noted in Chapter 5.

15 Between 1915 and 1919, although the Reform party had more MPs than the Liberals, the positions in the War Cabinet were shared equally between the two parties. The same pattern was repeated between 1931 and 1935 during the United/Reform coalition; although Reform had more MPs than United, each party had five ministers in the 10-person cabinet.

16 M. Schmidt, 'Two Logics of Coalition Policy: the West German Case', in V. Bogdanor (ed.), *Coalition Government in Western Europe*, p.46.

17 See I. Budge and M. Keman, *Parties and Democracy*, pp.89–131; I. Budge and M. Laver, 'Office Seeking and Policy Pursuit in Coalition Theory', *Legislative Studies Quarterly*, 11, 1986, p.494; H. Rommetvedt, 'Norwegian Coalition Governments', pp.246–50.

18 T. Mackie and B. Hogwood (eds), *Unlocking the Cabinet: Cabinet Structures in Comparative Perspective*, Sage, London, 1985, p.13.

19 See J. Boston, 'The Treasury and the Organisation of Economic Advice: Some International Comparisons', in B. Easton (ed.), *The Making of Rogernomics*, Auckland University Press, Auckland, 1989, pp.68–91.

20 Note that under current conventions the Governor-General appoints ministers on the advice of the Prime Minister. See *Cabinet Office Manual*, Ch. 2, Para. B4, Wellington.

21 See T. Mackie and B. Hogwood (eds), *Unlocking the Cabinet*, p.18; J. Blondel and F. Muller-Rommel (eds), *Cabinets in Western Europe*.

22 See Cabinet Office, *Cabinet Office Manual*.

23 See R. Andeweg, 'The Netherlands: Cabinet Committees in a Coalition Cabinet', and J. Christensen, 'In Search of Unity: Cabinet Committees in Denmark', both in T. Mackie and B. Hogwood (eds), *Unlocking the Cabinet*; R. Andeweg, 'The Netherlands: Coalition Cabinets in Changing Circumstances', S. Eriksen, 'Norway: Ministerial Autonomy and Collective Responsibility', A. Frognier, 'Belgium: a Complex Cabinet in a Fragmented Polity', F. Muller-Rommel, 'Federal Republic of Germany: a System of Chancellor Government', T. Schou, 'Denmark', all in J. Blondel and F. Muller-Rommel (eds), *Cabinets in Western Europe*; P. Harris and E. McLeay, 'The Legislature'.

24 State Services Commission, *Working Under Proportional Representation*, p.18.

25 See J. Christensen, 'Cabinet Committees in Denmark', in T. Mackie and B. Hogwood (eds), *Unlocking the Cabinet*; S. Eriksen, 'Norway', in J. Blondel and F. Muller-Rommel (eds), *Cabinets in Western Europe*, p.192.

26 R. Andeweg, 'The Netherlands', in T. Mackie and B. Hogwood (eds), *Unlocking the Cabinet*, pp.139–40.

27 J. Christensen, 'Cabinet Committees in Denmark', p.131.

28 The procedures for consultation and co-ordination with other political parties were revised by the Cabinet in mid-1995 in response to the changed political situation in Parliament. See Cabinet Office Circular, 'Consultation with Political Parties: Revised Procedures and New CAB 100 Form', CO (95) 8, 8 September 1995.

29 See A. Lijphart, 'Measures of Cabinet Durability: a Conceptual and Empirical Evaluation', *Comparative Political Studies*, 17, 1984, pp.265–79.

30 See E. Damgaard, 'Termination of Danish Government Coalitions: Theoretical and Empirical Aspects', *Scandinavian Political Studies*, 17, 1994, pp.194–97.

31 L. Dodd, 'The Study of Cabinet Durability: Introduction and Commentary', *Comparative Political Studies*, 17, 1984, p.160.

32 K. Strom, *Minority Government and Majority Rule*, Cambridge University Press, Cambridge, 1990, p.116.

33 E. Damgaard, 'Termination of Danish Government Coalitions', p.200.

34 B. Särlvik, 'Coalition Politics and Policy Output in Scandinavia: Sweden, Denmark and Norway', in V. Bogdanor (ed.), *Coalition Government in Western Europe*, pp.140–45. There is an extensive theoretical literature on the termination of coalition governments. See, for example, I. Budge and M. Keman, *Parties and Democracy*; L. Dodd, *Coalitions in Parliamentary Government*; E. Damgaard, 'Termination of Danish Government Coalitions'; B. Grofman and P. van Roozendaal, 'Towards a Theoretical Explanation of Premature Cabinet Termination', *European Journal of Political Research*, 26, 1994, pp.155–70; A. Lupia and K. Strom, 'Coalition Termination and the Strategic Timing of Parliamentary Elections', *American Political Science Review*, 89, 1995, pp.648–65; and H. Narud, 'Coalition Termination in Norway: Models and Cases', *Scandinavian Political Studies*, 18, 1995, pp.1–24.

35 See B. Särlvik, 'Coalition Politics and Policy Output in Scandinavia', in V. Bogdanor (ed.), *Coalition Government in Western Europe*, pp.131–33.

36 D. Butler, *Governing Without a Majority*, Macmillan, London, 1986, p.137.

CHAPTER 8

The public service and the new environment

In all the debates on electoral reform before the referendums in 1992 and 1993, very little public attention was given to the question of how changes to the electoral system might affect the role, operations, power and ethos of the public service. Even within the Wellington policy community, debate about the possible consequences of MMP was relatively muted and little preparatory work was done by the central agencies – the Department of the Prime Minister and Cabinet, the State Services Commission (SSC), and the Treasury. To be sure, there were some seminars on the subject, but few substantive papers were prepared.[1] Nor was much attention given to the possible impact of MMP on the new model of public sector management ushered in by the State Owned Enterprises Act 1986, the State Sector Act 1988, and the Public Finance Act 1989.[2]

Many, no doubt, simply assumed that the existing laws and conventions governing the conduct of public servants would continue to apply, and that it would be mostly business as usual. The composition of the House might change, as might the mode of policy-making and the mechanics of forming and sustaining governments, but the role and responsibilities of the public service would remain the same. Likewise, whereas the move to proportional representation was widely recognised as marking a shift away from the pure Westminster model – particularly the tradition of adversarial two-party politics, single-party majority governments, and executive dominance of Parliament – there was no expectation that the conventions of the Westminster model applying to public servants would be altered. Continuity, not change, would be the order of the day. Thus, public servants would still be expected to serve the duly elected government, regardless of its composition or ideological complexion, with equal dedication and vigour. They would similarly be expected to provide 'free and frank' advice, execute ministerial decisions and deliver public services in a professional, non-partisan and lawful manner.[3] Their role, in short, would remain that of obedient servant.

Since the referendum decision in favour of MMP in 1993, much more detailed consideration has been given to the possible implications of the new electoral system for the bureaucracy (and the executive as a whole).[4] Several senior public servants, including the Secretary of Cabinet and the State Services Commissioner, have visited countries with PR systems (primarily in northern Europe and Scandinavia) in order to gain a better understanding of how MMP might affect the conduct of politics and the operations of the executive. Numerous seminars and workshops for public servants have been held to furnish information about the new electoral system and its possible impact on the nature of their work. And new guidelines have been issued by the Cabinet Office and the SSC on the appropriate conduct of public servants in particular situations (e.g. during periods of caretaker government, providing evidence and advice to select committees, briefing opposition parties).

Perhaps most important, the SSC oversaw the preparation of a major report entitled *Working Under Proportional Representation: a Reference for the Public Service*. The product of a year's concentrated effort by a team of officials and external advisers, this document provides a thorough and systematic account of existing constitutional conventions and explores the possible ramifications of the new electoral system for the workings of the political process. It outlines the various kinds of executive–legislative relationships which may occur under MMP and the likely consequences of these for the public service. Many of the subjects addressed in this report are discussed below.

Since the report's publication, the SSC has continued its efforts to ensure that government departments and other public sector agencies are adequately prepared for the new MMP environment. Among other things, it commissioned Mel Smith (a former deputy-secretary in the Department of Justice) to examine how individual departments were preparing for MMP. As part of this exercise, interviews were conducted with most chief executives and various issues requiring further attention were identified. Overall, the conclusion was positive: 'the Public Service is preparing itself well for the demands to be placed on it . . . CEs were, to a person, together with their senior staff, interested and responsive to the emerging issues . . . Departments and ministries . . . are focusing on training and process development and many have appointed a senior officer as their project manager'.[5]

Types of government and the role of public servants

As with the cabinet, the impact of MMP on public servants is likely to depend on which of the four kinds of government outlined in Chapter 6 prevails (see Table 8.1). Under a single-party majority government – which, admittedly, is the least likely outcome – the role and operations of the public service should be little different from those under similar governments in the past.

Government transitions are likely to be straightforward and caretaker periods brief. By virtue of its majority, the government will not need to undertake extensive consultations or negotiations with other parliamentary parties on

Table 8.1. *Types of government and the possible implications for public servants*

	Likely continuities	**Possible changes and difficulties**
Single-party majority government	Key constitutional conventions of the Westminster model will continue to apply. Departmental officials will remain the government's principal source of policy advice.	Little change in role of public servants or in relationships between ministers and departmental advisers. Possibly greater scrutiny of public agencies by select committees under revised Standing Orders.
Multi-party majority government	Key constitutional conventions of the Westminster model will continue to apply. Departmental officials will remain the government's principal source of policy advice.	Tensions between coalition partners may pose difficulties for departmental chief executives in reconciling their obligations to the collective interests of the government and loyalty to their portfolio minister. More inter-party consultation and negotiation may generate demands for additional policy advice. Possible appointment of more political advisers, thereby creating a more contestable market for policy advice. Possibility of longer caretaker periods while coalition is being formed, or re-formed.
Single-party minority government	Key constitutional conventions of the Westminster model will continue to apply. Departmental officials will remain the government's principal source of policy advice.	Lack of government majorities on most select committees will expose public servants to greater parliamentary scrutiny. Departmental policy advisers will have much more contact with non-government parties. More inter-party consultation and negotiation may generate demands for additional policy advice. Possibility of longer caretaker periods while government is being formed. Possible changes to Budget cycle.

	Likely continuities	Possible changes and difficulties
Multi-party minority government	Key constitutional conventions of the Westminster model will continue to apply. Departmental officials will remain the government's principal source of policy advice.	Tensions between coalition partners may pose difficulties for departmental chief executives in reconciling their obligations to the collective interests of the government and loyalty to their portfolio minister. Departmental policy advisers will have much more contact with non-government parties. More inter-party consultation and negotiation may generate demands for additional policy advice. Possible appointment of more political advisers, thereby creating a more contestable market for policy advice. Lack of government majorities on most select committees will expose public servants to greater parliamentary scrutiny. Possibility of longer caretaker periods while coalition is being formed, or re-formed. Possible changes to Budget cycle.

legislative initiatives or budgetary matters. Hence, the relationship between public servants and opposition parties is likely to be much the same as under FPP.

By contrast, under each of the other three government types, various changes and new challenges can be expected.[6] Some examples are outlined in Table 8.1. Coalition governments, whether majority or minority, will bring a new political dynamic, and additional uncertainty, to policy-making (see Chapter 7). The process of forming the coalition and determining its policy agenda could be protracted, thereby giving rise to much longer periods of caretaker government. While the conventions surrounding such governments, as described in Chapter 6, are reasonably clear, any protracted caretaker period could generate problems for senior departmental officials (e.g. ensuring that adequate legal authority exists for incurring certain expenditures, handling requests under the Official Information Act, determining departmental work programmes, handling reforms which were barely under way at the start of the caretaker period, and responding to unexpected eventualities). As the SSC argues in *Working Under Proportional Representation*, during periods of caretaker government 'extra care' will need to be taken 'to distinguish between the political responsibility of the Ministers and the proper role of public servants in supporting the Government of the day'.[7]

In the event of a coalition being relatively unstable and perhaps deeply divided on important policy issues, various difficulties could arise for senior departmental advisers. For instance, if a department advocates a policy position which is similar to that of one of the coalition parties, it may open itself to the accusation of acting in a partisan fashion. That may undermine the relationship between the department and certain ministers, thereby adversely affecting intra-governmental communication and co-ordination. Similar difficulties could arise if there were major divisions within the coalition on strategic objectives, policy priorities, and the particular outputs (or key result areas) to be sought from various departments. In such situations, departmental chief executives will need to keep themselves well abreast of the political dynamics evolving within the coalition and try to ensure that their staff behave in a fully professional, non-partisan, yet politically sensitive manner. Astute judgement by officials will be required if the appropriate balances are to be struck.

Minority governments will pose additional challenges for public servants. As a result of the shift in the balance of power between Parliament and the executive, much greater consultation on policy issues will be needed with non-government parties – especially supporting parties, but also opposition parties – much as has happened during the transition to MMP. Under a minority regime, the government will be obliged to seek support from other parties on every legislative initiative. Also, since it will lack a majority on most, perhaps all, select committees, it will be obliged to negotiate with other parties on controversial matters. For public servants, such requirements will necessarily entail greater contact – at the request of ministers – with non-government parties, especially party leaders and select committee chairs. This has already been apparent during the transition to MMP. It will be crucial in these circumstances for officials to observe the various guidelines prepared by the cabinet, the SSC and individual departments setting out the proper role of public servants and the parameters within which they should work.[8]

Any increase in the level of dialogue between the government and other parties in Parliament will doubtless impose additional costs on departments, especially the central agencies. There will be a need, for instance, for departmental information to be more widely circulated, for officials to respond – at the direction of ministers – to policy proposals and ideas from the non-governing parties, and for more frequent attendance by officials at select committees and other policy-making forums. This has already been occurring during the transitional period.

An additional feature of minority government is the probability that select committees will subject departments (and other public bodies) to greater scrutiny and take a more independent line in their review of departmental expenditure. Although this may impose additional costs on the public service, it should also provide a spur for better performance and improve the political accountability of public agencies.

Finally, under minority government, certain changes to the budgetary process are likely – as, in fact, was highlighted by the preparation of the 1996/97 Budget. Budgets may take longer to prepare, inter-party negotiations will be more extensive, secrecy less intense, and parliamentary scrutiny more rigorous. For the public service there are obvious implications for the timing of the budgetary cycle, the need for longer planning horizons, and the provision of support for inter-party negotiations. Equally important, to the extent that minority government generates greater uncertainty over supply, 'Departments and other government agencies may need to be more accurate in the monitoring of their financial positions against authorisation, and may need to monitor more closely areas of potential fiscal risk'.[9]

Departmental officials and the process of government formation

One issue which may arise during the early years of MMP is what role, if any, public servants should play in the process of government formation, including the preparation of any coalition agreements which might be negotiated. In PR systems elsewhere it is not uncommon for officials, especially those in finance ministries and Prime Minister's departments (or their equivalents), to assist in various ways with the preparation of coalition agreements. After all, the politicians involved may be too busy to address every issue or prepare all the necessary policy papers. Normally, any assistance supplied by departments is limited to the provision of technical information, the costing of certain policy options, and the supply of relevant research data. Participation in the substance of the negotiations or the preparation of papers assessing the merits of particular policy proposals is rare. These are the responsibilities of politicians, not bureaucrats. Plainly, were departmental officials in New Zealand to be involved directly in the process of coalition formation there would be an inevitable risk of breaching the convention of political impartiality. Any participation, therefore, must be prudently managed. As the SSC has put it, 'The Public Service must not compromise its ability to work with future Governments, and this requires that care be taken to preserve and demonstrate neutrality at all times'.[10]

A more specific issue needing clarification is whether the post-election briefings (PEBs) prepared by departments in the period leading up to a general election should be available (at least in the first instance) only to the duly elected government once it has been sworn in, or whether they should be made more widely available straight after the election.[11] Under the latter option, for instance, all the parties represented in Parliament would be able to secure copies of all PEBs, thereby providing them with a valuable source of information and advice. Such material could prove very useful during ensuing coalition negotiations.

Both options have their drawbacks. If PEBs cannot be obtained by the parties until a new government is duly constituted, they will not be available during the preceding inter-party negotiations and policy deliberations. This means, in effect, that some key policy issues might be decided before the advice of officials is available. Moreover, if the caretaker period is protracted, some of the material in the PEBs may be dated by the time it becomes available. In each case, the utility of the briefings will be reduced. Against this, releasing all the briefings straight after the election also has disadvantages. One obvious risk is that the advice will be used in politically motivated ways and, as a result, the departments concerned may get caught up in the politics of government formation. This could ultimately prove damaging to the role and standing of the departments (or particular officials) in question, as well as undermining the tradition of public service neutrality. To avoid such outcomes, departments may be tempted to remove any potentially controversial material from their briefings. But, of course, if the briefings were 'sterilised' in this way their usefulness would be correspondingly diminished and the tradition of 'free and frank' advice called into question.[12]

Given the difficulties associated with each option, a third approach has been suggested: that departments release their briefings *before*, not *after*, an election. In our view, such a proposal is neither practical nor prudent. Departments would have an extremely limited time in which to prepare their briefings, especially in the event of a snap election. Further, releasing such briefings before an election would inevitably draw departments into the hurly-burly of the election campaign. Their policy prescriptions, rightly or wrongly, would be interpreted as favouring a particular party (or parties). Almost certainly this would generate allegations of political bias. Maintaining the Westminster tradition of political neutrality in such circumstances could be rendered impossible.

Politicisation of the public service?

The new electoral system may well generate a greater range of situations in which the political impartiality of departmental officials could be called into question. This in turn raises the question of whether MMP will, over time, increase the risk of the public service becoming (partially) politicised, especially at senior levels.[13] Under this scenario, some officials (including departmental chief executives, members of the senior executive service and policy advisers) would be openly acknowledged as supporters of a particular political party. Their employment within departments, or at least their tenure in sensitive advisory or management positions, would depend on which party (or parties) was in office. Hence, a change of government would result in personnel changes not merely within the cabinet but also within the upper echelons of the bureaucracy – as occurs to some extent, for instance, in Germany and Sweden, and to a much larger extent in the United States when a new President takes office.

Any significant and explicit politicisation of the upper echelons of the public service would represent a major departure from New Zealand's bureaucratic traditions. Its implications for policy-making, and the whole character of governance, could be far-reaching. Unlike the US, for instance, there is no alternative group of experienced policy advisers waiting in the wings to take office in the event of a change of government. Moreover, given the small size of the policy community and the virtual absence of policy think-tanks, it would be extremely difficult, as well as grossly inefficient, to imitate the American model. Fortunately, these constraints and drawbacks are understood by senior politicians and, to date, the idea of a more politicised bureaucracy has received little support from parliamentarians. Likewise, there is no evidence of senior public servants wishing to depart from the Westminster traditions in which they have been nurtured.

It is significant in this context that no government has so far exploited the opportunity provided by the State Sector Act 1988 (S. 35 [11]) to overturn the recommendations of the State Services Commissioner on the appointment of departmental chief executives and make its own appointment.[14] In fact, since 1988 only one of the commissioner's formal recommendations has been rejected, and in that instance the government, rather than making its own appointment, asked the commissioner to make another recommendation.[15] Unless there is a substantial change in the views of senior parliamentarians over the coming years, there is little prospect of 'political' appointments being made under the State Sector Act.

Bear in mind, too, that there is no direct causal relationship between electoral systems and bureaucratic traditions. Hence, countries with PR have diverse public service norms and practices. While some (e.g. Germany and Sweden) have a degree of politicisation (primarily at very senior departmental levels), others (e.g. Denmark and Ireland) have a long history of public service neutrality.[16] Moreover, even where the boundary between matters 'political' and 'bureaucratic' is more fluid than in Westminster systems, only a small percentage of those serving in government departments are in any sense 'political' appointees. Accordingly, there is no reason to believe that MMP necessarily signals the demise of a Westminster-style bureaucracy.

Yet, if the politicisation of the upper echelons of the public service is unlikely, officials will need to be comfortable with an environment in which policy decisions are more frequently driven by inter-party politics.[17] They will also need to accommodate a greater reliance by ministers on 'political' advisers (employed on short-term contracts). Some 60 percent of respondents in our survey (and over 80 percent of the senior public servants who completed the questionnaire) thought that non-departmental political advisers would have a 'greater role in the policy-making process' under MMP. Of course, some ministers already employ such people in their Beehive offices, and in recent years there has been a significant expansion in the public resources available to opposition parties for the employment of policy advisers. Under MMP the demand for politically tailored advice is likely to increase. Even here, however, major changes are improbable. There is little prospect, for instance, of each minister (or opposition party) having a substantial coterie of political advisers. Also, departments are still likely to appoint one or two staff to ministerial offices to undertake liaison functions. Overall, any changes to the number and role of 'political' advisers under MMP are likely to be modest and the impact on the public service correspondingly minor.

Other observers are less sanguine. Indeed, some believe that a degree of politicisation is already evident, and that this may gather momentum under MMP. In a speech in mid-1995, Helen Clark, the Leader of the Opposition, observed:

> Unfortunately over the last five years the few remaining major departments of state have become far too politicised. Treasury has been highly politicised even longer, from the time when Roger Douglas held sway. It does not, in my view, provide balanced advice. Now the virus has spread more widely so that, as in Treasury, it is felt by public servants at lower levels in some other departments that advancement is possible only if one subscribes to the prevailing orthodoxy. One wonders how such departments will fare with a change of government.[18]

Various issues raised here deserve comment. First, it is important to distinguish between, on the one hand, a shift in the philosophical or ideological framework within which policy advisers operate and within which advice is fashioned and, on the other, a bureaucratic context where only officials whose views are compatible with those of the incumbent government can aspire to high office. In New Zealand, a major intellectual revolution occurred during the 1980s and early 1990s with the result that the ideas currently in the ascendancy within the public service are very different from those which previously found favour. Even so, public service appointments and tenure remain virtually free of political influence (except perhaps in the case of departmental chief executives); merit, not patronage, is the overriding principle. Second, were a government to be elected that was strongly opposed to some of the key tenets of the new policy orthodoxy (e.g. an Alliance-led government), it would be bound to encounter some resistance from senior officials. Such officials would, however, be obliged to implement its policies. Any attempt to thwart the government's purposes would be incompatible with the Westminster tradition. If particular officials believe that the government is so misguided that they can no longer serve it with appropriate loyalty and dedication, then they should seriously consider resigning.

Systems and structures

Another issue is the possible impact of MMP on the new systems and structures of public sector management introduced over the past decade. Any administrative changes resulting directly from electoral reform are likely to be minor. Electoral systems are not a key determinant of bureaucratic systems and structures. Administrative traditions, management theories, the level of economic development, public expectations, and the degree of technological sophistication are much more important. Moreover, most of the recent reforms (e.g. human resource management, financial management, corporatisation, machinery of government) have secured multi-party endorsement.[19] There is thus little support for reversing the key reforms or, alternatively, embarking upon radical new directions. The only major exceptions relate to the commercialisation and/or privatisation of certain public services. Here the Alliance, and to a lesser extent Labour and New Zealand First, are generally opposed to further privatisation and prefer less 'user-pays', especially in education, health care and housing.

With regard to the machinery of government, one possible modification might be the establishment of an Office of the Deputy Prime Minister. In a two-party coalition, for instance, the leader of the smaller party may well be the Deputy Prime Minister, and in this capacity may have much broader co-ordination and policy responsibilities than hitherto. A more significant change to which MMP might give rise is the division of the Treasury into two separate departments, one responsible for economic policy and the other for expenditure control and financial management (as in Canberra and Ottawa). Under a two-party coalition government, the minor party may be reluctant to allow the analytical resources of both the Department of the Prime Minister and Cabinet and the Treasury to be vested with the major party. Conversely, the major party may be unwilling to give up either portfolio. In this situation, a division of the Treasury might be the most politically expedient solution.

In the new model of public management in New Zealand, departmental performance management systems have been extensively revised and upgraded. New forms of 'contracting' have been introduced with much more rigorous systems of performance specification, monitoring and enforcement.[20] Departmental chief executives, for instance, have annual performance agreements with ministers. These are reviewed by the State Services Commissioner, in consultation with the portfolio minister(s) and other central agencies. Additionally, a new system of strategic management has been introduced (see Chapter 7). Such initiatives have attracted substantial support from senior bureaucrats and politicians alike. Although the move to MMP may necessitate certain modifications to the new systems (e.g. to accommodate longer periods of caretaker government or the policy-making uncertainties associated with minority governments and unstable coalitions), the architecture of the new bureaucratic order seems robust enough to weather any political storms wrought by MMP.

The power of public servants

Some observers have suggested that one of the many unintended, and undesirable, consequences of MMP will be to enhance the relative power and influence of public servants, most notably those responsible for providing policy advice. The argument is that, if governments change more frequently and ministers correspondingly spend less time in their respective portfolios, the opportunity for senior bureaucrats to dominate the minister–adviser relationship will be enhanced. Hence, whereas the bureaucrats will be relatively permanent (albeit on fixed-term contracts), their political superiors will be increasingly transient. This will make it harder for ministers to master their departmental responsibilities, gain command of the policy issues within their portfolio, and see through major policy reforms. Ministers may also be required to devote greater attention to inter-party consultations and negotiations. In these circumstances, it is contended, departmental officials will be subject to less political control and may come to exert greater influence on policy formulation and long-term strategising.

Interestingly, almost a third of those surveyed in late 1995 thought that senior public servants would have a greater role in the policy-making process under MMP (see Table 8.2). Another third thought their role would be largely unchanged, while 26 percent expected them to have a reduced role. As Table 8.2 shows, the expectations of the various groups surveyed were markedly different. For instance, business leaders and MPs were much more likely to think that the role of senior public servants would be enhanced than were interest-group leaders and senior public servants themselves.

Table 8.2. *The expected role of senior public servants under MMP*

	Business	Interest groups	MPs	Public servants	All
Greater role	46.1	29.7	50.7	33.1	32.6
Unchanged	35.7	34.3	29.9	33.1	31.4
Lesser role	16.1	29.1	11.9	28.9	26.0
Don't know/ Not applicable	2.1	6.9	7.3	4.9	10.0
Total	100%	100%	100%	100%	100%

In our view, the claim that there will be a major increase in the role or power of senior departmental officials under MMP is open to doubt. Of course, measuring the relative power of different institutions and actors in the political arena is a complex and hazardous business, not open to precise, empirically based conclusions. Nevertheless, increased mandarin dominance under MMP is unlikely, for several reasons. First, as noted in Chapter 7, governments will not necessarily change more frequently in the future. Relatively enduring governments, especially majority coalition governments, are a realistic possibility, as the experience of some countries with PR systems demonstrates. Further, even if more regular changes of government become the norm, this will not necessarily entail the replacement of one entire cabinet line-up with another. In some instances, the changes will be characterised by the addition of a party to (or its subtraction from) the governing coalition. In this event, only some members of the cabinet will change. In short, a significant reduction in ministerial tenure is not an inevitable outcome of MMP.

Second, under minority governments, whether single party or multi-party, there will be a relative shift in the balance of power from the executive to the legislature. This shift will affect both the political and bureaucratic arms of the executive (as argued in earlier chapters). It should not, however, involve any change in the relative influence of ministers and their departmental officials.

Third, as a result of the state sector reforms of the late 1980s and early 1990s, the capacity of ministers to exercise control over their departments has been improved. Ministers are now involved more directly in the appointment and appraisal of departmental chief executives. They have a vital role not merely in setting the government's strategic result areas, but also in determining the key result areas for their departments. In addition, the Public Finance Act 1989 has strengthened ministers' ability to specify the departmental outputs they wish to purchase (including the matters on which they wish to secure policy advice), and enhanced their capacity to scrutinise departmental performance.

Fourth, if ministers under MMP make greater use of political advisers, the relative influence of departmental policy advisers may be diminished, not enhanced. Likewise, any moves to expand the independent advice available to select committees via the Select Committee Office (within the Office of the Clerk) and the Audit Office will pose an additional challenge to the position of departmental officials.[21] The greater the range and sources of advice, the harder it will be for departments to win policy debates.

Fifth, the increase in the size of Parliament under MMP will correspondingly widen the pool of individuals available to serve in cabinet. This may contribute to an improvement in the overall depth and breadth of talent within the cabinet, and should enhance the influence of ministers relative to the public service.

Finally, regardless of whether there is any change in the respective roles and overall influence of ministers and departmental officials under MMP, there will doubtless continue to be fluctuations in the relative standing of particular departments (and advisory bodies). Under governments of a centre-left disposition, for instance, the overall influence of the Treasury on public policy is likely to wane, while that of Education, Health, Social Welfare and Women's Affairs might be expected to increase. Of course, much will depend on the quality of the advisers in such ministries and the nature of the advice tendered.

The future role of the public service

The past decade has witnessed a significant reduction in the scope of the state's activities and major changes in the nature of its policy interventions. The activist and expansionary state of the early post-war era has been replaced with the more limited, streamlined and finely tuned state of the 1990s. The consequences of the 'great transformation' for the public service have been immense. Not merely has there been a huge reduction in the number of people employed in the 'core' public service (from over 80,000 in the mid-1980s to less than 35,000 in the mid-1990s) but virtually every public sector organisation has been restructured or 're-engineered'. Such 'revolutions' generally occur only once in a lifetime, if that. Irrespective of the kind of electoral system New Zealand has over the coming decades, therefore, further changes of a similar magnitude are most unlikely.

This is not to suggest that New Zealand is about to enter a period of bureaucratic stasis. Plainly, there will continue to be changes in the number, size, structure and management of public sector agencies. The nature and direction of such changes will depend on the ideological leanings of the governments in office. Under centre-left governments, public expenditure is more likely to rise than fall and further commercialisation and privatisation of public services will be limited. Any administrative reorganisations are likely to be in areas such as health care and housing where the current policy settings remain politically controversial. In the absence of another fiscal crisis, any further radical downsizing of the 'core' public sector is unlikely. A centre-left government may also renew the quest for a more genuinely bicultural public service – a quest begun in the mid-1980s by the fourth Labour government but which subsequently lost momentum under National.[22]

Under centre-right governments, by contrast, there will be continuing pressure for the state to review, and where possible reduce, its activities – particularly its roles as *owner* (e.g. of land, buildings, infrastructure) and as direct *provider* of services (e.g. in health care and education). Against this, the pressure on the government to reduce its role as *funder* may be less in evidence, especially if there are substantial fiscal surpluses. Accordingly, while there may be a reduction in public service employment due to the contracting-out or privatisation of various services (e.g. prisons, hospitals, tertiary institutions), there may be no corresponding reduction in overall levels of public expenditure.

Conclusion

Irrespective of the political complexion of governments under MMP, the role of the public service will be as vital as ever. It will remain the principal source of 'free and frank' advice to the cabinet. It will continue to ensure that the normal day-to-day responsibilities of the state are undertaken during periods of political uncertainty. It will continue to serve as a key facilitator of the democratic process, supplying high-quality information to the public and politicians alike, and assisting in the process of inter-party consultation and conflict resolution. It will remain accountable for its actions (or inactions) through the doctrines of individual ministerial responsibility and collective responsibility. While MMP will bring changes to certain bureaucratic procedures, systems and structures, and while parliamentary scrutiny may at times be more intense, it is unlikely to usher in another administrative revolution. Nor are there grounds for expecting the existing conventions governing public service conduct to be radically altered. In all probability, evolutionary rather than abrupt change will be the hallmark of bureaucratic life in the new politics of MMP.

Notes

1 One of the few articles to appear on the impact of MMP on the bureaucracy was by P. Carpinter, 'MMP and Coalitions: Possible Issues in the New Zealand Context', *Public Sector*, 16, 1, March 1993, pp.5–8, subsequently re-published as 'MMP and Coalitions: Possible Effects on New Zealand's Public Service', in G. Hawke (ed.), *Changing Politics? The Electoral Referendum 1993*, Victoria University Press, Wellington, 1993, pp.131–41.

2 The most comprehensive account of the new model of public management is J. Boston, J. Martin, J. Pallot and P. Walsh, *Public Management: the New Zealand Model*, Oxford University Press, Auckland, 1996.

3 For a brief exploration of these conventions and the possible implications of MMP, see G. Hensley, 'Free and Frank Advice to Ministers – Reappraising Ethical Fundamentals', *Public Sector*, 18, 3, 1995, pp.21–23.

4 The Cabinet established an ad hoc committee on the Implementation of Proportional Representation (IPR) to consider issues raised by the move to MMP, and to oversee and co-ordinate the work being done by officials in preparation for the first MMP election. This committee was serviced by an inter-departmental team of officials chaired by the State Services Commissioner, Don Hunn.

5 Mel Smith, 'Proportional Representation and Its Effects on the Public Service: Report to the State Services Commissioner', December 1995, p.13.

6 For a detailed analysis, see State Services Commission, *Working Under Proportional Representation: a Reference for the Public Service*, Wellington, 1995. See also J. Bolger, 'Address to Public Service Senior Managers Conference', 17 August 1995, Wellington; and J. Boston, S. Levine, E. McLeay and N. S. Roberts, 'Proportional Representation and the Public Service: Will MMP Make a Difference?' *Public Sector*, 18, 4, 1995, pp.24–27.

7 P.79. The conventions relating to caretaker periods and the conduct expected of public servants during them were clarified further in late 1995 in a Cabinet Office Circular (CO [95] 15).

8 See, for example, Cabinet Office Circular, 'Consultation with Opposition Parties', CO (94) 8, 21 March 1994; Cabinet Office Circular, 'Consultation with Political Parties: Revised Procedures and the New CAB Form', CO (95) 8, 8 September 1995; SSC, *Public Service Principles, Conventions and Practices*, Wellington, 1995; and Ministry of Health, 'Protocol for Opposition Party Briefings and Consultation', 1995. One area where further clarification may be required is the conventions applying to the boards and chief executives of Crown-owned entities. See Mel Smith, 'Proportional Representation and Its Effects on the Public Service', p.13.

9 State Services Commission, *Working Under Proportional Representation*, p.63.

10 Ibid, p.93.

11 For a discussion of these issues, see Mel Smith, 'Proportional Representation and Its Effects on the Public Service', pp.8–9.

12 To some extent 'sterilisation' is already occurring, with departments glossing over some of the more difficult and controversial policy issues in PEBs and dealing with them in separate reports.

13 Several thoughtful papers have been written on this subject in recent years. See, for instance, J. Martin, 'MMP and the Public Service: "Politicisation" and Professional Ethics', paper presented to an IIR Seminar, 24 March 1994, Wellington.

14 See Boston et al., *Public Management: the New Zealand Model*, pp.100–5.

15 The case in question involved the Commissioner's recommendation of Gerald Hensley as Secretary of Defence. See J. Boston, 'Public Sector Update: Appointing a Secretary of Defence', *Public Sector*, 13, 3, pp.5–6.

16 There is an extensive literature on public bureaucracies and the relationship between the political and administrative arms of the state in various jurisdictions. See, for instance, M. Dogan (ed.), *The Mandarins of Western Europe: the Political Role of Top Civil*

Servants, Sage, New York, 1975. For an account of the implications of a change of government on the public service in Germany, see Hans-Ulrich Derlien, 'Repercussions of Government Change on the Career Civil Service in West Germany: the Cases of 1969 and 1982', *Governance*, 1, 1, 1988, pp.50–78.

17 The changing attitudes of senior public servants towards the political process is important in this context. For recent work on this subject, see Robert Gregory, 'Post-Reform Attitudes of New Zealand's Senior Public Servants: a Follow-up Study', *Political Science*, 47, 2, 1995, pp.161–90.

18 Helen Clark, 'Relationships between politicians and public servants – as it has been and as it might be under MMP: one participant's observations', speech to Victoria University's Master of Public Policy Programme, Winter 'Downtown' Seminar Series, 12 September, 1995, Wellington, p.3.

19 See Boston et al., *Public Management: the New Zealand Model*, pp.350–66.

20 The new emphasis on contractualist modes of governance is examined in J. Boston (ed.), *The State Under Contract*, Bridget Williams Books, Wellington, 1995.

21 The issues relating to the provision of advisory services for select committees were canvassed in the recent Report of the Standing Orders Committee, *On the Review of Standing Orders*, House of Representatives, 1995, pp.45–48. Interestingly, Helen Clark argues that, 'It is not appropriate for the legislative arm of government to continue to rely so heavily on the executive for advice'. Accordingly, she maintains that government officials should cease to be advisers to select committees and that a separate advisory service should be built up within Parliament (presumably within the Office of the Clerk). See Clark, 'Relationships between politicians and public servants', p.6.

22 See Boston et al., *Public Management: the New Zealand Model*, pp.141–59.

CHAPTER 9

The dynamics of policy-making under MMP

Criticisms of New Zealand's policy process and outcomes have focused on three related problems. These have been attributed, at least in part, to the FPP electoral system:

- the policy process has been seen as too rapid, especially concerning the legislative process, thus detrimentally affecting the quality of decisions and legislation;
- policy formulation and political debate have been seen as unduly adversarial;
- public policy has been seen as being too much the product of small cabinet cliques rather than a response to the needs and wishes of the citizens. Parliament itself has been viewed as uninfluential, and also unrepresentative of the range of political parties and groups (especially Maori and women). Thus the official governmental policy agenda has not reflected the wider public agenda; cabinet has been an 'elective dictatorship'.[1]

This chapter explores how the shift to multi-party Parliaments and away from single-party, majority governments will affect the policy process. The characteristics of public policy formulation are fundamental to all five of the challenges to New Zealand's future political culture discussed in Chapter 1: forging processes that reflect New Zealand's political identity as a bicultural state and multi-cultural society; the participation of individual citizens, political parties and interest groups in policy-making; the fair distribution of resources among the people; the resolution of arguments about the extent to which the state should penetrate people's lives; and the extent to which the politics of policy-making is regarded as legitimate by political actors and citizens alike.

Because the FPP electoral system produced governments with relatively unconstrained power over the policy process, it was blamed by some for the three failings summarised above. Some opponents of electoral-system change, however, argued that these characteristics were, on the contrary, very positive aspects of FPP. This was why the status quo should be preserved. The powerful cabinet which could make clear policy decisions, act decisively in times of crisis and be held directly accountable for its decisions at the next general election were in fact systemic strengths. Political structures and institutions therefore do matter; they affect both policy processes and policy decisions.

MMP and the policy process: theoretical perspectives

Some perspectives on the policy process adopt 'society-centred approaches' and 'see policy as being determined by pressures within society'.[2] For example, a Marxist approach would view policy as a consequence of class clashes and the dominance of capitalist interests. Even modified Marxist versions would argue that Parliament, the primary focus of electoral reform, is largely irrelevant. Alternatively, a pluralist approach would view policy as the outcome of group struggles; this, in its classical form, sees the state as a mere arbitrator among competing interests. The neo-pluralist argument modifies the theory, attributing a great deal of influence to the dominance of capitalism and business interests, and according the state some autonomy.[3] Another approach to the policy process regards the policies themselves as the principal variables: issues create their own policy-making patterns. Thus Theodore Lowi distinguished between four types of issue: *regulative* issues (health and safety legislation, food standards), *distributive* issues (farm subsidies), *redistributive* issues (welfare), and *constitutive* issues (electoral laws). He argued that each type of issue generates its own pattern of conflict, taking place in distinctive arenas, and involving parties and/or interest groups.[4]

Here, however, we argue that constitutional frameworks and institutional practices do affect the ways in which policy decisions are made and the substance of the decisions which collectively comprise public policy. This approach does not deny that, for example, the requirements of modern capitalist economies are significant factors in the policy process, or that policies differ from one another according to the nature of the issues involved and the political arenas in which they are discussed and resolved – or, indeed, ignored and bypassed. Rather, as foreshadowed in our opening chapter, we argue that, in the context of the wider economic and social environment and political culture, the shape of our political institutions does affect New Zealand's public policy. Thus, the shift to MMP will have an impact on the policy process, although the effects ought not to be exaggerated.

FPP and the policy process

It is now widely recognised among political scientists that, as well as influencing the nature of the party system (see Chapter 4), there is a strong relationship between different types of electoral system and the nature and powers of government (although not, as we shall see, between types of electoral system and economic success and failure). Based on their comparative analyses, Bert Rockman and R. Kent Weaver have argued that electoral rules are related to certain types of regime. These types, in turn, are linked with the government's ability or inability to control the policy process. In particular, some systems are more able to produce innovative policies.[5] Single-member electorates and plurality systems (FPP), when combined with parliamentary government where cabinet is chosen from the legislature, facilitate majority party control of the legislature. The parties are cohesive and the political system often offers few veto points (such as a powerful second chamber) to obstruct policy. In such an environment, interest groups generally have limited access to government. Controversial policy initiatives can be imposed, but they can also be reversed by a new governing party. The doctrine of parliamentary sovereignty in New Zealand has helped preserve the prerogative of elected governments to make policy, for under this doctrine no Parliament can bind its successors.

Under FPP, therefore, policy innovation is feasible and elected governments can generally expect to govern for their whole parliamentary term. This produces policy and regime stability during their period of office. However, it needs to be remembered that the adversarial party politics which New Zealand's two-party system has produced can also foster instability in the policy process. This happens when parties lose power to their opponents. In 1990, for example, the Labour government passed the Pay Equity Act, then lost the general election the same year, and the new National government promptly repealed that legislation. Similarly, Labour's Runanga Iwi Act was repealed by the incoming National government.

The type of system New Zealand has had for so long has been labelled a 'responsible majority'[6] or 'majoritarian'[7] system. It is *responsible* because cabinet is drawn from the legislature and responsible to it for continuing to govern; it is called *majoritarian* because the governing party can generally guarantee the successful passage of legislation, through having a cohesive and enduring majority of votes in Parliament. Responsible party systems are notable for the strong links parties often have with particular interests (e.g. Labour with the unions and Maori, National with farming and commercial interests). In the past, parties operating in FPP systems have tended to offer policy packages to voters at election times, thus simplifying the choices citizens have to make when voting. The governing party is held responsible for its actions at election time, and can either be returned to power or rejected.

In the debate over MMP, therefore, criticisms of New Zealand's political system and policy process struck at the heart of its constitutional identity. For the reasons outlined above, New Zealand's electoral system always had the potential to produce majoritarian, radical, adversarial government. As explained previously, it was the actions of particular governments (especially since the early 1980s), intent on maximising the innovative characteristics of the political system they inherited, that placed the electoral system in disrepute and stimulated criticisms of the pace, radicalism, and quality of policy change. Governments that consulted widely among their own backbenchers, supporters and interest groups, even if they indulged in the politics of adversarialism, were regarded as democratically acceptable.[8] The extremes of responsible majoritarianism were in this way modified by political practice; the systemic tendencies were softened by a particular political culture. The fact that Parliament was not representative of the range of political parties and groups in New Zealand society was deemed less important simply because those interests were often brought into the policy process and their ideas incorporated into official policy agendas. Certainly this occurred with some of the environmental ideas advanced by the Values and Green parties.

MMP and the policy process

Proportional electoral systems such as MMP have also been associated with particular types of party, government and policy systems. Because PR produces multi-party rather than predominantly two-party parliaments, single parties seldom have a majority and hence cannot govern without help from supporting parties. Veto points are thus introduced into the policy process and can block policy initiatives. The existence of antagonistic parliamentary parties makes it necessary for governments to negotiate policies through the legislative process, either with coalition partners or non-government parties. This, of course, is precisely what happened in New Zealand with the minority governments since mid-1995. And when non-governing parties have real influence on legislation, especially through powerful select committees, interest groups tend to seek out parties to gain their support for or against policy measures.

When legislatures gain greater power over the passage of statutes – and cabinet power is thus constrained – the configuration of interest group/parliament relationships is thereby altered. This type of political system has been labelled variously as 'negotiated', 'consensual' and 'representational'.[9] Together these terms highlight two significant interlinked characteristics of PR systems: the wide range of parties and interests represented in the policy process; and the greater need to negotiate public policies rather than merely imposing them. We shall discuss each of these in relation to New Zealand's policy system, and then examine the likelihood of policy stability and change. First, however, in order to clarify how far electoral-system change can have an impact on public policy, we outline a model of the policy process and summarise the policy mechanisms available to governments.

The policy cycle and mechanisms

A summary of the policy cycle is set out in Table 9.1. This is an over-simplification of the political world, especially where it implies that policy formulation and implementation occur logically, in a similar way for all policies and proceeding in an orderly fashion over time. In fact, of course, among other difficulties, problem identification often occurs in the middle of the cycle, when difficulties become obvious, as well as at the beginning; democratic evalu-

Table 9.1. *The policy cycle under FPP and MMP*

Policy stage	FPP: key actors	MMP: key actors
Problem identification	All political parties Interest groups Mass media Public sector agencies	No change
Public agenda setting	All political parties Interest groups Mass media	No change
Government agenda setting	Governing political party (mainly cabinet but also government caucus) Favoured interest groups Public sector agencies, especially Treasury	Mainly cabinet but also caucus/caucuses of governing political party/parties Non-governing parliamentary parties Interest groups (working through the parties) Public sector agencies, especially Treasury
Policy decisions	Cabinet Public sector agencies	No change
Policy implementation	Cabinet Public sector agencies Affected interest groups	No change
Policy evaluation	Informal evaluation (e.g. citizens making democratic judgements): - all political parties - interest groups - mass media Formal policy evaluation: - public sector agencies	No change

ation of policies (and political processes) may take place at any point.[10] Nevertheless, Table 9.1 does serve to show how the impact of the new electoral system will be felt mainly at the stage where issues move from the public agenda to being taken up by official decision-makers and placed on the agenda of the government. In the past, under FPP, the government agenda and policy adoption stages were almost entirely in the hands of the cabinet working with departmental advisers. In the future, the range of parties and interests able to move issues onto the central political arena, and also to veto policy moves, will be wider. Much, however, will depend on the composition of particular governments (coalition majority, coalition minority, single-party minority), and the attitudes and goals of the parliamentary parties which support and oppose the government.

The actual policy mechanisms available to governments of the future will not differ from those available at present, although the way in which several are used will alter. New Zealand governments can enact their policies broadly in two different ways: through legislation, and through administrative (executive) action.

Enactment of legislation

Much of New Zealand's public policy is made through statutes.[11] The Cabinet Manual, together with Parliament's Standing Orders, sets out the processes by which legislation is proposed and drafted (see Chapters 5 and 7). Ministers must consult all affected departments, any measure that involves expenditure must have a Treasury report attached, and any proposal that affects Maori, women or youth must also take note of comments from the relevant ministries. The views of interest groups affected are sometimes solicited. The proposal goes to one of the cabinet committees for discussion and amendment, and then to full cabinet for ratification and, sometimes, further amendment. Caucus is also informed and may be involved to an extent in initial policy formulation and amendment of detail, particularly when governing parties have a slim majority. The Legislation and House Business Cabinet Committee is responsible for scrutinising drafts and ordering priorities. The legislation then goes to Parliament (see Chapter 5), and finally to the Governor-General for formal assent.

The Budget is a vital part of the policy process, since it authorises the primary decisions about supply and resource distribution. It is subject to a similar process, although the process of inter-agency advice and consultation is usually more complex than with other sorts of policy change.[12]

Already, in the transition to MMP, there have been incremental adjustments to the legislative process. Some of these have been formalised under the new Standing Orders, which provide for new legislative and financial reporting cycles (see Chapter 5). Others have arisen out of political events. After National lost its formal majority in the House in September 1994, it incorporated into the normal policy process consultation on certain measures with other parties, mainly RoC (later the Conservatives), United and the Christian Democrats. After the coalition with United was formed in early 1996, the two partners agreed to consult each other on policy and the legislative process (see Appendix 4). The 1995–96 budgetary process involved considerable inter-party discussion of such issues as the proposed (and promised) tax cuts. After the 1996 general election, the consultative process is likely to become even more complex because the minor parties which manage to gain parliamentary representation will have larger contingents than during the 1993–96 Parliament. The processes of consultation and negotiation (see below) will be particularly complicated if there are minority coalition governments. The actual process of formulating legislation, however, will continue to go through the established stages. This brings us to the other major mechanism for policy formulation and implementation: executive policy decision-making.

Executive decision-making

Policy may be changed by ministers acting under delegated legislation. Under specific statutes – the Health and Education Acts, for example – ministers may act unilaterally and with little or no discussion with colleagues. Ministers also have a great deal of flexibility in that they can alter decision-making processes to suit their own goals. For example, they can use consultants to write reports and advise on change; this device has been commonly employed, especially (but not only) during the 1990–91 changes in health, accident compensation and housing policy. Other recommendations can be implemented under the umbrella of existing legislation. Much structural change, designed to affect policy outputs and outcomes, can be achieved in this way. Interdepartmental committees can be established both to develop policy and to oversee its implementation. Sectoral working parties can be set up with similar purposes. Ministers can decide to agree on outputs from agencies that do not require legislation. All these mechanisms will remain available to future governments, although wise ministers in coalition governments will consult their coalition partners in order to secure cabinet consensus for even mildly controversial actions.

Governments which do not have a majority in Parliament, and which therefore face having their legislation vetoed, may prefer (where possible) to use non-legislative mechanisms (i.e. regulations) to implement their policies. Executive decision-making may be constrained by the new Parliament, however, armed with its traditional powers, the new Standing Orders, and a reconfigured party balance. Government departments and ministries can change regulations and thus implement policies made at the ministerial and departmental levels. But in some circumstances proposed policy changes can be opposed. In January 1996 it was reported that the Ministry of Education had changed its staffing regulations, abolishing about 800 specialist manual teacher jobs. The adviser to the Post Primary Teachers' Association, Sir Geoffrey Palmer, was reported as saying that 'regulations were being used not to just limit Crown liability, but also to alter the structure of the teaching system and livelihoods of many teachers'.[13] The unions requested the Regulations Review Committee to disallow the changes. In return, ministry officials denied the union's claims and, in order to limit expenditure, threatened to make the controversial bulk-funding of schools compulsory. The Regulations Review Committee could have overturned government policy made in this way because it did not have a majority of National MPs at the time.[14] This provides an excellent example of the potential scope provided by a multi-party Parliament, with a minority government, to exercise select committee powers to restrain the actions of the executive, responding in this case to an issue brought onto the agenda by an interest group.

Parties and the political agenda

Although the 1993–96 Parliament to some extent demonstrated future patterns under MMP, in other ways this experience provides a misleading model (e.g. in terms of the number of parties and their relative balance). Nevertheless, it is clear that, when there is a government with a precarious or no majority and a range of other parliamentary political parties, the policy agenda alters.

Overall, the initiative during the transition to MMP remained with National. Under Standing Orders (until 1996) the government has had the sole power to initiate expenditure. As noted in Chapter 5, the new Standing Orders open up unprecedented opportunities for law-makers to introduce legislative proposals with financial implications.

So long as it remains in office, the government remains the sole constitutional source of advice to the Governor-General. The formation of the United party in 1995, generally sympathetic towards National's policies, helped the government first as a supporting party and then as a coalition partner. Nevertheless, the non-governing parliamentary parties did have an impact on public policy. It is doubtful, for instance, whether the National government would have taken quite such strong measures against the French nuclear tests in the Pacific during 1995 (especially sending a naval vessel to the test area) had not the other parties helped to keep the issue in the public eye, and lobbied the government to act.[15] In an altogether different policy area, the revisions made to the Electoral Act in 1995 restricted party expenditure on the promotion and advertising of the national party lists, contrary to National's own preference.

By being represented in Parliament, parties gain opportunities to influence the public agenda, if not always the government's agenda. Parties are better resourced (with press officers, research assistants, etc) and have a greater prospect of attracting attention to their views. They are also provided with a public, legitimate debating forum in which to promulgate those ideas. Thus, a more representative Parliament will certainly affect the character of the policy agenda and the nature of government decisions.

Groups, interests and the political agenda

Political structure affects the relationship between interest groups and the policy process. In all democratic systems, whatever the nature of the electoral rules or the characteristics of the state bureaucracy, there are 'insider' groups with well-established links between elected and public sector officials. These groups tend to be either employees of the state (teachers, police officers) or economically significant sector groups (employers, farmers). There are also 'outsider' groups beyond the normal policy circles, either through choice (civil liberties groups), through ideological belief (Marxist groups), or because they espouse uncomfortable causes (such as Maori sovereignty).[16] The basis of this analytical distinction is their legitimacy in the eyes of political decision-makers. The strategy of interest groups themselves is an important, separate component which contributes to the group's influence and is more under their control.[17] We return to this point shortly.

Some groups have relatively easy access to political decision-makers. Access is particularly straightforward when the groups and the decision-makers are in ideological sympathy with one another, as between 1984 and 1990 with certain Labour politicians and public servants, and with the Business Roundtable between 1986 and 1990. Another example was the close involvement between the anti-smoking lobby, the Department of Health and the Minister of Health during the formulation of the smoke-free legislation in 1990.[18] Similarly, the Employers' Federation was closely involved in the formulation of the Employment Contracts Act in 1990–91. Traditional ideological closeness does not guarantee permanent insider status, however, as the trade unions found when faced with the imposition of the State Sector Act 1988.[19]

The relationships between governments and the interest groups have been called by policy analysts 'policy networks' (or sometimes 'policy communities').[20] Analysis of policy based on examination of group–institution relationships, or 'networks', facilitates comparative analysis between states, between sub-central government units (e.g. the states of the US or Australia) and within states over time, making this approach especially useful for monitoring changes in New Zealand. Some of the aspects that interest researchers are: the extent of professional networks; how far policy networks are closed or open to new and different groups and bodies; whether they are independent of other networks; whether they have continuity of membership; and the pattern of resource distribution.

Some evidence that structural change affects policy networks has already come from New Zealand's experience between 1984 and 1990, when the restructuring of the state left many interest groups without their former state agency contacts (formal and informal). Groups rather suddenly lost important access points to the political system, and were forced to rebuild their contacts and rethink their strategies if they were to continue to represent their members and have any influence over policy directions. The new parliamentary politics will similarly affect established policy networks; political decision-makers and interest-group leaders will have to adapt to a changed policy and institutional environment. One likely impact is an expansion of policy networks, at least in some sectors, as pressure groups become more active within the parliamentary arena. It is not surprising, in this context, that 72 percent of participants in our survey (see Chapter 3) thought that interest groups would have a 'greater role in the policy-making process' under MMP.

Although some groups are more regularly involved in the policy process than others, whatever the composition and power configuration of the legislature and executive, New Zealand's majoritarian political system has enhanced the discretion of decision-makers as to whom they wish to involve in consultation and negotiation. This is a matter of incentives and disincentives – the constitutional factors that make it necessary or unnecessary to involve interest groups. Cabinet's unequivocal power has meant that it has not had to consult, let alone negotiate, except where the government wants to legitimate its action, to gain information, and/or to simplify the policy implementation process. This is why 'outsider groups' feel it necessary to use 'noisy' means to get their issues and concerns onto the government agenda.[21] Examples include the Maori land march in 1975, the Waitangi Day protests in 1995, and the Unemployed Workers' Association protests at the World Bank conference in 1995.

States which have parliaments with more effective power than the New Zealand House of Representatives have exhibited different patterns of interaction. When Parliament can exert influence over policy outcomes, it is worthwhile for groups to focus their attention on the parliamentary parties rather than concentrating only on ministers and public servants. There is evidence that New Zealand interest groups have been planning their strategies for the new policy environment. Interviews in 1995 with representatives of six interest groups found that they were already striving to improve their links with political parties. This will entail ensuring that their resources can cope with the additional demands of lobbying a wider range of political actors.[22] Sir Geoffrey Palmer has suggested that pressure groups:

> are going to be more influential in the policy making process but how influential will not depend so much on their political clout, as on their policy making sophistication – their ability to craft policy changes that are acceptable to a Parliament which is broadly representative of the public and not peddle their own particular interests ahead of those. If they can subordinate their private interests for a wider set of interests, pressure groups are likely to be much more effective in the policy making process than they are now.[23]

Thus, in Palmer's opinion, structure will affect the policy process, but perceived legitimacy and strategy will continue to be significant factors in determining how far interest groups influence public policy.

Negotiating decisions: towards consensus?

We have used the terms 'consultation' and 'negotiation' as essentially interchangeable in the discussion so far. However, they require more precise usage if they are to clarify future relationships between governments, political parties and interest groups. Indeed, the Cabinet Office now distinguishes between three levels of consultation. The first is 'a policy briefing, consisting of a simple explanation of a policy position'. The second, called 'consultation', is 'a briefing on the issue and an opportunity for others to put forward their thoughts and ideas'. The third level is a 'negotiated accord or agreement, consisting of formal processes established to reach a multi-party agreed position on a particular issue'.[24]

Here, 'consultation' is used to describe situations where political actors communicate with one another about their policy views, but have no incentive actually to heed the other players' ideas. In this situation the main goal of consultation is usually to legitimate policy decisions that are in principle already made, by being seen to follow the correct formal processes or widely understood established practices. The decision-makers need not respond to the views of those they consult because the power resources are unequal; the consulted – whether they are interest groups, ethnic minority groups, or opposition political parties – have no means either to veto decisions or to refuse to implement them. For example, the National government in 1994 and 1995 consulted with few Maori before announcing details of the subsequently much-criticised 'Fiscal Envelope'. With no way of blocking change, the only options for Maori unhappy with both the content of the Fiscal Envelope and the absence of consultation were discussions and protest.[25]

Negotiation occurs when those in political authority not only consult but also heed the voices of the consulted. This typically occurs when the political actors involved all have some important political resources, which may include the following:

- information which official decision-makers need (say, knowledge about the spread of infectious diseases held by public health experts);
- strategic positions in the economy, making their views and reactions essential for feasible and effective policy implementation (e.g. financial institutions' influence on interest rates);
- constitutionally sanctioned power, as when the members of a select committee decide to alter legislation and have enough votes in the committee and in Parliament to do so.

Systems which provide incentives for negotiation have been regarded as appropriate for societies with profound cleavages based on such characteristics as ethnicity or language.[26] It has been argued that minority rights and values are more easily incorporated into consensual representative systems than into majoritarian ones, because of their formal incorporation into the former through parliamentary representation. For example, under MMP, Maori might in due course have their own political party represented in Parliament, and there may be more Maori in Parliament as a result of their placement on the party lists (see Chapters 3 and 5). While MMP will not make Maori an equal partner with the government in policy discussions, it will enable Maori concerns and issues to play a larger part in the legislative policy agenda. In the long run, an MMP Parliament increases the likelihood of Maori gaining an improved negotiating position on issues of Maori concern – a result both anticipated and preferred by the royal commission.

Although *consultation* can be seen as a characteristic of government under FPP, and *negotiation* as more typical of MMP, such a straightforward equation is too simplistic. Governments in the past have had to negotiate in order to appease powerful interests and implement policies. MMP governments in the future will often consult rather than negotiate, simply because they are pursuing particular lines of policy, or because urgency prohibits extensive negotiation.

Moreover, the characteristics of the power relationships between official decision-makers and interested political parties and groups are not the only factors in whether official decision-makers consult or negotiate. Hitherto, in this section, we have assumed that the retention of political power is the key motivation of political decision-makers. Hence, it has been supposed that they will consult and/or negotiate only as far as they absolutely have to in order to achieve their policy goals – which might themselves be modified in order to retain office. This has certainly happened in New Zealand. The Holyoake government, and even the Muldoon government, negotiated with key sectoral groups such as farmers and unionists in order to keep the economy functioning, employment high and to avoid overt conflict. Until the early 1980s these governments had no problems with their parliamentary majorities. Note, too, how the National government in 1994 and 1995 merely consulted the medical profession about the ongoing problems of the restructured health service, particularly in mental health; the major reforms were in place and there was no real need to negotiate. On the other hand, National during 1995 and 1996 negotiated the major points of the 1996 Budget with the supporting minor parliamentary parties, especially United, during the planning period. Of course, after the National/United coalition was formed – with United's Peter Dunne as Minister of Revenue in a finance portfolio – the Budget was more likely to have a safe passage through Parliament.

But the retention of political power is not the only goal of politicians. On the contrary, there is considerable empirical evidence that political decision-makers also have ideological views that are identified with their parties, and these views are expressed in specific policy proposals that are essentially non-negotiable. Giving up these policies, or modifying them in some way, can result in governments losing the support of their own backbenchers, support that is crucial in minority government situations. It was therefore highly unlikely that the National government, in power from 1990 but in a minority position from May 1995 until February 1996, and again from April 1996, would have substantially altered the Employment Contracts Act. Indeed, if faced with a Parliament that repealed key parts of that legislation, National may have felt obliged to call an early general election, not because constitutionally such a defeat would automatically represent a vote of no confidence in the government, but because some aspects of that legislation are integral to National party policy. As a non-negotiable issue in the view of key National decision-makers, defeat would discredit the party in the minds of its supporters, and political commentators.

Conversely, many issues in politics are seen by those in government as negotiable. Often issues such as the details (but not the principles) of taxation legislation are the subject of negotiation as well as consultation, in the interests of enacting more feasible policy. This also happened with the Resource Management Act 1991, which went through a long and complex formulation process, formally beginning in 1988, and straddling two administrations.[27]

Thus, characteristics of political structures and the nature of the parliamentary party system are not the only important aspects determining the extent to which governments consult and/or negotiate. But they are significant for the policy process and outcomes, because of the ways in which they organise and allocate power, and influence and distribute incentives and disincentives to behave in particular ways. MMP, and the resulting multiparty Parliament, will affect the patterns of policy negotiation. Tables 9.2 and 9.3 summarise the situation.

The 'consensual politics' which theorists have associated with proportional representation systems implies that decision-makers must negotiate with other players in order to implement policy. Thus 'consensual' here refers to the processes of policy-making, to situations where groups and parties bargain with one another and where differences are worked out through discussion and compromise. But 'consensual politics' has also been applied to other situations. One is where there is substantial agreement over a country's constitutional framework, including the procedures for voting and choosing a government.[28] We return to this aspect at the end of the chapter. Another use of the term is based on the fact that, in countries such as New Zealand, most people are loyal to various cross-cutting groups – ethnic, occupational, religious, political. Elites should therefore promote policies that have a general appeal, not an appeal to special interests only.[29]

A recent example of policy-making in New Zealand encapsulates several of these different interpretations of consensual politics (policy process and policy agreement). The Prime Ministerial Taskforce on Employment was set up in 1994 to examine education and training as well as the interrelationship between social benefits and wages, and employment opportunities. The taskforce, which reported in November 1994, was a multi-party working group, involving National, the Alliance and Labour (New Zealand First declined involvement, and no other parties were represented in Parliament when it was established). It received a wide variety of submissions from interest groups.

Consensualism, it has been suggested, can adversely affect our polity. It can eventuate in 'non-decisions', either deliberately or because the parties involved cannot reach agreement. As a result, policy paralysis can occur. Alternatively, 'log-rolling' can be a characteristic of a system where consultation and negotiation are institutionalised, producing deals that give some payoffs to all the players involved but really please nobody, and might actually produce perverse effects (e.g. increases in public expenditure that the country cannot afford). Furthermore, where political will is hard to exert, it may be difficult to achieve policy innovation or impose 'losses' (especially of a financial nature) on powerful sector groups.[30] A common question asked by critics of consensual politics is: how could governments which lack a clear

Table 9.2. *Incentives and cabinet consultation and negotiation: governments under FPP*

Focus	Positive incentives	Negative incentives
Caucus of governing party	To retain MPs' loyalty when there is a narrow government majority. To comply with party norms to consult with colleagues.	When the government majority is safe, cabinets have little incentive to consult because they can rely on the personal ambitions of MPs for promotion, and their party loyalty. Even when the parliamentary majority is narrow, cabinet can dominate caucus through sheer weight of numbers. Generally easier to make decisions first and consult after, relying on backbenchers' loyalty for parliamentary support.
Opposition parties	To avoid damaging internal party splits over some moral issues, 'conscience votes' are sometimes permitted, involving cross-party discussions and even negotiations (e.g. abortion, capital punishment). To achieve policy change that can be implemented effectively, at select committee stage of legislation there is some incentive to discuss and negotiate over details of legislation, usually as a result of expert submissions (e.g. taxation and environmental legislation).	Because the government has an automatic majority in Parliament, there is no need to consult the MPs and leaders of other parties to get legislation passed; governments do not have to compromise on their policy principles, and seldom on the details (e.g. State Sector Act 1988, Employment Contracts Act 1991).
Interest groups	To achieve feasible, effective policy change, governments have consulted with sector groups at (a) pre-parliamentary planning stage and (b) select committee stage (depending on party policy and attitudes of particular governments towards groups affected and interested). Internal cabinet disagreements can provide incentives for ministers to consult sectoral groups in order to bolster particular ministerial views.	Consultation with groups can delay policy change when government might prefer to act quickly. Advice from pressure groups can be conflicting. Advice from pressure groups can be self-interested.

Table 9.3. *Incentives and cabinet consultation and negotiation: governments under MMP*

Focus	Positive incentives	Negative incentives
Caucus (or caucuses) of governing party (or parties)	Under single-party minority governments and minority coalitions, parties must retain their MPs' loyalty because every vote is important. To comply with party norms to consult with colleagues.	Under single-party minority governments and minority coalitions, there are no disincentives to consultation and negotiation (even when a minority government is small enough for the cabinet to dominate caucus through weight of numbers, the risk of alienating MPs through non-consultation and hence threatening the government itself far outweighs the costs, in delays and policy modification, of consultation).
	Under majority coalitions, leaders of coalition parties need to negotiate with their caucuses to secure and continue stable policy agreements with coalition partners.	Under majority coalitions, priorities of maintaining the coalition and fulfilling coalition agreements may override the normal incentive to consult with caucuses.
Supporting and opposition parties	Minority single-party governments and minority coalitions need to negotiate with representatives of other parliamentary parties to ensure legislation and budgetary measures are passed. Supporting parties more significant than opposition parties. (Coalition parties have to negotiate with one another, although joint meetings of the caucuses of coalition parties are unusual.)	Under single-party minority governments and minority coalitions, there will be some limitations to inter-party consultation and negotiation because of some non-negotiable issues, where compromise might threaten unity of individual parties.
	Under majority coalitions there are no incentives to consult and negotiate beyond those existing under FPP (see Table 9.2).	No incentives to negotiate under majority coalitions because they have a secure parliamentary majority.
Interest groups	Minority single-party governments and minority coalitions need to negotiate with sector groups at (a) pre-parliamentary planning stage, and (b) select committee stage in order to acquire legitimacy for government initiatives, and hence the	Minority single-party governments and minority coalitions may have non-negotiable issues that will limit consultation with some groups, as negotiation with those groups could threaten internal party support and support of allied parties.

Focus	Positive incentives	Negative incentives
Interest groups *(continued)*	government itself (always faced with a potentially hostile Parliament). Consultation will be partly the consequence of non-government party links with particular groups.	
	Majority coalitions will be in a similar position to majority single-party governments (see Table 9.2). But note that parties in a coalition will bring with them associated groups with whom consultation might be required.	Majority coalitions will be in a similar position to majority single-party governments (see Table 9.2), although complicated by groups associated with each coalition partner. Note that all government consultation with groups may be limited by governments' perception of conflicting and self-interested advice.

majority of parliamentary seats deal with the sort of economic crisis Labour inherited when it took office after the 1984 election?

Consensual decision-making can undoubtedly be slow. But the politics of negotiation and consensus are inclusive of groups and interests. Moreover, 'Majoritarian governments may be able to make decisions faster than consensus governments, but fast decisions are not necessarily wise decisions'.[31]

Policy stability and change

Voters, interest-group leaders, politicians, and media commentators all tend to focus on political change. They either favour particular policy reforms which they see to be in their own or New Zealand's interests, or comment on political change in the pursuit of newsworthy items or political point-scoring. Yet most public policy – that is, the pattern of decisions in particular policy sectors (health, education, industry, welfare, and so forth) – is inherited from past decisions. These historically developed policies often have involved public servants and interest groups with strong attachments to them. This was the case with agriculture in New Zealand before subsidies were removed under the fourth Labour government. That was why politicians like Roger Douglas advocated rapid, radical policy change, allowing little time for opponents to rally themselves to obstruct it.[32]

There is a second important factor in the politics of policy change. Established policies can be difficult to alter because they develop their own momentum. One example is the Resource Management Act 1991, fruit of a

1984 Labour government manifesto promise to reform New Zealand's environmental statutes. Yet the 1990 National government took the bill on and saw it through its last legislative stages. This occurred for at least four reasons: (i) the process of institutional reforms in conservation, environment and local government restructuring had already gone so far that there could be no major backward steps; (ii) the principles of the Act were not controversial in partisan terms; (iii) by 1990–91 there was an elite consensus on the measure; and (iv) it 'was written in such a way as to leave many issues undecided', thereby helping its acceptance.[33] Thus decisions of the past influence those of the present. Government under MMP is not going to alter this.

Third, the structure of the New Zealand public service has some conservatism built into it. The advocates of restructuring public agencies (especially the Treasury) believed that administratively separating out the policy, regulatory and delivery functions would help protect public agencies from policy capture, particularly by interest groups but also by bureaucrats seeking to expand their administrative budgets and empires. Several unintended consequences have followed. Policy co-ordination has been problematic because the multiplicity of relatively autonomous agencies has made policy formulation and implementation more complex. Consequently, policy innovation is also more complex, as the authors of the 1991 Budget changes found.[34]

The fractionated public service has created numerous points of institutional policy development and protection; each agency has its policies to propose and protect. Thus there could be an in-built structural feature to the New Zealand state that inhibits policy change. A further consequence, perhaps not unintended, has been that the Treasury, well resourced with policy experts and strategically placed in its role and function, stands out as the single most important agency player. The Treasury, of course, is doctrinally wedded to protecting both the state architecture it helped design and build and the economic policies of the past decade.

Fourth, the new electoral system places a considerable obstacle in the path of a political party with radical policies. It will be difficult for any new parties to enter Parliament, given the five percent threshold (or minimum of one electorate seat) requirement (see Chapters 2 and 4).

Conclusion: electoral change and the future policy agenda

It is likely that incremental rather than radical change will characterise the future policy agenda. This would seem to advantage the centre–right rather than the centre–left of the political spectrum, for 'non-decisions' have historically favoured conservatives and the structural characteristics of political power can easily favour and freeze existing social and economic arrangements. This will certainly be the case in New Zealand if the centre–left remains as fractured as it has been in recent years. By the same token, the increasingly fractured right might inhibit further radical reductions in the role of the New Zealand state in welfare issues.

Nevertheless, the modern world, and New Zealand itself, is sufficiently turbulent for new socio-economic crises to eventuate and new policy ideas to develop. A multi-party Parliament, plus active and involved interest groups and new social movements, might well be able to place new policies on the official policy agenda. These are aspects of policy change which, while challenging the dominant elite policy consensus (see Chapter 3), do not challenge the operating values of New Zealand's democratic system. Thus, parliamentary parties might unite to restore elected area health boards, reduce tertiary fees, and lower rents in state houses. They might even repeal significant sections of the Employment Contracts Act and alter the Reserve Bank Act so that goals such as employment and investment might take an equal place with price stability – although, interestingly, major changes in these two Acts are not anticipated by participants in our survey (see Chapter 3).

Against this, there is little prospect of 'anti-system' parties becoming sufficiently strong to change the nature of New Zealand's political system by, say, passing laws against the freedom of speech or the right to vote. The five percent threshold should preclude this. Overseas research has found that, when tiny, anti-system parties are excluded by electoral thresholds, then the polity itself is more likely to be stable.[35] The factors contributing to policy continuity or discontinuity are summarised in Table 9.4.

The question of stability has also been related to New Zealand's future economic performance. There are several aspects to this issue. The first relates to the sorts of question discussed above. The market economy depends upon a settled political environment, since investment decisions are best made when the polity's rules concerning the operations of the macro- and micro-economy are well understood and are expected to operate steadily in the future. (This, of course, is the key attraction of both the Reserve Bank Act and the Fiscal Responsibility Act.)

Second, there is the question of the long-term impact of MMP on New Zealand's economic growth and prosperity. What does the public policy literature tell us about the relationships between different kinds of electoral systems and economic outcomes? The answers here are inconclusive. Certainly, PR systems appear to perform no worse on commonly used measures – such as economic growth, public debt, inflation, and unemployment – than do FPP systems.[36] Research using OECD data and comparing four FPP parliamentary democracies with nine PR democracies found 'a uniformly better record for the PR than for the plurality [FPP] countries'. But none of the differences was statistically significant.[37]

Table 9.4. *Policy continuity and discontinuity*

Factors contributing to policy continuity	**Factors contributing to policy discontinuity**
Exogenous factors* Influence of financial markets, including their impact on interest rates, inhibits governments from increasing state expenditure because they fear adverse impact on (a) NZ international credit ratings, and (b) capital investment. Internationalisation of world economy, including agreements such as GATT and CER, constrain government options in agricultural and industrial policies, fostering market-type mechanisms. Key producer and financial sector groups lobby for low public debt, low fiscal deficit, low social expenditure, low tax rates, and privatisation of various government services. Citizen electoral conservatism might inhibit growth of new, radical political parties which might challenge economic policy consensus.	**Exogenous factors** World crises (e.g. war, depression, environmental catastrophe) might compel radical policy change. New social movements might develop in New Zealand that radically challenge dominant policy consensus (radical left-wing or right-wing movements, radical Maori nationalism, environmental protest, etc). Increased immigration might have impact on accepted social policies.
Endogenous factors High degree of inter-party agreement on need for open, competitive economy and necessity of operating successfully and conventionally within world capitalism. High level of inter-party agreement on repayment of public debt as key government goal. Moderately high degree of satisfaction among party elites with architecture of the new state set in place between 1984 and 1994 (State Owned Enterprises Act 1986, State Sector Act 1988, Public Finance Act 1989, Fiscal Responsibility Act 1994). High level of bureaucratic elite socialisation in new public management ethos, thus predisposing public servants to support primary features of new state architecture. Many major policy changes 1984–94 difficult and expensive to undo (e.g. privatisation, public sector accounting systems). Policy continuity might be entrenched by Parliament dominated by right-wing and centre-right parties.	**Endogenous factors** Significant levels of discontent among groups in community (women, unemployed, Maori) who have not shared in economic recovery may influence some parties to force policy changes - especially to key aspects of new state architecture (Reserve Bank Act 1989, Employment Contracts Act 1991) and taxation and social policies. New Zealand parties may try to adapt their policies to perceived preferences of voters in attempt to create electoral market niches, thus shifting policy directions. Interest groups, parliamentarians and bureaucrats may create new policy networks in particular policy sectors (e.g. health, education, employment, housing, Treaty of Waitangi issues), which may influence policy directions.

* 'Exogenous' refers to factors outside the central policy-making institutions. 'Endogenous' refers to factors inside those institutions (i.e. Parliament, cabinet, public service and public sector agencies, 'insider' pressure groups).

Third, there is the question of whether the shift from one electoral system to another will unsettle the relationships between state and economy so much that the economy will suffer. Again, some aspects of the discussion above are relevant. At the time of writing (in April 1996) it was evident that New Zealand's political and economic elites were already adapting to the new politics of MMP. They have learned that minority governments, for example, are not necessarily unstable or powerless, and that government can continue in times of uncertainty and when a general election does not produce a clear winner. New Zealand's move to a new electoral system is certainly a challenge for the polity, but to date there have been few signs of the transition generating serious economic repercussions.

Arguably, the real threat to New Zealand's economic and political security is from any members of the economic and political elite who might seek to destabilise the new politics before they have been tested. Whether or not New Zealand's future policy processes and outcomes are the product of consensus, there ought to be agreement about supporting – at least for the next two terms of government – the fundamental rules of the game, as decided by referendum and Parliament. Consensus over the basis of our constitution is essential if the new politics are to be given the opportunity to create a successful policy environment.

Notes

1 R. Mulgan, 'The Elective Dictatorship in New Zealand', in H. Gold (ed.), *New Zealand Politics in Perspective*, 3rd edn, Longman Paul, Auckland, 1992, pp.513–32.

2 Martin J. Smith, *Pressure, Power and Policy: State Autonomy and Policy Networks in Britain and the United States*, University of Pittsburgh Press and Harvester Wheatsheaf, Pittsburgh, 1993, p.1. See particularly Chs 2 and 3, pp.15–75.

3 See, for example, P. Dunleavy and B. O'Leary, *Theories of the State: the Politics of Liberal Democracy*, Macmillan Education, London, 1987, especially pp.271–318.

4 T. Lowi, 'American Business, Public Policy, Case Studies, and Political Theory', *World Politics*, 16, 1964, pp.677–715, and 'Public Policy and Bureaucracy in the United States and France', in D. E. Ashford (ed.), *Comparing Public Policies: New Concepts and Methods*, Sage, Beverly Hills, California, 1978, pp. 177–97.

5 R. K. Weaver and B. A. Rockman (eds), *Do Institutions Matter? Government Capabilities in the United States and Abroad*, The Brookings Institution, Washington, 1993, especially pp.445–81.

6 G. Bingham Powell Jr, 'Party Systems and Political System Performance', *American Political Science Review*, 75, 1981, pp.861–79.

7 A. Lijphart, 'Democracies: Forms, Performance, and Constitutional Engineering', *European Journal of Political Research*, 25, 1994, pp.1–17.

8 R. Mulgan, 'The Democratic Failure of Single-Party Government: the New Zealand Experience', *Australian Journal of Political Science*, special issue on Party Systems, 30, 1995, pp.82–96.

9 See A. Lijphart, 'Democracies', and G. Bingham Powell Jr, 'Party Systems and Political System Performance', respectively.

10 For a good critical discussion, see T. Buhrs and R. Bartlett, *Environmental Policy in New*

Zealand: the Politics of Clean & Green, Oxford University Press, Auckland, 1993, pp.19–30.
11 See Chs 5 and 6 of E. M. McLeay, *The Cabinet and Political Power in New Zealand*, Oxford University Press, Auckland, 1995, for a discussion of the roles of cabinet and ministers.
12 For an analysis of the particularly ambitious 1991 budgetary process, see the essays in J. Nethercote et al. (eds), *Decision Making in New Zealand Government*, Federalism Research Centre, Australian National University, Canberra, 1993.
13 C. Bell, 'Bulk-funding threat over teachers' staff dispute', *Dominion*, 25 January 1996, p.3.
14 The Regulations Review Committee consisted of Bill English and Robert Anderson (National), Richard Northey and Martin Gallagher (Labour) and Peter Hilt (United). United and National formed a coalition on 28 February 1996, thus giving the committee a government majority.
15 J. Henderson, 'MMP. The Implications for New Zealand Foreign Policy', paper presented at New Zealand Political Studies Association Conference, Wellington, 30 August 1995.
16 W. Grant, 'Insider Groups, Outsider Groups and Interest Group Strategies in Britain', Working Paper No. 19, University of Warwick, Warwick, 1978.
17 W. Maloney et al., 'Interest Groups and Public Policy: the Insider/Outsider Model Revisited', *Journal of Public Policy*, 14, 1994, pp.17–38.
18 J. Deeks, 'Who's Choking Smoking? Advertising, Sponsorship and Government Regulation of the Tobacco Industry', in J. Deeks and N. Perry (eds), *Controlling Interests: Business, the State and Society in New Zealand*, Auckland University Press, Auckland, 1992.
19 P. Walsh, 'Industrial Relations and Personnel Policies under the State Sector Act', in J. Boston et al., *Reshaping the State: New Zealand's Bureaucratic Revolution*, Oxford University Press, Auckland, 1991.
20 See, for example, D. Marsh and R. Rhodes (eds), *Policy Networks in British Government*, Clarendon Press, Oxford, 1992.
21 P. Harris, 'Pressure Groups and Protest', in H. Gold (ed.), *New Zealand Politics in Perspective*, 2nd edn, Longman Paul, Auckland, 1989, pp.295–311.
22 S. Redward, 'Policy-making under MMP: an Examination of the Potential Behaviour and Role of Interest Groups in the Policy-Making Process', Master of Public Policy Research Paper, Victoria University, Wellington, 1995.
23 G. Palmer, interview with Kim Hill, National Radio, 16 January 1996 (transcript).
24 Cabinet Office, 'Consultation with Political Parties: Revised Procedures and New CAB Form', Cabinet Office Circular, CO (95) 8, 8 September 1995, Wellington. These three levels had been outlined by the Prime Minister in early 1994. See 'Consultation with Opposition Parties', Cabinet Office Circular, CO (94) 8, 21 March 1994.
25 See W. Gardiner, *Return to Sender: What Really Happened at the Fiscal Envelope Hui*, Reed, Auckland, 1996.
26 The extent to which systems of proportional representation facilitate the better management of potentially divisive social cleavages is examined in R. K. Weaver and B. A. Rockman (eds), *Do Institutions Matter?*, see esp. pp.272–344.
27 See T. Buhrs and R. Bartlett, *Environmental Policy in New Zealand*, esp. Ch. 5, pp.113–34.
28 See D. Kavanagh, *Political Science and Political Behaviour*, Allen & Unwin, London, 1983, pp.20–21.
29 Ibid.
30 For an excellent analysis of the problems of imposing losses on powerful groups under different institutional arrangements, see P. D. Pierson and R. K. Weaver, 'Imposing Losses in Pension Policy', in R. K. Weaver and B. A. Rockman (eds), *Do Institutions Matter?*, pp.110–50.

31 A. Lijphart, 'Democracies', p.12.

32 R. Douglas, 'The Politics of Successful Structural Reform', paper delivered to the Mt Pelerin Society, 31 November 1989.

33 T. Buhrs and R. Bartlett, *Environmental Policy in New Zealand*, p.124. Also, the extensive consultative process served to legitimate the bill.

34 See the articles in J. Boston and P. Dalziel (eds), *The Decent Society? Essays in Response to National's Economic and Social Policies*, Oxford University Press, Auckland, 1992; E. McLeay, *The Cabinet and Political Power in New Zealand*, pp.101–7.

35 See Powell, 'Party Systems'; and *Report of the Royal Commission on the Electoral System*, pp.57–58.

36 See R. Rose, *What Are the Economic Consequences of Proportional Representation?*, Electoral Reform Society, London, 1992; F. Castles, 'The Policy Consequences of Proportional Representation: a Sceptical Commentary', *Political Science*, 46, 2, 1994, pp.161–71; and Alan Bollard, *The Economic Consequences of Electoral Reform*, New Zealand Institute of Economic Research, Discussion Paper 38, Wellington, 1993.

37 A. Lijphart, 'Democracies', p.8.

CHAPTER 10

MMP: an enduring experiment?

The choice of MMP was in many respects a response by electors to their perception that New Zealand's political parties had failed to meet the challenges of governance. A nation whose self-image involved 'leading the world' – away from racial prejudice, class inequalities, the outdated barriers of gender – had lost its way. The late 1970s and 1980s eroded the sense that somehow history was on New Zealand's side. In 'race relations', land marches and court cases were something of a rude awakening for many non-Maori. The grief and grievances of Maori cultural and economic loss were on the agenda again: previously 'settled' issues were back on the table for discussion and resolution. As for economic affairs, despite a Prime Minister with a reputation for economic wizardry, the decades of full employment came to an end. In short order New Zealanders learned that there were no longer any 'guarantees' – not of employment, nor prosperity, nor even much of a 'safety net' to ensure that the gap between the affluent and the 'less fortunate' was of modest proportions. Without such relative equality, where was the notion of the essential dignity of the human person? And without a commitment to equality, realised in practice as well as in rhetoric, what was New Zealand? What was the country to be? What had it become?

Attitudes towards New Zealand's parties and support for MMP

There have been many challenges to the legitimacy of the established order since the onset of British settlement in the nineteenth century.[1] The loss of confidence in New Zealand's two alternating parties of government, National and Labour, is the most recent, and is largely responsible for the momentum which brought the once-obscure topic of 'electoral reform' to the top of the national agenda. As suggested above, the failure of National and Labour to protect the commitment to economic and social justice – to cherish, in office, both freedom *and* equality – was in conflict with features of New Zealand's national identity and, as a result, deprived each of them of some of the legitimacy, of the 'right to govern' which they had held for much of this century. There is ample survey evidence to show that New Zealanders became interested in a new electoral system, and were more inclined to support change, the more thoroughly they rejected the two main parties.[2]

This background of disenchantment has, of course, far-reaching implications for voter choice under MMP. As we have noted (see Chapters 2 and 4), the two-vote system – itself a novelty for New Zealanders, used to having only one vote at their disposal – will be exercised in an environment populated by a multitude of new parties. Some of them will have candidates standing in constituencies around New Zealand. Almost all will field party lists, comprising a range of would-be parliamentarians. Many will have both electorate candidates *and* party lists on offer. A potentially bewildering array of choices faces conscientious voters.

Party identification and MMP

In the past, many New Zealand voters have simplified an already streamlined system even further by relying on a basic loyalty to party for their cue as to how to vote. Party identification began to decline, however, as public confidence in the competence of New Zealand governments began to erode.[3] For many, as a result, the absence of an ongoing link with a particular party's outlook and philosophy, its central message and purpose, meant that voting choices became less automatic, and thus more difficult. The proportion of 'floating voters' grew; New Zealand elections were more apt to be examined for their volatility than for the stability associated with persistent patterns of party identification. What politicians had to say about particular issues and problems seemed to acquire greater salience for voters.[4]

With MMP – and the opportunity to use two votes, one to reward a party, the other to select a particular constituency representative – the area of voter discretion expands considerably. Indeed, many voters are likely to vote for two different parties: one party for the party list, and another for a constituency candidate with a different party affiliation. In such circumstances, it will be much more difficult to assert without qualification (as has often been done in the past) that party identification is the primary factor behind voting choice when there are so many New Zealanders considering 'split ticket' voting.[5]

It is not only how voters regard New Zealand's parties which is in flux. The way parties regard voters is also evolving steadily. Certainly, the first MMP election will see major changes to campaign strategy. Even 'safe' seats (i.e. electorates which have traditionally supported one or other party when electing the local MP) are important for all parties: there is always that 'other' vote, the party vote, to compete for. It is also possible that, in some 'safe' seats, voters committed to one party by habit and inclination may be encouraged to keep that affiliation in the *party* vote but to use their *constituency* vote in a more independent manner. This would allow electors to maintain an allegiance to their preferred party while choosing the local person considered most qualified or most likely to do the best job for the community. In this respect, because 1996 is the first MMP election and there has been a reduction in the number of electorates from 99 to 65, there will be some especially interesting head-to-head battles between incumbent MPs. These include:

- Auckland Central – Sandra Lee (Alliance) v. Judith Tizard (Labour);
- Banks Peninsula – David Carter (National) v. Ruth Dyson (Labour);
- Invercargill – Mark Peck (Labour) v. Eric Roy (National);
- Nelson – John Blincoe (Labour) v. Nick Smith (National);
- New Plymouth – Harry Duynhoven (Labour) v. Roger Maxwell (National);
- Otaki – Judy Keall (Labour) v. Roger Sowry (National);
- Rimutaka – Peter McCardle (New Zealand First) v. Paul Swain (Labour);
- Whanganui – Peter Gresham (National) v. Jill Pettis (Labour).

Such choices will permit National party supporters in New Plymouth, for example, to vote for Labour's Harry Duynhoven while at the same time giving their party vote to National. Of course, the reverse may also happen: some voters may decide that loyalty to party really involves support for the party's local candidate. This could mean that the new, unfamiliar voting choice, for a nationwide party list, then becomes the vehicle for more independent action. If that happens in significant numbers, the party with which they most closely identify but which they desert in the party-list vote is going to do less well than might have been expected.[6]

The concept of party identification, so important in the international and New Zealand voting literature, is thus certain to be subject to further strain and confusion under MMP. This is probably long overdue. There was a time when most New Zealand parties were based on large memberships and grew out of what political scientists and sociologists refer to as 'organic' communities. The parties, in other words, actually represented groups of people with ongoing links to one another. In some communities the National party was Anglican church membership in another guise. At other times it was simply the local farmers wearing different hats and boots. The Labour party, similarly, was an expression of working-class solidarities and experiences in another form and setting. There was therefore a genuine association between the *ideas* of a party, the *people* taking part in its affairs, the *interests* being represented, and the *voters* themselves. In recent times all of these networks have deteriorated, becoming artificial and losing their effectiveness. Few New Zealand parties any longer have large memberships – yet only two decades ago this was another area in which it could have been said that New Zealand 'led the world'.

Parties and political entrepreneurs

More common in the MMP environment will be parties which serve (in effect) as the vehicle for a prominent personality.[7] This is especially true of the newer parties, of course. New Zealand First is just such a party: established by, and for, Winston Peters, it remains centred primarily on him and owes its political survival and its fortunes largely to Peters' own popularity.

The pre-election changes to the party system have almost all revolved around particular individuals in Parliament, some of them 'famous for 15 minutes', serendipitously 'prominent' only because of their decision to defect from the party under whose banner they were elected. Peter Dunne established the Future New Zealand party and subsequently walked away from it; it never grew – and so hardly withered – but, with his departure, it effectively died. Similarly, Ross Meurant set up Right-of-Centre, saw it renamed the Conservative party, grew restive, and left it, staying on in Parliament as an independent. A third MP, Graeme Lee, announced the establishment of the Christian Democrats as a means for promoting a point of view on social and moral issues not entirely in keeping with the outlook of his National caucus colleagues. This has now become part of the Christian Coalition.

Even mooted parties (those which lived and died without ever leaving the hothouse of the parliamentary press gallery) have focused on the political ambitions of particular people. Will Mike Moore set up a centrist party? Will John Banks establish another Christian or conservative party? Would Michael Laws organise a separate political vehicle for himself? All these media-driven questions centre on individual MPs – would-be political entrepreneurs – rather than on that wider network of social and economic interests which parties are traditionally assumed to reflect and represent.

Even the larger or more established parties have lost much of their ideological and communal cohesion, becoming more detached from New Zealand society while at the same time trying to sustain a uniform national appeal. The Alliance, for instance, though a working coalition of five distinct political entities, is often regarded largely as Jim Anderton's political vehicle, and not without justification. He has been able to leave, and return to, its leadership almost at will, and its fortunes in the polls seemed to ebb and flow with his presence at the helm and with popular perceptions of his leadership and ability. As for the Labour party, it has shed much of its trade union connections, though in a period when the unions themselves have lost much of their power. The National party maintains much of its strength in farming communities, but its heyday as the 'natural' party of business – both large and multi-national, as well as small and insular – would seem to have passed.[8]

The 1996 election, as the first under MMP, may attract more interest and attention from New Zealanders than has recently been the case. Will the multitude of new parties, and the greater flexibility of political choice in the two-vote system, mean that more New Zealanders will register and vote? Is there likely to be a greater turnout at political meetings?[9] Are the parties' televised advertisements going to be watched with greater interest? In a sense the success or failure of MMP – as the royal commission's criteria (set out in Chapter 2) suggest – will depend on whether in due course there develops a renewed sense of confidence in the effectiveness of New Zealand's parties, in their capacity to represent the views of New Zealanders and to develop constructive social and economic policies. MMP was designed, ultimately, to persuade New Zealanders that participation at the ballot box was a *meaningful* social act – that there was a point to voting. New Zealand's older parties, and its many new ones, are each, in their own way, committed to reversing the levels of disquiet and distrust in the political system.[10] If they succeed in doing so, their own legitimacy, as well as that of MMP, will be strengthened and consolidated.

Models of democracy

Although all systems of democratic government owe some of their effectiveness to the existence of political parties and elections, these are only part of the overall political and policy-making process. While the basic principles of democracy are clear and concise – government by consent of the governed, with majority rule limited by respect for the rights of minorities – there are various ways in which democratic principles can be carried out in practice. This should be especially clear in New Zealand: we have gone from one electoral system, FPP, to another, MMP, and each (notwithstanding its respective strengths and weaknesses) represents a procedure for measuring consent – to candidates, parties and policies – which is consistent with democratic values and is found in democratic societies.

The New Zealand system of government used to be described as perhaps the purest form of the 'Westminster model': i.e. cabinet government, with its members accountable to Parliament. (The other principal 'model' of democratic government is the presidential form, with the elected head of government neither a member of, nor accountable to, the legislature.)[11] The Westminster model in New Zealand before MMP was characterised by:

- a concentration of executive power, with only one political party represented in cabinet;

- a fusion of power between the executive and Parliament, with the cabinet dominant;
- a single-chamber Parliament;[12]
- a two-party system;
- a one-dimensional party system in which parties essentially reflect a single cleavage (i.e. the parties are ranged along a socio-economic continuum);
- a plurality (i.e. FPP) system of elections;
- unitary, centralised government (i.e. all other tiers of government, such as local and regional authorities, owe their legal existence and their powers to Acts of Parliament; there are no state or provincial governments);
- an unwritten constitution, whose meaning is subordinate to Parliament (and, in practice, the executive) under the doctrine of parliamentary sovereignty;
- a representative democracy augmented by occasional referenda.[13]

Which of these features will change under MMP? The electoral system, of course, has already changed, and has been the starting-point for further developments. The number of parties is already growing, and their character seems to be changing as well. Some are narrower than we have had in the past: the recent profusion of Christian and Maori parties, for instance, or parties deliberately 'conservative' or 'right-of-centre'. In contrast to those seeking to appeal to a more focused political market, there are others striving to attract a broader audience. While its ideological message may be far from all-encompassing, the Alliance as a concept, as a coalition of many parties (Maori, environmentalist, working-class, provincial, and liberal), is by default and definition seeking to be multi-dimensional in its outlook and even in its rules and selection practices.

It is likely that New Zealand's Westminster model of government under MMP will be a mix of change and continuity, characterised by:

- a concentration of executive power, but with the likelihood of more than one political party represented in cabinet;
- a fusion of power between the executive and Parliament, with the cabinet *generally* dominant;
- a single-chamber Parliament;
- a multi-party system;
- a multi-dimensional party system, with a mix of parties reflecting a wider variety of social, ethnic and political cleavages;
- a proportional (i.e. MMP) system of elections;
- unitary, centralised government;
- an unwritten constitution;
- a representative democracy augmented by non-binding, citizens-initiated referenda (CIR).

How closely does the new model reflect public aspirations for 'consensus' government? Arend Lijphart has suggested that there are essentially eight elements to consensus government:

- executive power-sharing, sometimes through 'grand coalitions' (i.e. of the major parties, rather than of one major party with one or more smaller partners);
- a separation of powers and responsibilities between the executive and the legislature;
- a two-chamber Parliament, with a balance of powers and responsibilities and effective provisions for minority representation;
- a multi-party system;
- a multi-dimensional party system, reflecting the social, ethnic and political cleavages of a genuinely plural (i.e. multi-cultural) society;
- a proportional system of elections;
- an effective dispersal of powers and responsibilities from the central government to quasi-autonomous and in some respects co-equal territorial authorities;
- a formal, written constitution, superior to and binding on Parliament and the executive, with effective legal and political protections for minorities.[14]

It seems clear that under MMP New Zealand will begin to embrace some of the elements of the consensus model, but not all of them. Grand coalitions (between Labour and National, for instance) are possible but unlikely. A separation of powers between the executive and Parliament along the lines of the presidential model is altogether improbable; however, greater attention may be given to suggestions that some cabinet ministers should be drawn from people who are not members of Parliament, and that others, on appointment to the executive, temporarily resign their seats in Parliament (see below).

A bicameral Parliament, however, is doubtful, despite support for the idea (at times) from Prime Minister Bolger and some interest in it as well from various Maori leaders. There is also little likelihood of effective decentralisation from Wellington (privatisation, rather than redistribution of power to other units of government, is more in keeping with present thinking), while further moves towards institutionalising restrictions on government through a supreme constitutional document seem remote.

Consensual democracy aims at restraining majority rule by requiring, or encouraging, the sharing of power between the majority and minorities; and dispersing power away from the central government, and towards other institutions, levels of government, parties and groups. On this measure it appears that, despite the rhetoric, New Zealand's experience of 'consensus' government will be somewhat limited. There may be some disappointment, therefore, with some of the fruits of MMP, and thus some interest in further refinements to the New Zealand style of government and politics.

Possible constitutional changes

Our survey of opinion leaders brought out a number of ideas for further modifying the New Zealand system of government (see Chapter 3). Some of these are: providing for a 'constructive vote of confidence' (i.e. permitting Parliament to bring down a Prime Minister only when there is an absolute majority in favour of a successor)[15]; giving the Prime Minister the sole prerogative to call elections, irrespective of whether the government has a majority; providing for a fixed term of Parliament (e.g. either three or four years); changing the role of the Governor-General; reforming the cabinet; and moving from a constitutional monarchy to a republic. It is not possible to examine all these matters here. However, brief comment on some of them is in order.

Changing the role of the Governor-General

As discussed in Chapter 6, there is a greater likelihood under MMP that Governors-General may be called upon to use their 'reserve powers' (i.e. in relation to the appointment of Prime Ministers and the dissolution of Parliament). This has prompted several concerns. The first, and most fundamental, relates to the desirability of such powers being retained by the Governor-General in the new MMP environment. Some argue that the present arrangements – which enable, in certain circumstances, a Governor-General to act in the absence of, or even contrary to, the advice of an incumbent Prime Minister – give the Governor-General too much power. Also, were this power to be exercised unwisely (as it was, according to some, in Australia in 1975), it might undermine public respect for the office of the Governor-General, if not raise questions about the legitimacy of the prevailing constitutional order. To avoid such outcomes, it has been suggested that the current discretionary powers available to the Governor-General should be removed. Of course, if this were done, other procedures would need to be established to deal with situations of potential constitutional uncertainty. For example, another person – perhaps the Speaker, as in Sweden – could be given the task of resolving the question of who should be appointed Prime Minister. Similarly, uncertainties over the Governor-General's role regarding the dissolution of Parliaments could be resolved either by the introduction of a fixed parliamentary term or by giving Prime Ministers the right to call elections at any stage in the parliamentary cycle, irrespective of whether the government had a majority of the seats in Parliament.

If the current constitutional arrangements are retained, it has been suggested that there should be some formalisation of the processes through which a Governor-General secures expert advice on constitutional issues. As it stands, the Governor-General is advised by the Prime Minister. But, of course, were issues of a constitutionally sensitive nature to arise, the Governor-General would also be likely to discuss such issues with constitutional experts. Under current arrangements, there is no formal panel of experts and Governors-General are entirely free to decide with whom they consult. This provides insufficient accountability for the advice which might be tendered (and which, in certain circumstances, could influence a Governor-General's actions). One possible remedy might be for the government to appoint a panel of experts from whom Governors-General could seek advice on constitutional matters. Such a panel could include senior academic lawyers, the President of the Law Commission, and the Chief Justice.

The reform of cabinet

As emphasised throughout this book, major changes to an electoral system – such as the move from FPP to MMP – can have potentially significant implications for the role and operations of a nation's key political institutions, especially Parliament and the executive (i.e. the cabinet). While New Zealand legislators have already begun to reform the way Parliament conducts its business in order to accommodate the new political environment (see Chapter 5), much less thought has been given to the reform of the cabinet, the most powerful component in our polity.[16] Of course, coalition governments will necessarily alter the way cabinet operates (as discussed in Chapter 7), and the cabinets of minority governments – whether single party or multi-party – will invariably have less power than their majoritarian counterparts. Nevertheless, in the wake of the introduction of MMP, there may well be a case for considering changes, not just to the day-to-day operations of the cabinet, but also to its overall size and structure, the nature of its membership, and the relationship between ministers and Parliament.

Various suggestions have been made over the years for reforming the cabinet and its operations.[17] Some proposals have been intended primarily to enhance the cabinet's effectiveness as a decision-making institution; others have been prompted by concerns about the unrepresentative nature of most New Zealand cabinets (especially in their lack of gender and ethnic balance), together with concerns over the poor calibre of some ministers; yet others have been geared at improving the accountability of the executive to the legislature.

Perhaps the least radical of the various proposals would be simply to restructure the cabinet along the lines advanced by Prime Minister Bolger in late February 1996. Under this option (as mentioned in Chapter 7), the cabinet would be reduced in size to around 12–14 members, but there would be more ministers *outside* the cabinet. Essentially, this would amount to the creation of an 'inner cabinet', surrounded by a wider 'ministry'. This is not unlike the system used by governments in Australia – although the cabinet there is usually slightly larger than that proposed by Bolger (with 15-17 members and a full ministry of around 30). To the extent that smaller cabinets are better (e.g. in operational efficiency), this proposal may have merit. At the same time, changing the structure of the cabinet does not, in itself, alter its representativeness or accountability. Moreover, it does little, if anything, to lighten ministerial workloads or reduce the burdens of constituency work.

Another idea which has attracted interest from time to time is to enable Prime Ministers to appoint a certain number of people to the cabinet who are not MPs.[18] This is currently prohibited by Section 6 of the Constitution Act 1986. The Act does provide, however, for ministers (and other members of the Executive Council) who lose their parliamentary seats at an election to remain in their portfolio for 28 days. Elsewhere in the world – particularly in countries with proportional representation – there are provisions for ministers to be selected (usually by the Prime Minister) from outside the legislature. In some cases such provisions are used extensively. In the early 1990s, for instance, there were three non-MPs in the Danish cabinet, six in the Swedish cabinet, and 11 (more than half) in the Norwegian cabinet. Ministers who are not MPs typically have most of the same powers and privileges as their counterparts who are MPs. Hence, they are able to speak in Parliament and answer MPs' questions, present bills and other policy proposals, and appear before select committees. They are not, however, able to vote in Parliament.

Various reasons can be advanced for amending the Constitution Act to enable non-MPs to be appointed to the cabinet. This would:

- facilitate the appointment of people with specialist skills not otherwise available to the government, thereby increasing the depth and breadth of talent within the cabinet;
- enhance the representativeness of the cabinet (e.g. by facilitating the appointment of more women or Maori ministers), especially where the caucus of the governing party (or parties) lacked an appropriate gender or ethnic balance;
- strengthen Parliament by enabling the governing party (or parties) to place some of their more able members on select committees rather than in ministerial portfolios;
- enable minority governments – which might otherwise struggle to find sufficient competent personnel within their parliamentary ranks to fill all relevant cabinet posts as well as their allocation of select committee places

– to recruit a portion of the cabinet from other sources (e.g. the business community, the universities, the public service, and so on).

Critics of such a reform have raised various objections, the most serious being that ministers appointed from outside the House are likely to be less politically sensitive, less in tune with the needs and concerns of voters, and less democratically accountable for their actions.[19] Admittedly, ministers appointed from outside the House would not have to seek re-election; but the government of which they are a part most certainly would. Also, Parliament would remain sovereign. The passing of legislation and budgetary proposals would remain the province of Parliament; these would not become the responsibility of a non-elected oligarchy.

An even more radical approach to the reform of cabinet would be to follow the example of several parliamentary democracies (e.g. the Netherlands, Norway and Sweden) which have a much more clear-cut separation of the legislature and the political executive. Under this model, MPs who join the cabinet are required to vacate their parliamentary seats for the period during which they hold a ministerial portfolio, their place being taken by another person from the same party (e.g. selected via the party's list in the relevant multi-member constituency). Such people are sometimes referred to as 'alternates' or 'substitutes'. Under this approach, provision could also be made (as in the Netherlands, Norway and Sweden) for non-MPs to be appointed to the cabinet. However, that is not an essential feature of this particular model. Ministers would enjoy speaking rights in Parliament but would not be able to vote.

It is important to stress that this approach to separating the executive from the legislature within a parliamentary system of government is very different from the formal separation of powers under a presidential system like that of the United States. Under a parliamentary system, the cabinet remains fully responsible to Parliament. If it loses the confidence of the legislature, it must resign. Under the American system, by contrast, the President is not directly accountable to Congress, and there are separate elections for the President and the members of the Senate and the House of Representatives.

Some argue that a strict decoupling of the executive and the legislature would enhance both institutions, because it would:

- enable ministers to focus fully on their cabinet responsibilities, with the main burden of constituency work being undertaken by their substitute; and
- enhance the accountability of the executive to the legislature, since ministers would not in fact be sitting in judgement upon themselves and would have less capacity to dominate Parliament's proceedings and decisions.

Against this, such a reform would impose additional costs (i.e. the salaries and support services for substitute MPs). A more serious problem would be selecting substitutes. In the case of list MPs who became cabinet ministers, it would be a relatively straightforward process: their places in Parliament (i.e. for the duration of their period in cabinet) would be taken by people further down the relevant party list.[20] In the case of constituency MPs who became cabinet ministers, it is not clear how substitutes might best be chosen. Sir Geoffrey Palmer suggests that by-elections should be held.[21] But this would raise all kinds of difficulties, not the least being the possibility of a candidate from another party winning the seat. An alternative would be to select people from further down the party list. But this might result in a person resident in one part of the country ending up as a substitute MP for a constituency in a very different part of the country. This is unlikely to be acceptable to voters. A further complication would arise in finding substitutes to fill vacancies in Maori constituencies. In short, MMP, unlike some other systems of PR, does not readily lend itself to the kind of formal separation of the executive and legislature advocated by Palmer.

Judging from the results of our survey, the prospects for significant changes to the system of cabinet government in New Zealand are not good. Although some 33 percent of respondents supported the inclusion of non-MPs in the cabinet and 39 percent supported the separation of the executive and Parliament, less than 20 percent thought that either change was likely to occur within the next decade. This is probably a realistic assessment. Apart from a few constitutional reformers, such changes have very few advocates. Furthermore, parliamentarians are likely to be preoccupied with making MMP workable; they will have little incentive to pursue potentially contentious reforms. This is not to suggest that the cabinet will remain in its present form. But if changes are made, they are much more likely to affect its size and structure rather than its composition or relationship to Parliament.[22]

Will the experiment endure?

The electoral system . . .

Electoral systems are, in essence, devices for converting votes into seats, and there is no such thing as the perfect voting system. FPP in New Zealand was not static and unchanging: it was altered in several ways.[23] Changes were made to the 1993 Electoral Act even before the first MMP election was held under it (most notably, as already discussed, to the ballot paper); and, if MMP remains the basis for the way in which New Zealanders vote, it could well be altered further. Such changes could include:

- the introduction of regional party lists;

- adopting open party lists;
- the abolition of by-elections;
- compensating the other parties in Parliament if any parties win more constituency seats than their proportion of the party-list vote entitles them to hold in Parliament.

Under the 1993 Electoral Act, all the political parties seeking party votes have to field rank-ordered, nationwide lists of candidates. The lists of candidates for whom electors in Northland can vote will be identical to the lists facing voters in Southland.[24] By contrast, in Germany separate lists are drawn up state by state. Regional pressures may well develop in favour of local lists in New Zealand. After all, the Labour party, National, and the Alliance all adopted separate regional lists of candidates prior to melding them into single lists for the country as a whole for the first MMP election. Dissatisfaction among party activists at the treatment of local favourites during selection processes at higher levels could serve to unite sentiment for regional lists across party lines.

Voters may also feel that the head offices of the political parties in New Zealand have too much power under MMP, and they may thus begin to demand more say in the choice of their list MPs. This is not impossible: electoral systems overseas have various ways which permit voters both to vote for a party list and, at the same time, to cast a 'personal vote' for one or more of that party's list candidates.[25] If the party's lists under MMP seem too remote, unrepresentative, or contrived, pressure for change may be hard to resist even for the party hierarchies (who would be surrendering some of their control over the composition of the party list, and hence of the party in Parliament, if voters could choose from among the candidates on the list).

One of the lesser-known characteristics of the MMP system is that, if a list MP resigns or dies during the life of a Parliament, there will not be a by-election. The person will simply be replaced by the next available candidate on the party's list. On the other hand, in comparable circumstances involving an electorate MP, a by-election will be held. This means that a seat could change hands and – possibly – a government fall following the departure of one type of MP (i.e. an electorate MP), whereas party numbers and fortunes will be unaffected by the death or resignation of the other type of MP (i.e. a list MP). This discrepancy could be avoided by providing that *all* seats made vacant be replaced by members from party lists. If an electorate MP were to die or resign, the replacement would simply be the next available person on the appropriate party list. Objections that the new MP could be from an entirely different part of the country would be overcome, at least in part, if there were regional party lists.

Another feature of MMP is that parties may win more electorate seats than their overall share of the party vote entitles them to in the House. For example, if Labour were to win 36 electorates but at the same time received only 21 percent of the party-list vote, entitling the party to, say, 26 seats in Parliament, Labour would (as mentioned in Chapter 2) retain all its 36 constituency seats (but receive no list seats whatsoever). The size of the House of Representatives would be increased by 10 to 130 until the next election. If this were to happen, the over-representation of Labour and the consequent under-representation of the other parties in Parliament would give rise to concerns about the lack of proportionality in the overall election result. Under this scenario, Labour would have 28 percent of the seats in Parliament, and there would probably be calls to compensate the other parties so they could match the 'extra' seats gained by Labour.[26]

Whatever changes are made or proposed to the new electoral system, it is unlikely that New Zealand will revert to FPP. For a start, extensive changes have already been made to the party, parliamentary, and governmental systems in this country. They have been the theme of this book. There is, indeed, a new politics in New Zealand. The pre-MMP status quo has been considerably altered; it would be difficult to go back to it. Formerly small parties are set to become relatively large ones under MMP, and their MPs are unlikely to consent to the wholesale dismantling of the system responsible for their presence in Parliament. The most that is likely to occur is that New Zealand either adopts a PR system based on STV (especially if it is used for local body elections), or moves some time in the 21st century to a modification of MMP, whereby the party vote determines the distribution of only the list seats in Parliament (and not the whole of Parliament). The latter would be a supplementary member (SM) electoral system along the lines of those recently introduced in Italy and Japan (as well as in Russia).[27]

. . . and the governments it produces

Irrespective of any changes which may be made to the composition of cabinet or the rules governing MMP, whether MMP endures in its current form will, in the final analysis, depend on the quality and character of governments formed as a result. The relative merits of different institutional arrangements, as considered by Kent Weaver and Bert Rockman, provide a useful starting-point.[28] Their comparative study of government performance identifies 10 tasks which all governments need to carry out (and, in effect, 10 criteria by which they may be judged):

- 'to set and maintain priorities among the many conflicting demands made upon them so that they are not overwhelmed and bankrupted;
- to target resources where they are most effective;
- to innovate when old policies have failed;

- to co-ordinate conflicting objectives into a coherent whole;
- to be able to impose losses on powerful groups;
- to represent diffuse, unorganised interests in addition to concentrated, well-organised ones;
- to ensure effective implementation of government policies once they have been decided upon;
- to ensure policy stability so that policies have time to work;
- to make and maintain international commitments in the realms of trade and national defense to ensure their long-term well-being;
- and, above all, to manage political cleavages to ensure that the society does not degenerate into civil war.'[29]

New Zealand advocates of proportional representation were confident that MMP governments would be superior to FPP ones in their ability to meet some of these objectives. It was argued that greater representation for smaller parties, and the need for governments to consult more widely with them over policies and budgets, would lead to a more equitable ordering of priorities, particularly in social welfare. Consultation with affected groups was also expected to lead to more 'effective implementation of government policies', avoiding the 'blitzkrieg' approach by which excluded sectors of the community had policies sprung on them without notice.[30]

On the other hand, the transition to MMP has seen concern grow about the influence of smaller parties, whose behaviour may appear selfish or even capricious. For instance, United MP Peter Dunne has revealed that his party was prepared to unseat National and form a coalition with Labour – i.e. to go to the Governor-General with an assurance that National lacked a parliamentary majority, but that no election needed to be held since Labour/United could govern together – but that the Labour party 'didn't show any interest'. If Dunne's claim is correct, it is only fortuitous that New Zealand has been governed by National since mid-1995, for, on its own admission, a small party which did not even exist at the time of the 1993 election, and on which National has had to rely for support in order to stay in office, was equally content to support the principal opposition party, Labour; it is only 'circumstances' which put one party (National) in office rather than another.[31]

The possibility that coalitions may shift from one group of parties to another, possibly without intervening elections being held, means that 'policy stability' and the keeping of 'international commitments' cannot be entirely guaranteed. When control of the Treasury benches changed from National to Labour (or vice versa) under FPP, however, there was also an inevitable loss of policy continuity – which is not always a bad thing, and in some instances precisely what electors voted for.

Furthermore, Weaver and Rockman rightly point out that 'effectiveness

. . . is not the sole purpose of government'.[32] In the United States, for instance, it is correct to observe that 'effectiveness was not the exclusive or perhaps even central objective for the Framers of the American Constitution'.[33] Seymour Martin Lipset argues that the American way of life entails a commitment to five core values: liberty, egalitarianism, individualism, populism and laissez-faire[34] – effective government is not one of them.

New Zealand also recognises these five values. By the mid-1990s, however, each of them had become more closely associated with one or other political party, rather than with the country's overall identity: the commitment to freedom with ACT; equality with the Alliance; individualism with National; populism with New Zealand First; and free market politics together with a smaller, restructured state (laissez-faire) with the proponents of market liberalism in National, Labour, ACT and United. This is perhaps another way of noting the absence in New Zealand of that elusive political entity, the genuinely 'centre' party, for at least in democratic societies such parties span the most divisive cleavages (and hence often have few truly passionate enthusiasts), their main ideology embracing those values most closely associated with a country's underlying sense of itself. A truly enduring centre party, contributing to a stable and effectively functioning MMP system, would be widely recognised as encompassing all these values, thus fulfilling the wider-ranging criteria for 'effectiveness' (which include 'fairness' towards minorities), stressed by the royal commission (see Chapter 2), as well as strengthening the capacity of governments to fulfil the broad objectives of politics summarised in our opening chapter.

Conclusion

As MMP begins in New Zealand, MPs and the public appear ready for a pause, for another of those 'breaks for a cuppa' recommended by Prime Minister Lange as an interval during the Rogernomics reform period. But no political system stands still; as we suggest above, there are likely to be pressures on cabinet to modify its procedures. Other long-established institutions are also apt to face calls for change as New Zealand voters and decision-makers deepen their experience with MMP, including Parliament, the party caucuses, the role of the Governor-General, the public service, the courts, and even MMP itself.

When the American Constitution (the oldest still in force) had been drafted, Benjamin Franklin was asked what sort of government had been established. The tenor of his reply, 'a republic – *if you can keep it*', holds for any group of people embarked on an historic course of political institution-making. The introduction of MMP was intended primarily to 'remedy major defects in [FPP]' and was considered the 'best voting system for New

Zealand's present and future needs'.[35] As we approach the first MMP election, there is a potentially more equitable and more genuinely effective electoral system in place in New Zealand, a form of proportional representation designed to be both 'fair' and 'effective' – if we can keep it.

Notes

1 These have included, among others, the emergence of various spiritual and political movements among Maori, and the rise of the trade union movement and its parliamentary/electoral wing, the New Zealand Labour Party.

2 See, for instance, S. Levine and N. S. Roberts, 'The New Zealand Electoral Referendum of 1992', *Electoral Studies*, 12, 2, 1993, pp.164–66; S. Levine and N. S. Roberts, 'The New Zealand Electoral Referendum and General Election of 1993', *Electoral Studies*, 13, 3, 1994, pp.249–50.

3 See E. P. Aimer, 'Travelling Together: Party Identification and Voting in the New Zealand General Election of 1987', *Electoral Studies*, 8, 2, 1989, pp.131–42; S. Levine and N. S. Roberts, 'Sore Labour's Bath: the Paradox of Party Identification in New Zealand', in M. Clark (ed.), *The Labour Party After 75 Years*, Victoria University, Wellington, 1992, pp.50–72; and J. W. Lamare, 'Party Identification', in M. Holland (ed.), *Electoral Behaviour in New Zealand*, Oxford University Press, Auckland, 1992, pp.51–70;

4 See S. Levine and N. S. Roberts, 'Policies and Political Perspectives: the Importance of Issues and Problems in New Zealand Electoral Behaviour', in M. Holland (ed.), *Electoral Behaviour in New Zealand*, pp.71–93; and J. Vowles and P. Aimer, *Voters' Vengeance: the 1990 Election in New Zealand and the Fate of the Fourth Labour Government*, Auckland University Press, Auckland, 1993, Chs 5 and 11.

5 J. Vowles, P. Aimer, H. Catt, J. Lamare, and R. Miller, *Towards Consensus? The 1993 Election in New Zealand and the Transition to Proportional Representation*, Auckland University Press, Auckland, 1995, Ch. 11.

6 Fear that this would occur was the primary reason for Labour and National's decision to co-operate in Parliament and change the form of the MMP ballot paper before the first MMP election had even been held. All the minor parties – both in and out of Parliament – opposed the change.

7 See N. Frohlich, J. Oppenheimer and O. Young, *Political Leadership and Collective Goods*, Princeton University Press, Princeton, 1971.

8 The strong support given to the fourth Labour government by the business community at the time of the 1987 general election is an instance of this.

9 There is clear evidence internationally that voter turnout is higher in countries with PR. See, for example, J. Elklit and N. S. Roberts, 'A Category of Its Own? Four PR Two-Tier Compensatory Member Electoral Systems in 1994', *European Journal of Political Research*, 30, 2, 1996; and R. W. Jackman and R. A. Miller, 'Voter Turnout in the Industrial Democracies', *Comparative Political Studies*, 27, 4, 1995.

10 See Vowles et al., *Towards Consensus?*, Ch. 8.

11 See, e.g., A. Lijphart, *Democracies*, Yale University Press, New Haven, 1984; A. Lijphart (ed.), *Parliamentary Versus Presidential Government*, Oxford University Press, Oxford, 1992; and M. Palmer, 'Collective Cabinet Decision Making in New Zealand', in M. Laver and K. Shepsle (eds), *Cabinet Ministers and Parliamentary Government*, Cambridge University Press, New York, 1994.

12 New Zealand abolished its upper house, the Legislative Council, in 1950. See W. K. Jackson, *The New Zealand Legislative Council: a Study of the Establishment, Failure and Abolition of an Upper House*, University of Otago Press, Dunedin, 1972. Despite some suggestions (particularly from Prime Minister Bolger) that a restored second chamber

might be an alternative or an adjunct to electoral reform or parliamentary reform, there has been little public enthusiasm for the idea.

13 A. Lijphart, *Democracies*, pp.16–20.

14 Ibid, pp.23–30.

15 A procedure like this operates in Germany: see A. N. Dragnich and J. Rasmussen, *Major European Governments*, 6th edn, Dorsey, Homewood, Illinois, 1982, pp.404–5.

16 'The New Zealand Cabinet, acting through the sovereign power of Parliament, effectively holds the supreme position in political decision making': E. McLeay, 'Selection Versus Election: Choosing Cabinets in New Zealand', in H. Clarke and M. Czudnowski (eds), *Political Elites in Anglo-American Democracies: Changes in Stable Regimes*, Northern Illinois University Press, DeKalb, 1987, p.279; see also E. McLeay, *The Cabinet and Political Power in New Zealand*, Oxford University Press, Auckland, 1995.

17 See, for instance, J. Boston, 'Electoral Reform in New Zealand: the Implications for the Formation, Organisation and Operations of the Cabinet', *Australian Quarterly*, 66, 3, 1994, pp.67–90; G. Palmer, *New Zealand's Constitution in Crisis: Reforming our Political System*, John McIndoe, Dunedin, 1992; State Services Commission, *Working Under Proportional Representation: a Reference for the Public Service*, Wellington, 1995; and M. Waring, 'Revitalisation of Cabinet, Parliament and Parties', in J. S. Hoadley (ed.), *Improving New Zealand's Democracy*, New Zealand Foundation for Peace Studies, Auckland, 1979.

18 A fuller treatment of this proposal is in J. Boston, S. Levine, E. McLeay and N. S. Roberts, 'The Future Development of the Executive', paper prepared for a conference on New Zealand's constitution, Wellington, 24–25 May 1996.

19 Other criticisms are set out in ibid.

20 To make it attractive for candidates further down a party's list to act as 'substitute' MPs for those appointed to the cabinet, some guarantee would have to be given that the individuals in question could return to their former jobs in the event that their parliamentary services were no longer required (e.g. due to a cabinet reshuffle or a change of government).

21 Palmer, *New Zealand's Constitution in Crisis*, p.173.

22 Predictably, MPs taking part in the survey were overwhelmingly opposed to proposals to include non-MPs in the cabinet or for a clearer separation between the executive and the legislature. They were also highly sceptical whether either idea would be implemented.

23 For example, the 'country quota' (the permitted discrepancy between the size of rural and urban electorates) was abolished in 1945; the number of South Island electorates was stabilised (at 25) in 1965; the voting age was lowered from 21 to 20 in 1969 and from 20 to 18 in 1974; the number of Maori electorates was allowed to 'float' in 1975, although the provision was never implemented and the system reverted to a fixed number (i.e. four) a year later.

24 Although the names of list candidates will not appear on ballot papers, they have to be displayed in polling places.

25 The Danish ballot paper is a good example of a voting paper on which electors are able to vote both for a party list and for an individual candidate on that party's list. See, for example, J. Elklit and A. B. Pade, *Parliamentary Elections and Election Administration in Denmark*, Ministry of the Interior, Copenhagen, 1996, pp.14–15 and 36.

26 This would be difficult to accomplish in view of the lack of public support for even more seats in Parliament.

27 Australian political scientist Malcolm Mackerras advocates this reform as an appropriate model for New Zealand.

28 R. K. Weaver and B. A. Rockman, 'Assessing the Effects of Institutions', in Weaver and Rockman (eds), *Do Institutions Matter? Government Capabilities in the United States and*

Abroad, Brookings Institution, Washington, DC, 1993, p.6.

29 Ibid.

30 See B. Easton, 'How Did the Health Reforms Blitzkrieg Fail?', *Political Science*, 46, 2, 1994.

31 *Dominion*, 11 April 1996, p.2.

32 Weaver and Rockman, 'Assessing the Effects of Institutions', p.7.

33 Ibid.

34 S. M. Lipset, *American Exceptionalism: a Double-Edged Sword*, W. W. Norton, New York, 1995.

35 *Report of the Royal Commission: Towards a Better Democracy*, Government Printer, Wellington, 1986, pp.63–64.

APPENDIX 1

Key political events 1993–96

6 November 1993	General election. National wins with a majority of one seat. Second, binding referendum on the electoral system approved with 54 percent support.
29 November 1993	National cabinet sworn in. Rob Storey and Graeme Lee lose their ministerial posts. Ruth Richardson is replaced by Bill Birch as Minister of Finance.
1 December 1993	Helen Clark replaces Mike Moore as leader of the Labour party by a caucus vote of 26 to 19.
21 December 1993	Peter Tapsell (Labour) sworn in as Speaker.
15 February 1994	Maori enrolment option commences. Controversy surrounds the official publicity campaign intended to explain the implications of Maori enrolment choices for the number of Maori seats.
14 July 1994	Ruth Richardson resigns from Parliament, necessitating a by-election in Selwyn.
13 August 1994	David Carter (National) wins the Selwyn by-election.
29 August 1994	A claim by Maori against the Crown begins in the High Court, asserting that the Crown acted unlawfully in its conduct of the Maori option. In the subsequent decision the case is lost, although the Minister of Justice is mildly reprimanded.
11 September 1994	Ross Meurant leaves National and launches the Right-of-Centre party. The distribution of seats in Parliament becomes National: 49, Labour: 45, Alliance: 2, NZ First: 2, RoC: 1.
12 October 1994	Peter Dunne leaves the Labour party. The new distribution of seats is National: 49, Labour: 44, Alliance: 2, NZ First: 2, Independent: 1, RoC: 1.
7 November 1994	The Court of Appeal begins hearing the appeal of the High Court decision on the implementation of the Maori electoral option.
10 November 1994	Jim Anderton announces he is stepping down as leader of the Alliance and will retire from Parliament at the next election.
16 November 1994	Peter Dunne launches the Future New Zealand party. The consequent distribution of seats in Parliament is National: 49, Labour: 44, Alliance: 2, NZ First: 2, Future NZ: 1, RoC: 1.
23 December 1994	The Court of Appeal upholds the High Court ruling, dismissing the Maori claim against the conduct of the electoral option.
17 February 1995	ACT New Zealand registers with the Electoral Commission as a political party – the first non-parliamentary party to register.

27 April 1995	The Report of the Representation Commission is tabled, giving the boundaries of the new 16 South Island and 44 North Island general electorates, and five Maori electorates. As a result, any future general election has to take place under MMP rules.
8 May 1995	Jim Anderton returns as leader of the Alliance.
9 May 1995	Graeme Lee leaves the National party and launches the Christian Democrats (CD). This alters the seats in Parliament to National: 48, Labour: 44, Alliance: 2, NZ First: 2, CD: 1, Future NZ: 1, RoC: 1.
8 June 1995	Jim Anderton moves a vote of no confidence in the government, thus ending the Alliance support of National on confidence issues in Parliament.
10 June 1995	Trevor Rogers leaves National and joins RoC. The composition of Parliament is now National: 47, Labour: 44, Alliance: 2, NZ First: 2, RoC: 2, CD: 1, Future NZ: 1.
28 June 1995	The United New Zealand party is launched, consisting of four National MPs (Bruce Cliffe, Pauline Gardiner, Peter Hilt and John Robertson), two Labour MPs (Clive Matthewson and Margaret Austin) and Peter Dunne. Matthewson is leader, and Cliffe the deputy. As a result, the distribution of seats in Parliament is National: 43, Labour: 42, United: 7, Alliance: 2, NZ First: 2, RoC: 2, CD: 1.
19 July 1995	Following consultations with leaders of the other parties in Parliament, the government reverses its stance and announces it will send the New Zealand Navy research ship *Tui* to Mururoa as a support vessel for the peace flotilla.
8 August 1995	The government decides to contest French nuclear testing in the South Pacific at the International Court of Justice.
28 August 1995	Ross Meurant is dismissed from his position as parliamentary under-secretary.
19 September 1995	State Services Commission launches *Working Under Proportional Representation: a Reference for the Public Service*.
20 September 1995	The government is defeated on two votes in Parliament on the introduction and referral to select committee of the Teacher Registration Bill introduced by opposition MP Trevor Mallard.
25 September 1995	The Radio New Zealand Bill (No. 2) passes as a result of consultations between United and National.
23 November 1995	Parliament passes the Electoral Reform Bill providing for disclosure of donations, new limits on campaign spending, and for voters to enrol up to polling day.
27 November 1995	The Christian Democrats undertake an unsuccessful court challenge against the right of Parliament to amend provisions of the Electoral Act 1993.

6 December 1995	Electoral Amendment Bill (No. 2) is passed amending the ballot paper so that the party vote and electorate vote are directly alongside each other. Labour and National support the amendments but all the minor parties in Parliament oppose them.
23 January 1996	United party leader Clive Matthewson and finance spokesperson Peter Dunne announce that working with National offers the best prospects for stable government.
31 January 1996	Ross Meurant leaves the Conservative party (formerly RoC). The distribution of seats becomes National: 43, Labour: 42, United: 7, Alliance: 2, NZ First: 2, CD: 1, Conservatives: 1, Independent: 1.
15 February 1996	Alliance leader Jim Anderton rules out any coalition deal with the Labour party.
20 February 1996	Parliament meets under the new Standing Orders for the first time.
21 February 1996	The National party executive confirms it will not stand a candidate against Peter Dunne in the Ohariu-Belmont electorate in the upcoming general election.
25 February 1996	Michael Laws announces he is leaving the National party. The seats in Parliament are now National: 42, Labour: 42, United: 7, Alliance: 2, NZ First: 2, CD: 1, Conservatives: 1, Independents: 2.
27 February 1996	Trevor Rogers (Conservative) announces the end of his party's formal support for the government.
28 February 1996	National and United sign a formal coalition agreement (see Appendix 4). Peter Dunne joins cabinet as Minister of Internal Affairs and Minister of Revenue.
6 March 1996	Michael Laws joins New Zealand First. The composition of Parliament is thus National: 42, Labour: 42, United: 7, NZ First: 3, Alliance: 2, CD: 1, Conservatives: 1, Independent: 1.
29 March 1996	Christian Democrats and Christian Heritage parties reach an electoral accommodation under the auspices of the Christian Coalition.
3 April 1996	Peter McCardle quits the National party, and Jack Elder leaves the Labour party. Both MPs join New Zealand First. The composition of Parliament is thus National: 41, Labour: 41, United: 7, NZ First: 5, Alliance: 2, CD: 1, Conservatives: 1, Independent: 1.
29 April 1996	Michael Laws resigns from Parliament. The distribution of seats is National: 41, Labour: 41, United: 7, NZ First: 4, Alliance: 2, CD: 1, Conservatives: 1, Independent: 1.

Illustrating the Sainte Laguë formula using the results of the 1993 New Zealand general election

Under MMP, the number of seats a party wins in Parliament will be determined directly by the number of votes it receives. If political parties win *either* at least five percent of the party vote *or* at least one electorate seat, then their party votes will be used to ascertain precisely the overall number of seats they are entitled to in the House of Representatives. As mentioned in Chapter 2, the Sainte Laguë formula is used to decide how many seats each party has in Parliament (as well as the order in which seats are allocated to the parties).

Parties may win fractions of the vote, but MPs cannot be cut into pieces and parties must, therefore, win whole seats, not parts of a seat: 12.3 percent of the votes cannot be turned into 14.8 seats in Parliament. The Sainte Laguë formula ensures that parties will win whole seats (no fractions or remainders are left over). It also ensures that the number of seats allocated to a political party is in close proportion to its overall share of the party vote. Indeed, the share of the seats each party wins will be *very* close to the precise share of the qualifying votes it won (i.e. after excluding votes for parties which did not qualify for seats in Parliament).

This appendix illustrates how the Sainte Laguë formula works by applying it to the results of the 1993 general election. Of course, people would have voted in different ways had there been a different electoral system in 1993. (For a start, they would have been able to 'split their tickets' by casting votes for different parties on the party-list and electorate halves of the ballot paper.) The value of this appendix is that it uses real parties and real numbers. It is more tangible and meaningful than an appendix based on mock parties and hypothetical statistics.

Had the 1993 election been held under MMP, only four parties would have qualified for list seats in Parliament. They are National, Labour, the Alliance, and New Zealand First – each won more than five percent of the votes and each won at least one electorate. All the other parties contesting the 1993 election would have failed to qualify for seats in an MMP Parliament. As a result, in this example the Sainte Laguë formula is applied only to the votes for National, Labour, the Alliance, and New Zealand First. The actual number of votes received by each party is divided by successive odd numbers – 1, 3, 5, 7, 9, 11, 13, etc. (In this example, of course, it is the total number of votes won by the parties in every electorate they contested; in a real MMP election, on the other hand, it would be the number of party votes won throughout the country as a whole by each party.)

As is shown below, National has 44 of the 120 highest quotients[1] stemming from these successive divisions, Labour 43, the Alliance 23, and New Zealand First 10. The number of electorate seats won by each party is also shown.[2] National would have won

29 of the 65 electorates in 1993, Labour 33, the Alliance 1, and New Zealand First 2. In each case, the number is less than the party's overall seat entitlement; and the number of list seats awarded to each party thus represents the difference between the party's overall entitlement and the number of electorates it won. In National's case, the party is entitled to 44 seats in the 120-member Parliament. It won 29 electorates and is, therefore, awarded an additional 15 list seats (44–29 = 15).

The 120th highest quotient – which is, of course, the lowest quotient to win a seat in a 120-member Parliament – was 7,745. The 121st highest quotient was 7,689. (This is the figure obtained by dividing New Zealand First's total of 161,481 votes by 21.) This means that National would have won its 44th seat narrowly and New Zealand First just missed out on an 11th seat. If New Zealand First had won 1,185 more votes throughout the country as whole (that is, if it had gained an average of 19 more votes in each of the country's 65 electorates) and if National had won 1,185 fewer votes, then New Zealand First would have picked up the 120th seat in Parliament and National would have lost it (and in this scenario Parliament would have seen Labour and National with 43 seats apiece, the Alliance with 23 seats, and New Zealand First with 11). Because New Zealand First narrowly missed winning the last seat to be distributed to the parties, it would have been very slightly under-represented in Parliament if 1993 had been an MMP election. It won 8.4 percent of all the valid votes cast and 8.7 percent of the votes which qualified for seats in Parliament, but 'only' won 8.3 percent of the 120 seats in Parliament.

Party vote divided by	National		Labour		Alliance		NZ First	
1	673,892	(1)	666,759	(2)	350,064	(3)	161,481	(6)
3	224,630	(4)	222,253	(5)	116,688	(9)	53,827	(17)
5	134,778	(7)	133,351	(8)	70,012	(14)	32,296	(28)
7	96,270	(10)	95,251	(11)	50,009	(20)	23,068	(41)
9	74,876	(12)	74,084	(13)	38,896	(25)	17,942	(53)
11	61,262	(15)	60,614	(16)	31,824	(30)	14,680	(64)
13	51,837	(18)	51,289	(19)	26,928	(35)	12,421	(75)
15	44,926	(21)	44,450	(22)	23,337	(39)	10,765	(86)
17	39,640	(23)	39,221	(24)	20,592	(45)	9,498	(97)
19	35,468	(26)	35,092	(27)	18,424	(50)	8,499	(110)
21	32,090	(29)	31,750	(31)	16,669	(56)	7,689	
23	29,299	(32)	28,989	(33)	15,220	(61)		
25	26,955	(34)	26,670	(36)	14,002	(67)		
27	24,958	(37)	24,694	(38)	12,965	(72)		
29	23,237	(40)	22,991	(42)	12,071	(78)		
31	21,738	(43)	21,508	(44)	11,292	(83)		
33	20,420	(46)	20,204	(47)	10,608	(88)		
35	19,254	(48)	19,050	(49)	10,001	(93)		
37	18,213	(51)	18,020	(52)	9,461	(99)		
39	17,279	(54)	17,096	(55)	8,976	(104)		
41	16,436	(57)	16,262	(58)	8,538	(108)		
43	15,671	(59)	15,506	(60)	8,141	(114)		
45	14,975	(62)	14,816	(63)	7,779	(119)		
47	14,338	(65)	14,186	(66)	7,448			
49	13,752	(68)	13,607	(69)				

Party vote divided by	National		Labour		Alliance	NZ First
51	13,213	(70)	13,073	(71)		
53	12,714	(73)	12,580	(74)		
55	12,252	(76)	12,122	(77)		
57	11,822	(79)	11,697	(80)		
59	11,421	(81)	11,301	(82)		
61	11,047	(84)	10,930	(85)		
63	10,696	(87)	10,583	(89)		
65	10,367	(90)	10,257	(91)		
67	10,058	(92)	9,951	(94)		
69	9,766	(95)	9,663	(96)		
71	9,491	(98)	9,390	(100)		
73	9,231	(101)	9,133	(102)		
75	8,985	(103)	8,890	(105)		
77	8,751	(106)	8,659	(107)		
79	8,530	(109)	8,439	(111)		
81	8,319	(112)	8,231	(113)		
83	8,119	(115)	8,033	(116)		
85	7,928	(117)	7,844	(118)		
87	7,745	(120)	7,663			
89	7,571					
Total seat entitlement in Parliament:	**44**		**43**		**23**	**10**
General electorates						
* South Island	7		8		1	0
* North Island	22		21		0	1
Maori electorates	0		4		0	1
Total electorates	29		33		1	2
Therefore, number of party-list seats for each party	15		10		22	8
Equals the party's total seat entitlement in Parliament:	**44**		**43**		**23**	**10**
Share of seats in Parliament (%)	*36.7*		*35.8*		*19.2*	*8.3*
Share of the votes of parties qualifying for seats in Parliament (%)	*36.4*		*36.0*		*18.9*	*8.7*
Share of all the valid votes in the 1993 election (%)	*35.0*		*34.7*		*18.2*	*8.4*

Notes

1 Only whole numbers have been used in this example. (If necessary, the divisions can obviously be made to several decimal places.)

2 These calculations are based on data in '1993 Final Results Redistributed into the 1995 MMP Electoral Districts', in Alan McRobie, *The 1995 Electoral Redistribution*, MC Enterprises, Christchurch, 1995.

APPENDIX 3

List of political parties registered with the Electoral Commission as at 30 April 1996

No.	Party name	Abbreviation	Component parties	Date registered
1	The New Zealand National Party	National		02/12/94
2	New Zealand Conservative Party	Conservatives		02/12/94[1]
3	New Zealand First Party	NZ First		20/12/94
4	ACT New Zealand			17/02/95
5	New Zealand Labour Party	Labour Party		17/02/95
6	Christian Heritage Party of New Zealand	CHP		06/03/95
7	The Alliance	Alliance	Mana Motuhake (Inc), New Zealand Democratic Party (Inc), NewLabour Party, The New Zealand Liberal Party (Inc), The Greens	17/03/95
8	The Republican Party Incorporated	Republican Party		19/05/95
9	The McGillicuddy Serious Party	McGillicuddy Serious		13/07/95
10	Te Tawharau			10/08/95
11	Advance New Zealand Party Inc	Advance NZ		10/08/95
12	The New Zealand Democratic Party Incorporated	Democrats		10/08/95
13	United New Zealand Party	United NZ		10/08/95
14	The Greens, The Green Party of Aotearoa/ New Zealand	Green Party		17/08/95
15	Christian Democrats	CD		17/08/95
16	Accord Seniors and Youth			14/09/95
17	Aotearoa Party			16/11/95
18	Natural Law Party	Natural Law		01/12/95
19	Christian Coalition		Christian Heritage Party of New Zealand, Christian Democrats	01/02/96
20	Progressive Green Party	Progressive Greens		01/02/96

Note

1 On 16 November 1995, the commission approved an application to change the registered name and abbreviation of this party from 'Right of Centre' and 'RoC' respectively.

Coalition agreement between the New Zealand National party and the United New Zealand party

Date: 28/2/96

Preamble

1 Each party to this agreement wishes to work with the other as a coalition government until the next general election with the purpose of maintaining political stability and promoting sound economic and social policies.

2 In furtherance of these objectives, the parties will co-operate with each other in respect of parliamentary activity, consulting closely and operating with mutual respect.

3 Notwithstanding the above, each party will preserve its separate identity and operating procedures in every respect.

Agreement

1 Parliamentary activity

a) In advance of legislation being introduced to Parliament after the coming into effect of this agreement, the parties will agree their positions in respect of such legislation and other related issues. The parties note that commitments in respect to legislation announced by United New Zealand Party prior to this agreement do not form part of this agreement.

b) The whips of each party will consult as required to monitor vote availability, including proxies, and manage voting requirements as necessary to ensure that the coalition is not defeated in Parliament on matters that each party has agreed to support.

c) Notwithstanding anything covered by paragraphs a) and b) above, United New Zealand agrees to support issues nominated by the Prime Minister as ones of confidence as previously discussed by the Prime Minister with the leader of United New Zealand.

d) With the exception of confidence issues any disagreements shall be referred for resolution to a Disputes Group comprising the leaders and deputy leaders of each party.

e) In respect of proposed government legislation, the appropriate minister will brief the caucus or caucus representatives of each coalition partner.

2 Working relationship

a) United New Zealand may, at any time, put forward to National any policy initiative and full discussion on such initiative will occur.

b) There will be fair and equitable representation of each coalition party in all parliamentary processes including questions, speaking opportunities, committees and other matters arising out of parliamentary activities.

c) The leaders of each party shall meet on a regular basis to discuss any matters arising out of this agreement or other matters as the case may be.
d) The parties recognise that other coalition arrangements either exist or may be agreed and each party will consult the other about them to preserve a reasonable consistency and compatibility of policies and principles.

3 Electoral representation

a) Each party will conduct the election campaign as a separate party with its own policy platform and acknowledges that there will be competition with the other party for voter support.
b) Notwithstanding the above, National will not stand a constituency candidate in the Ohariu–Belmont electorate at the 1996 general election.

4 Membership of the executive

United New Zealand will be entitled to one position as a member of the executive. As a condition of participation that member will comply with the requirements of the Cabinet Office Manual and associated Cabinet Office circulars, in particular the conventions of collective cabinet responsibility and cabinet confidentiality. With the concurrence of the Prime Minister as chair of cabinet the United New Zealand member of the executive may share and disclose information obtained as a member of the executive with the leader of United New Zealand. It is expected that the leader of United New Zealand would observe the necessary confidentiality, and accord appropriate security to any such information including written material.

5 Duration of agreement

This agreement will continue until the next general election.

Signed for and on behalf of the New Zealand National Party

Rt. Hon. J. B. Bolger
Leader

Mr G. W. F. Thompson
President

Signed for and on behalf of United New Zealand Party

Hon. Clive Matthewson
Leader

Mr Brian Wilcox
Chairman

Index